HOW TO

Buy the Home You Want, for the Best Price, in Any Market

Also by Terry Eilers

How to Sell Your Home Fast, for the Highest Price, in Any Market

HOW TO

Buy the Home You Want, for the Best Price, in Any Market

FROM A REAL ESTATE INSIDER WHO KNOWS ALL THE TRICKS

TERRY EILERS

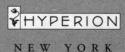

HYPERION

NEW YORK

All names of companies, products, street addresses, and persons contained herein are part of a completely fictitious scenario and are designed solely for illustrative purposes.

Some of the information contained in this book may be affected by changes in interpretations of the law or deviations in market conditions in specific geographic areas. This book should not be used as a substitute for legal, tax, investment, accounting, or similar professional services. If such services are required, publisher and author recommend that the reader secure the services of a competent professional.

Copyright © 1997, Terry Eilers

Library of Congress Cataloging-in-Publication Data

Eilers, Terry (Terry Lynn), 1948–
    How to buy the home you want, for the best price, in any market: from a real estate insider who knows all the tricks / Terry Eilers—1st ed.
        p.   cm.
    Includes bibliographical references and index.
    ISBN: 0-7868-8225-5
    1. House buying—United States. 2. Residential real estate—United States—Purchasing. 3. Mortgage loans—United States.
    I. Title.
    HD225.E37   1997
    643' .12—dc20   96–38667
                                        CIP

Designed by Robert Bull Design

FIRST EDITION

10 9 8 7

ACKNOWLEDGMENTS

To Janice Labbé, who labors so unselfishly whether the task is research, writing, editing, or data input. There seems to be no challenge too great for this lady.

To A. Richard Barber, agent extraordinaire, for his superb guidance and handling of our publications. His expertise, honesty, patience, wit, and dedication are immeasurable.

To Roger Smith, for sharing his thirty years of financing knowledge with the readers of this book. Also, to Roger, his staff and his company, a huge "THANK YOU" from the over 50,000 homeowners for whom they have provided loans to purchase properties.

To Laurie Abkemeier, Senior Editor, and all of the staff at Hyperion. They are truly the magicians who transform all of the ideas, thoughts, and information into lucid, readable book form.

C O N T E N T S

CONTENTS

CONTENTS

CONTENTS

FIGURES

CONTENTS

APPENDIX FIGURES

Where's the best place

I've ever stayed?

Home. I always know

they have to take me in there,

whether I've got my credit card

or not.

—George Burns, 1896–1996

INTRODUCTION

In 1955, the federal government conducted a survey across the United States questioning interviewees about their views and aspirations of the future. These people were chosen randomly with no regard to race, religion, or marital status. The interviewees were all thirty years old or younger and all living as financially independent individuals or families.

All interviewees were asked to list five things that they truly wanted in their lifetime. They were asked to be specific and not to give vague answers such as health, wealth, and happiness. The five most common answers provided by these people in the mid-1950s were:

1. To have a family of their own
2. To have a good, long-term job
3. To own a home
4. To travel
5. To live a long, healthy life

In 1995, an independent research company conducted the same survey as the federal government had forty years prior. It interviewed over 5,000 people nationwide, asking the same question: What five things do you truly want in your lifetime? The answers were slightly different from the previous survey. The following were the most common five answers given by the interviewees ages twenty-five to thirty:

1. To have a good job/career and to be financially secure
2. To be healthy, and if they eventually had a family, for them to be healthy as well
3. To own a home or property

4. To have the money to retire and enjoy life at a fairly young age
5. To have a job that allows the person time to enjoy the things they like to do

It is interesting to see how some of the answers changed. However, as the cliché states: Some things never change. The number-3 answer from both surveys was to own a home.

Without a doubt, the concept of home ownership has become a major part of the Great American Dream scenario, and with the major tax code revision in 1987, home ownership has become a necessity if a person or family is to achieve tax relief on income earned. Most important, home ownership is not limited only to persons who have large incomes or perfect credit. Because there are so many ways to buy, nearly everyone in the United States who has a steady income and the desire to own a home can do so.

This book will guide you step-by-step through the intricacies of buying the home that will best meet your needs and desires. Most important, this book will help you *purchase* that home quickly and for the best possible price.

HOW SHOULD YOU USE THIS BOOK?

Utilize *How to Buy the Home You Want, for the Best Price, in Any Market* to give you a solid understanding of home buying and as a reference throughout the entire home-buying process. This book provides a step-by-step, simple, concise plan to obtain the right home, at the right price, in the shortest possible time. From the beginning of your home search until long after the close of your transaction, *How to Buy the Home You Want, for the Best Price, in Any Market* will be your home-buying bible.

Throughout the book, many Smart Tips are highlighted. Pay close attention to these tips because they are especially important to you as a buyer.

SMART TIP:
Chapter 20 includes techniques to use to save money when buying a home. Also, the last pages of the book contain a complete glossary of real estate and lending terms.

How to Buy the Home You Want, for the Best Price, in Any Market is the only publication that you will ever need to understand the buying process and effectively and efficiently complete the purchase of a home.

THE LANGUAGE OF REAL ESTATE

Every industry has a language practically all its own. If you speak to professionals in the field of computers, they might throw out such terms as *bit-mapped, DOS, threshold, batch out, image filtering, line attributes, object menus, color palettes*. Whew, what in the world does all of that mean?

To the average person who does little more on his or her personal computer than write letters, all of that specialized jargon sounds like a foreign language. However, to the computer graphic artist, it all is very simple to understand. Unfortunately, when the average potential home buyer first begins searching for a home, the language of real estate and lending can be just as confusing.

One afternoon I overheard Roger Smith (one of the advisors for this book and a financing specialist) on the telephone speaking to one of his subordinates. His conversation went something like this: "Remember the margins remain the same at 1.5 for the first 5. On the 30-year rate it is tied to the 5th District Fed. There is a cap of 6 and after 5 the rate is fixed at a blend of the last 12, 48, to 60, and remains the same throughout the last 25."

Confused? Don't be. It doesn't matter whether you are dealing with people in the lending field like Roger or the computer graphic artist, terminology can be the most frightening aspect of the business.

If you have had conversations with real estate salespeople and they nonchalantly threw out terms like MLS, landlocked, assessments, appurtenance, amortized, discount points, great deed, liens, prime rate, title search, variance, and it all sounds like Latin ... just relax.

Think of all the terms that you use in your own field. If you sail, you know that the right is starboard and left is port. If you are a bowler, you know that a strike is knocking all the pins down with one ball and a spare is knocking down all of the pins with two consecutive balls. If you ride horses, you know that the cinch strap holds the saddle on the horse. To a fly fisherman, a Royal Coachman is a very common trout fly.

Since you have become interested in owning a home, you probably will begin to learn the most common terminology used in real estate and lending. Keep in mind, however, that you do not need to become an expert in real estate to own a home. Your goal is to learn to use the knowledge of the experts in the real estate and lending fields to help you achieve your goal: to purchase the home that you desire at the best possible price.

HOW DO YOU GET THERE?

How successful do you think a person would be who attempted to drive across the United States from San Francisco to New York City, and his or her only plan was to point the vehicle toward the east and hope to take the proper highways? Unless the driver has unlimited financial resources and time, most probably the trip would be very long, very expensive, and extremely frustrating. It would make much more sense for that traveler to use the services of a travel agent or a travel club and keep maps and guide books close at hand. By so doing, the journey would be much easier and more enjoyable, and the traveler would reach his or her destination in a timely manner.

Unfortunately, many potential home buyers simply point themselves in the direction of home ownership. Lacking guidance, their journey ultimately is very long and difficult. Oftentimes they become frustrated and turn back before they ever arrive at their ultimate destination: owning a home.

If you follow the process in this book that directs you toward home ownership, you will arrive at your destination comfortably, in a timely manner, and with great financial savings.

HOW TO

Buy the Home You Want,
for the Best Price,
in Any Market

CHAPTER ONE

A Brief Overview

In just a few short hours, you will have many of the right answers when it comes to the methods and procedures involved in buying a home. Bear in mind that almost everyone, regardless of his expertise, has an opinion about the home-buying process. Learn to question the novice opinions and trust those experts who have a proven track record of positive results.

When discussing the search for the right answers, I am reminded of a friend who became a glider pilot while living in the Riverside, California, area. Many afternoons when he went up in his engineless, PT-2 glider, it was very easy to find the updrafts near the San Bernardino Mountains (due to severe smog that blows in from Los Angeles). Because the air was so laden with brown smog, Gary could actually *see* the updrafts rolling up near the hillsides. He could simply glide over, catch the upward-moving air, and keep his glider in the air for two or three hours. However, when Gary was transferred to the San Francisco Bay area, he discovered very quickly that since the air was much clearer, finding the updrafts sometimes was difficult. Worse yet, if he wanted to fly for two or three hours, he might have to be towed back into the air by a powered plane as many as four times during his flight period . . . at $30 per tow.

Gary's best action would have been to talk to local expert glider pilots to learn which flight patterns would provide the best updrafts. But he was too embarrassed to ask. Eventually he thought he had found the answer on his own. One afternoon he noticed that seagulls would float for hours without ever flapping their wings and they seemed to just feel and know where the updrafts were. He glided over and positioned himself near the seagulls. Just as he expected, the birds knew where the updrafts were. They would float back and forth in the air movements. Gary was elated. No more being towed three or four times per flight at $30 a pop and no more loss of flight time.

But things are not always as they seem. Gary's excitement soon turned to disappointment when he discovered that if he followed the seagulls' flight patterns exactly, everyday at around 5:00 P.M. he would be gliding in circles around the garbage dump!

Remember, when buying a home, you are not just looking for answers—you are looking for the right answers. These answers must come from the experts in the field who are accomplishing what you want to accomplish. Don't end up gliding around the garbage dump.

SO YOU
ARE THINKING
OF BUYING A HOME?

Since the first settlers arrived in North America, almost everyone has shared the dream of home ownership. Owning a home provides security and permanence, not to mention pride of ownership.

Most important, maybe you are like so many renters who reach a point in their lives when they are just plain sick of making someone else's mortgage payment. But how do you make that big move from renter to home owner? How much money do you need to buy a home? Can you get a home loan? How do you find the right home? Who will handle all of the paperwork? What about the escrow/closing, title, insurance, and inspections?

Okay, maybe it does sound a bit overwhelming, but just take one step at a time. How do you think a honeybee would feel if it crawled out of its hive every morning and said to itself, "I've got to pollinate 2,000 flowers today!" It probably would crawl back inside and go back to sleep. Instead it just moves, flower to flower, effectively and efficiently, until it has pollinated an average of 2,000 blooms per day.

WHAT ARE THE ADVANTAGES
OF HOME OWNERSHIP?

When asked about the advantages of home ownership, most home owners mention enormous tax savings and point out the equity they have accumulated during the ownership period.

Another major financial reward of home ownership is that there is no worry about rent increases. One renter and potential home purchaser with whom we spoke in New York City explained that her rent had increased from $1,200 per month to over $1,900 in only five years. That $700 rent increase paralleled almost exactly her income, which had increased by $740 per month in that same period.

Lastly, a financial reward could occur if you decided to convert your home to a rental, which can provide a supplement to your income or retirement. One man we spoke with in Reno, Nevada, explained that he had purchased four homes over a twenty-year period. Each property had been financed with a fifteen-year loan. When he retires at age fifty-five, all of the homes will be paid for and the rental income will total $6,000 per month. After twenty years as an insurance agent, his retire-

SMART TIP:
In tax write-offs alone, the average home owner in the United States deducted between $6,400 and $6,600 annually, according to the 1995 IRS statistics. For home owners who have owned their home for five years or less, the average deduction figure was just over $8,900. Some other deductions that may be written off are nonrecurring closing costs, loan fees, and escrow/closing charges.

SMART TIP:
Although fixed-rate home loans usually remain the same throughout the term of the loan, adjustable-rate mortgages (ARMs) often have increases in the payments if or when the interest on the loan adjusts upward. For example, if the interest rate on an ARM were to increase from 7.5 percent to 8 percent on an original $100,000 principal loan amount with twenty-nine years left to pay on a thirty-year original term of the loan, the monthly payment would increase from $699.21 to $733.12 (not much of an increase). Of course, the interest rate on an ARM also may decrease, thereby reducing the monthly payments.

ment will only be about $3,000 per month. The extra $6,000 per month will make a big difference in the lifestyle this man and his family will enjoy.

Although financial rewards are certainly a major advantage of home ownership, the following excerpt from a letter I received from an eighty-four-year-old home owner explains the most distinct advantages of owning a home:

> *Each morning I spend time weeding my garden, always mindful of the fact that these carrots and radishes are truly mine, grown in my dirt and on my piece of land. I have owned my home for thirty-five years and after 360 payments it is free and clear. I only pay a small tax burden each year. Whether I am cooking in the kitchen or repairing a hinge on the gate, I thank the Lord each day that I have had the opportunity to experience, for all these years, the pride and comfort of owning and enjoying my own property. The feeling that home ownership gives an individual is not about tax write-off or equity. The true advantage is the feeling of permanence and security and the fact that you know it is your home for as long as you wish.*

Thank you, Mrs. Brown. I couldn't have said it better myself.

WHAT ARE THE DISADVANTAGES OF HOME OWNERSHIP?

Anyone who saw the 1986 Steven Spielberg film *The Money Pit* with Shelley Long and Tom Hanks may feel immediate trepidation when they think of buying a home. In that hilarious spoof, everything went wrong with the home that the couple had purchased—from the plumbing exploding, to the electrical wiring catching fire, to entire floors caving in. Soon the would-be dream home became the "home from hell."

But bear in mind, for the most part, that is Hollywood. The script was written as a comedy based on the famous Murphy's Law, which states: Anything that can go wrong will go wrong! Remember, Hollywood would also have you believe that there are "Terminators" in our midst, giant worms below the earth's surface causing "Tremors," and "Jaws" haunting every shoreline.

You may in fact experience some problems with the home you purchase. By having all the proper inspections, spending time in the neighborhood, talking to the experts in the area, obtaining the necessary warranties, and generally covering all of your bases, you probably will never face a catastrophe like *The Money Pit*.

Another disadvantage of home ownership might be the possibility of natural disasters causing financial loss to your property. For example, the 1994 Southern California earthquake caused over $3 billion in damage to property, and it was estimated that only about 5 percent of that figure was covered by insurance. Many uninsured home owners simply walked away from their homes because they owed more than the property was worth. They just could not afford the repair bills.

Another disadvantage to consider when moving into the new home is the substantial additional costs usually incurred for new furniture, repairs, remodeling, new window coverings, and the like. New home buyers need cash reserves if they want to make changes.

Possibly the biggest disadvantage to home ownership is the responsibility that accompanies the home purchase. The home owner is "on the hook" for the payments, the insurance, the taxes, the upkeep, and any other expenses that might be required to maintain the

> **SMART TIP:**
> Over time neighbors move, areas change, and what once was a quiet, *Leave It to Beaver* neighborhood can evolve into a semicommercial area with increased traffic, congestion, noise, and crime. Make sure that you examine how the area is evolving. If you want a guarantee of peace and quiet for the next twenty years, maybe you should consider a property in a rural area with a commute into the hustle and bustle of the city.

property. Although some landlords require long-term leases, in most cases a renter can give thirty days' notice and be gone. A much higher level of responsibility comes with home ownership.

All things considered, the advantages of owning a home far outweigh the disadvantages. Seldom will you hear a person say, "I'm so glad I rented my whole life."

CAN YOU OBTAIN A LOAN?

In a word, "Yes!"

Most people think that the loan process is very complex and difficult, when in fact it is quite simple. Most often difficulties occur in the loan process when potential borrowers are not prepared to or cannot provide a lender with all of the requested information.

Most potential home buyers are unaware of the hundreds of loans available in today's market. Potential borrowers with perfect credit and a large down payment may find it easy to obtain a loan at the lowest available interest rate. However, a person with less-than-perfect credit and a small down payment still has several loan options available, although he or she may pay slightly more interest. As I said earlier, there is a home and a loan for nearly everyone who has the desire to own a property.

HOW DO YOU FIND
THE RIGHT HOME?

The best way to find the right home for you is to first be prequalified or preapproved by one or more lenders, then identify areas where you can afford and want to buy, and, finally, narrow down your choices to the homes that best meet your needs and desires.

Always keep in mind that, to find the right home at the best price, during all aspects of the transaction you must be patient, be reasonable, and be focused.

Ask everyone questions. Find out about the schools. Check the traffic patterns. Find out if there are any proposed zoning changes in the area. Obtain the figures of crime rates in the area. Remember, you are not just buying a home, you are buying an entire neighborhood that will become a major part of your life. Above all, remember to trust the opinions of the people who are or have been successful in accomplishing what you are attempting to achieve.

WHAT CHALLENGES CAN
YOU EXPECT WHEN BUYING?

The biggest challenge for home buyers (especially first-timers) appears to be the frustration they experience while waiting for each facet of the transaction to unfold.

First is trying to find the right property. Second is waiting for the offer or counteroffer to be accepted. Third is waiting for the inspections to be completed and the reports filed. Fourth is the wait for the appraisal to be done. Fifth is the wait for the final title exam and report. Final loan approval also takes time. Then there is the closing and waiting for all the paperwork to be completed, including the recording of the ownership documents; then is the wait for the sellers to move—on time, it is hoped.

And throughout the entire process, everything always takes longer than you anticipated.

Buyers must learn to relax and understand completely a property transaction takes time, especially if everything is done properly. Remember, in most cases, the home is the largest and most important investment a person will ever make.

Another challenge for a home buyer will be choosing the right agent or broker with whom to work. Chapter 5 provides a detailed explanation of how to choose the best professional for your needs. Don't choose an agent just because he or she handed you a card in a grocery line. Find out about that salesperson and make sure he or she has the ability, experience, ethics, and determination to give you the results that you desire.

One of the toughest challenges home buyers face is obtaining all of the information about a property in which they are interested. This information includes: What problems have occurred with the property? What repairs have been made? Has the upkeep on the property been satisfactory? Are there leaks? Are there wiring problems? Are the plumbing fixtures old?

Proper inspections can detect many areas of concern. However, buyers should not rely just on written professional reports. They should never be afraid to ask neighbors, service or maintenance people who have worked on the property, agents or brokers who worked on the sale of the home, or even the current owners themselves what problems exist or have occurred with the property.

Although you face a myriad of challenges when purchasing a home, at each turn there will be professionals who can competently guide you through the entire process.

> **SMART TIP:**
> In all states except Alabama, Arizona, Kansas, and Tennessee, sellers are required by law to disclose to buyers any potential defects of which sellers are aware and that could affect the value of the home. The following Seller Disclosure Statement is an example of a form used in one state for the purpose of disclosing potential problem areas in a home.

FIGURE 1.1 >

SELLER DISCLOSURE STATEMENT

OTHER THINGS TO CONSIDER

Some other points to consider before deciding to purchase a home include whether:

1. You have a fairly secure job and a reasonable expectation that your income will continue at its current level or increase.
2. Now is a good time for you to buy based on your own personal financial position and the local area economy.

> **SMART TIP:**
> Buyers need to be aware not only of changes occurring in the neighborhood where they are considering a purchase but also of any changes in the entire area that might adversely affect home values. If there is a good chance that a large employer in the area may be closing down, investing in that area might not be wise, at least until the economy begins to stabilize.

Although there is no best time to buy, potential home owners

REAL ESTATE SELLER DISCLOSURE STATEMENT

Property Address:_____ Inspection Date:_____
The following aspects of the above-referenced property have been personally inspected by the undersigned buyers and their condition noted accordingly on this form.

The disclosure statement concerns the real property situated in the city of _____ , county of _____ , State of California, described as _____ . This statement is a disclosure of the condition of the above described property in compliance with section 1102 of the Civil Code as of _____ , 19_____ . It is not a warranty of any kind by the seller(s) or any agent(s) representing any principal(s) in this transaction, and is not a substitute for any inspections of warranties the principal(s) may wish to obtain.

Coordinate with Other Disclosure Forms: This Real Estate Transfer Statement is made pursuant to Section 1102 of the Civil Code. Other statutes require disclosures, depending upon the details of the particular real estate transaction (for example: special study zone and purchase-money liens on residential property).

Substituted Disclosures: The Seller disclosures have or will be in connection with this real estate transfer, and are intended to satisfy the disclosure obligations on this form, where the subject matter is the same: _____
_____
_____

Seller's Information: The Seller discloses the following information with the knowledge that even though this is not a warranty, prospective Buyers may rely on this information in deciding whether and on what terms to purchase the subject property. Seller hereby authorizes any agent(s) representing any principal(s) in this transaction to provide a copy of this statement to any person or entity in connection with any actual or anticipated sale of the property.

The following are representations made by the Seller(s) and are not the representations of the agent(s), if any. This information is a disclosure and is not intended to be part of any contract between the Buyer and Seller. Seller ❏ is ❏ is not occupying the property.

A. The subject property has the items checked below:

❏ Range	❏ Oven	❏ Microwave	❏ Dishwasher	❏ Trash Compactor
❏ Garbage Disposal	❏ W/D Hookups	❏ Window Screens	❏ Rain Gutters	❏ Burglar Alarm
❏ Smoke Detector(s)	❏ Fire Alarm	❏ TV Antenna	❏ Satellite Dish	❏ Intercom
❏ Central Heating	❏ Central Air Conditioning	❏ Evaporators Cooler(s)	❏ Wall/Wind Air Cond.	❏ Sprinklers
❏ Public Sewer System	❏ Septic Tank	❏ Sump Pump	❏ Water Softener	❏ Patio/Decking
❏ Built-in Barbecue	❏ Gazebo	❏ Sauna	❏ Pool	❏ Spa/Hot Tub
❏ Security Gate(s)	❏ Garage Door Opener(s)	❏ Attached Garage	❏ Not Attached Garage	❏ Carport
❏ Pool/Spa Heater—Gas	❏ Pool/Spa Heater—Solar	❏ Pool/Spa Heater—Electric	❏ Water Heater—Gas	❏ Water Heater—Solar
❏ Water Heater—Electric	❏ Water Supply—City	❏ Roof—Age_____	❏ Fireplace	

B. Are you (SELLER) aware of any significant defects/malfunctions: If yes, list/describe:
_____
_____
_____
_____

C. Are you (SELLER) aware of the following:

1. Substances, materials, or products that may be an environmental hazard such as, but not limited to, asbestos, formaldehyde, radon gas, lead-based paint, fuel or chemical storage tanks, and contaminated soil or water on the subject property.	❏ Yes	❏ No
2. Features of the property shared in common with adjoining landowners, such as walls, fences, and driveways, whose use or responsibility for maintenance may have an effect on the subject property	❏ Yes	❏ No
3. Any encroachments, easements, or similar matters that may affect your interest in the subject	❏ Yes	❏ No
4. Room additions, structural modifications, or other alterations or repairs made without necessary permits.	❏ Yes	❏ No
5. Room additions, structural modifications, or other alterations or repairs not in compliance with building codes.	❏ Yes	❏ No
6. Landfill (compacted or otherwise) on the property or any portion thereof.	❏ Yes	❏ No
7. Any settling from any cause, or slippage, sliding, or other spoil problems.	❏ Yes	❏ No
8. Flooding, drainage, or grading problems.	❏ Yes	❏ No
9. Major damage to the property or any of the structures from fire, earthquake, floods, or landslides.	❏ Yes	❏ No
10. Any zoning violations, nonconforming uses, violations of "setback" requirements.	❏ Yes	❏ No
11. Neighborhood noise problems or other nuisances.	❏ Yes	❏ No
12. CC&R's or other deed restrictions or obligations.	❏ Yes	❏ No
13. Homeowners' Association that has any authority over the subject property.	❏ Yes	❏ No
14. Any "common area" (facilities such as pools, tennis courts, walkways, or other areas co-owned in undivided interest with others).	❏ Yes	❏ No
15. Any notice of abatement or citations against the property.	❏ Yes	❏ No
16. Any lawsuits against the seller threatening to or affecting this real property.	❏ Yes	❏ No

Seller certifies that the information herein is true and correct to the best of the Seller's knowledge as of the date signed by the Seller.

Seller:_____   Date:_____

need to be aware that there are certainly better times to buy. Chapters 4 and 6 offer more on this subject.

Most important, buyers need to recognize that throughout their entire home-purchase process, they always should attempt to create win-win situations. An unhappy seller and/or a disgruntled broker or lender can become a major stumbling block to all parties during a home sale. Buyers who are sincere, honest, and direct will most probably experience a very successful transaction with few problems and little frustration.

Understanding the Buying Process

FIGURE 2.1

**PROCESS
OF BUYING
A HOME**

Make a decision to rent or buy.

Figure out how much you can afford.

Decide what kind of home you want.

Most important be
pre-qualified or better yet pre-approved.

Find a good real estate agent.

Find the right neighborhood.

Begin house hunting.

Inspect the homes.

Make an offer.

Apply for a mortgage.

Have the professional
inspections.

Close the transaction.

Move into your home.

Figure 2.1 depicts the process of buying a home. However, in the real world, each of those simple steps will be expanded into a complete process of its own.

It is very important for potential home buyers to understand that a structured plan is necessary for them to achieve the goal of successfully purchasing a home that best suits their needs at the best possible price.

This book will help you formulate and implement your own personal "perfect plan" to purchase a home. That strategy includes:

- Where to start
- How to determine what is right for you
- How to choose a real estate agent
- How to find your specific home
- Understanding proper pricing
- How to view and inspect homes properly
- Understanding financing and terms
- How to choose a lender
- How to make and have an offer accepted
- How to get a home loan
- How to negotiate with agents and sellers
- How to close the transaction
- What must you do after you close the transaction
- How to save money when you buy a home

First, and most important, buyers must understand that in real estate, *everything is negotiable*. If things don't work one way, then try another way and another way and another way, until everyone who is a party to the transaction says, "Yes, I'm happy with the deal!"

◄ FIGURE 2.1 **PROCESS OF BUYING A HOME**

WHEN IS THE BEST TIME TO BUY?

Oh, probably around 3:00 P.M. That way you won't have to get up too early and you'll be done with your purchase before dinnertime. I'm just kidding, I know what you mean. The answer is that there is no best time to buy, but there are better times to buy, just as there are better times to sell.

Almost everyone has heard the terms "buyers' market" and "sellers' market." Basically, these terms mean exactly what they say. A "buyers' market" is a good time to buy; a "sellers' market" is a good time to sell. But what factors help to make either of these markets exist? The following checklist helps to define and compare some of the important aspects of buyers' and sellers' markets.

BUYERS' MARKET	SELLERS' MARKET
High inventory of homes for sale	Lower inventory of homes for sale
Lower interest rates	Lower or reasonable interest rates
Unstable or weak local economy	Strong local economy
Less population influx into the area	High population influx into an area
Lower home prices	Increasing home prices
Narrow area economic base	Diverse area economic base
Decreasing area employment base	Increasing area employment base

Some factors that help to predicate the type of market include: weather; special interest in areas by specific groups of people such as retirees; spiritual affiliations; special recreation availability; artistic activities; or simply a heightened interest in an area.

One very important statistic that buyers need to be aware of is that nationwide, more homes are sold from May through September than are sold in the other seven months of the year. Why? For one thing, weather is generally better in the higher-selling months, so it is easier for potential buyers to be out looking for homes and ultimately to move. Second, families prefer to move when their children are out of school. And third, many sellers have been led to believe that homes sell faster and at a higher price in the summer months, so more homes are offered at this time.

Does this mean that you should wait to buy until it is a buyers' market? The answer is no—unless it is a "hot sellers' market," which means that few homes are for sale, there are very low interest rates, employment is climbing dramatically, and the area's population is growing at an astronomical rate. In that case, a knowledgeable buyer will be able to find a good deal any time of the year and virtually anywhere in the country. So, what does this all mean to you as a potential home buyer? Basically, this information is just a small but integral part of your own "Personal Buying Strategy." After you have finished this book, you will know not just how to buy a home, but how to "buy smart."

Here's an example: Suppose you want to purchase a home in Duluth, Minnesota. Since there probably will be a substantial snow cover in January and February, those months might be a good time to look at homes that are on the market but are not selling quickly (the sellers may be anxious or even desperate because few people are viewing their homes) and to use one or more of the letters from Chapter 16 to contact sellers who have not yet put their homes on the market.

Buyers must learn to use all of the advantages in a sale area to create the most lucrative purchase situation.

> **SMART TIP:**
> Sometimes smart buyers can make a great deal on a property by allowing the sellers to stay there on a rental basis for a specified period of time after the close of the sale. It may be to allow the sellers' children to finish the school year or simply for the weather to improve for ease of access.

HOW MUCH DOWN PAYMENT WILL YOU NEED?

The best answer to this question is somewhere between zero and as much money as you have to use as a down payment.

Yes, there are ways to buy a property with no money down. However, this is not recommended except under special circumstances, which will be explained in Chapter 11.

For the most part, down payments will vary upward from about 3 percent of the sale price. (This would be $3,000 on a $100,000 sale price, plus closing costs, of course.) In some areas, subsidized loans are available with as little as 1 percent down. Generally speaking, the larger the down payment buyers can provide, the better loan they can obtain.

WHAT TYPES OF LOANS AND FINANCING ARE AVAILABLE?

The list of types of loans and financing that are available to potential buyers is almost endless. Unfortunately, most potential home buyers never realize that hundreds of financing options are available on almost every home sold in today's market.

Table 2.1 shows several loans that were available to borrowers in the Pacific Northwest at the time of publication. Note that the higher the down payment, the lower the interest rate. Also, not shown is the fact that the qualification requirements were less stringent for borrowers as the down payments increased.

TABLE 2.1
LOANS AVAILABLE

Type of Loan	Loan Fee (%)	Points	Down Payment (%)	Interest Rate	Term (Years)
Conventional Fixed Rate	½	0	20	8.65	30
Conventional Fixed Rate	1	1	10	9.0	30
Conventional Fixed Rate	1	2	5	9.25	30
Conventional ARM	½	0	20	7.8	30
Conventional ARM	1	1	5	8.25	30
FHA	1	2	3	8.75	30
VA	1	2	0	8.75	30

Chapters 9, 10, 11, 12, 13, and 15 are dedicated to helping you determine the best type of financing available, to help you choose the proper lender, and to guide you through the entire loan process.

WHAT IS THE DIFFERENCE BETWEEN QUALIFYING FOR AND BEING ABLE TO AFFORD A HOME?

Home buyers need to be aware that oftentimes they will qualify *on paper* to purchase a home but may not actually be able to afford the property. As an example, North Carolina home buyers Carol and Mark shared their story with us.

In January of 1993, Carol and Mark had made the decision that, after graduating from college and three years of marriage, they were finally in a position to purchase a home.

The couple had saved nearly $20,000 and both were employed in good, stable positions. They had been renting a two-bedroom house near a lake outside the city where they were employed. Their rent was $750 per month. Both Carol and Mark enjoyed water sports, and they wanted to remain in the same rural area where they currently lived. However, properties were quite expensive near the water, and they had resigned themselves to the fact that they would probably have to move away from the lake.

When the couple applied at the bank where they had done business for almost five years, they were astounded to discover that they qualified for a home loan for as much as $217,000. At the current interest rates of 8 percent, the couple's monthly payments could be as much as $2,100, including principal, interest, taxes, and insurance. Prior to being prequalified, Carol had analyzed their financial position and had determined that they should have payments on a home of no more than $1,500 per month.

When the couple began to look at homes, they quickly discovered that they would have to pay approximately $230,000 for any of the homes in the area where they preferred to live. Carol was stubborn at first and did not want to consider the responsibility of payments of over $2,000 a month.

However, the real estate salesperson with whom the couple had been working convinced them that it would be in their best interest to "Buy as much home as you can possibly qualify for, for two reasons: one, you will have a much nicer house, and, two, the bank knows what they are doing and would not allow you to obtain a loan that you were not capable of repaying."

Unfortunately, the salesperson was Mark's brother, and Mark was insistent that they purchase the large home they really wanted and simply cut back on some of their other expenses. Carol finally agreed.

In October, Mark and Carol moved into their four-bedroom, three-bath, 2,900-square-foot, lakeview home. Closing the transaction took $23,280, so Mark borrowed $3,000 from his parents and agreed to repay the money within a year. The couple, having no money left in their savings, moved themselves with a borrowed truck.

Once these home owners had their possessions in their new house, they realized just how empty the home was. They had three vacant bedrooms, an empty formal dining room, a living room of 24 by 30 feet with only a chair, coffee table, end table, and love seat, numerous blank walls, and many large picture windows without drapes or blinds. There were also beautiful wood floors in three rooms that needed decorative area rugs. Also, the exterior of the home needed landscaping. The home Mark and Carol purchased looked quite different from the beautifully decorated and appointed model home on which they had based their buying decision.

It took Mark and Carol almost two and a half years to completely furnish and decorate the house to their satisfaction. Unfortunately, just after they finished the improvements on the home, Mark was transferred to Atlanta, Georgia. According to the couple, they felt as if they had struggled just to exist in a half-empty home the entire time they owned the property. Both buyers said that in the future, any home they buy will be a home that they can truly afford.

(One caveat to the story is that Mark's brother lasted only eleven months in the real estate business. In Chapter 5 we discuss how to choose the right agent or broker—that person may not turn out to be your brother or your best friend.)

WHAT CLOSING COSTS
WILL YOU HAVE TO PAY?

When you purchase a home, you will be asked to pay certain closing costs in addition to the required down payment.

> **SMART TIP:**
> Everything in a real estate transaction is negotiable. A seller or other parties to the transaction may pay some of the buyer's closing costs—it never hurts to ask.

Who pays certain closing costs varies from area to area through-out the country. What has become customary in an area is usually what the loan representatives and real estate agents assume you should pay. In Chapter 20, you will learn how to negotiate effectively and ultimately pay only the clos-ing costs that are absolutely necessary. For now, the following is an explanation of almost all of the closing costs that usually are asso-ciated with the purchase or sale of the home.

Brokerage Fee

The seller almost always pays the brokerage fee, which usually is somewhere between 5 percent to 7 percent of the sales price of the home. Some exclusive buyers' agents collect a fee from the buyer (or both the buyer and seller); however, this is rare and legally must be disclosed to all parties to the transaction.

Title Insurance
and Title Guarantee

Title insurance and title guarantee are different from most policies in that they are risk-elimination insurance rather than risk-assump-tion coverage. These policies guarantee that new buyers will own their property free of any liens or encumbrances that have not been disclosed by previous sellers. The seller often pays this fee, which is based on the sale price of the home.

Lender Title Insurance Policy

Lender title insurance simply is an additional title insurance policy specifically for and protecting the interest of the lender. The buyer often pays this fee, which is based on the loan amount. It is not required in every state.

Escrow/Closing Fee

The escrow/closing fee is charged by an uninvolved third party (escrow/closing company) to see that all documents, payments, inspections, recordings, and other required actions have been made or completed by all parties. The buyer and the seller usually split this cost evenly; it is based on the sale price of the home.

Subescrow Fee

The subescrow fee is charged to handle payoffs to the lenders or other parties to close the transaction. It is a set fee varying between $100 and $200 and usually is paid by the seller.

Home Warranty

Sellers often pay for a home warranty to encourage the sale of a home; it is always negotiable. The fees vary from approximately $200 to $900 depending on locales, coverage, and terms of coverage.

Home Inspection Fee

Professional inspectors charge to inspect and report on any problem areas that exist in the home. These fees vary from approximately $200 to $900, and are paid by either the buyer or the seller.

Roof Inspection Fee

The roof inspection fee is charged to inspect the roof for damage or necessary repairs. It is always negotiable, but varies from approximately $100 to $250, and is typically paid by the seller.

Termite Inspection Fee

A fee is charged to inspect the home for any termites, rodents, or other infestation, or water damage. (Yes, water damage is one of the main focuses of a termite inspection.) The fee, which varies from approximately $125 to $225, usually is paid by the seller.

Document Preparation Fee

The document preparation fee usually is paid by the party for whom the documents are being prepared and varies from approximately $25 to $100 (often waived upon request).

Recording Fee

The recording fee is charged to record documents at county, parish, state, or federal recording offices. This is usually paid by the party for whom the document is recorded. The fee varies from approximately $5 to $15 per page of the document recorded. (Typical home sale recordings cost approximately $50.)

Tax Service Fee

The tax service fee is charged to change tax records from the name of the sellers to the name of the buyers. The buyers usually pay the fee, which varies from approximately $20 to $50.

Bonds and Assessments

Bonds and assessments will be disclosed in the title report provided for all parties to the transaction. This fee usually is paid by the seller but sometimes is assumed by the buyer. Some bonds or assessments cannot be paid but are levied against the property owners to earn interest on the land or assessment amount.

Attorney Fee

Attorneys are not required to participate in real estate property transactions in most states, so this fee is usually paid by the party requesting the attorney's services. The fee varies in different areas and for the different services performed.

SMART TIP:

For most properties five years old or newer, home inspections or roof inspections are not always necessary. However, in areas where there is more severe weather, natural disasters, or other inclement conditions, these inspections should be done on all homes except new construction. Termite inspections also should be done on all properties except new construction.

Notary Fee

A notary public charges a fee to verify that parties are who they say they are. This fee varies from $5 to $15 per notary.

Lender Fees, Charges, and Required Payments

Although most lender fees, charges, and required payments are usually paid by the buyer, it is not uncommon for a seller to pay some or even all of these charges, especially if a strong buyers' market exists. (However, some lenders require that buyers pay a portion of their own lender fees.)

Points

Points are more appropriately called "discount points." This fee is either a prepayment of interest that increases the return on money loaned by the lending institution, or it may help to pay a mortgage broker who arranges the loan for the lender. Each point is equal to 1 percent of the loan amount. As an example, if you were to obtain a loan of $120,000 and you paid two points to obtain the loan, these points would equal $2,400. If you were paying 9 percent interest on the loan, your actual or true annual percentage rate (APR) would be higher than 9 percent for the first year, because you had prepaid 2 percent to obtain the loan.

> **SMART TIP:**
> The Truth in Lending Law requires that the Annual Percentage Rate (APR) or true interest rate be disclosed to every borrower obtaining a loan. The APR is calculated using the interest rate charged on the loan plus all costs to obtain the loan, spread over the loan term. (Chapter 9 presents a more detailed explanation of APR.)

Loan Origination Fee

The loan origination fee is usually one-half to 1 point of the loan amount (on a $150,000 loan, typically $750 to $1,500). Often a portion of the fee is paid to the loan or sales representative who originates the loan. Many lenders do not charge this fee but instead pay their loan representatives from the points charged.

Loan Application Fee

The loan application fee varies greatly, from $100 to $600. Many lenders lump several charges into one fee that may cover the cost of credit reports, mailing and handling costs for verifications of employment or deposits, property inspections, and even the appraisal fee. Many lenders do not charge this fee but charge individually for the services performed.

Credit Report Fee

A fee of $25 to $125 is charged to obtain credit report. This fee varies in areas and in reporting agencies, but often it is paid up front when the prospective buyers/borrowers complete the loan application.

Appraisal Fee

An appraiser charges to provide a written evaluation and a determination of fair market price for a property. This fee varies per lender and is usually $200 to $400, but some lenders that have appraisers on staff do not charge this fee.

OTHER COSTS TO CLOSE
THE TRANSACTION

Impounds

As a buyer, you may be asked by the lender to pay in advance a portion or all of the first-year premium for your home owner's insurance. (Normally, fire and casualty coverages are required, but most buyers include a liability package with their insurance.)

Home owner's insurance varies in price from company to company. In certain areas of the country, lenders may require special coverages for earthquakes, floods, and the like, which might dramatically increase the cost of the insurance.

Another cost that may be required as an impound (impounds will be discussed later), up-front charge may be a portion of the property taxes owed during the first year of ownership.

Essentially, the lenders do not totally trust the new home owners to keep the taxes and insurance current. With an impound account in place, the lender or a designated escrow agent (sometimes an escrow account is used instead of an impound account) can make the payments for these costs and be sure that they are paid. Taxes vary from area to area, but your real estate professional should be able to give you an estimate of what the taxes will be on properties in your area.

Each month as the home owners make their payments, if the taxes and insurance are included in these payments, the amount designated for this will be paid into the impound account. This will keep the amount in the account sufficient at all times to pay any tax or insurance bills that are due. If home buyers put less than 20 percent down on the purchase of their property, most lenders will require impounds to be collected. Conversely, if home buyers put 20 percent or more down on their property, impounds probably will not be required and the home owners will be responsible to keep their taxes and insurance current on their own.

Mutual Mortgage Insurance (MMI)
for Government Insured Loans
and
Mortgage Insurance Premium (MIP)
for Conventional Loans

MMI and MIP are required by the lender to ensure that the home buyers/borrowers do not default on their loan. The cost for this coverage is between ¼ to ½ percent additional interest rate. (If your interest rate was 8 percent and ¼ percent was added for MIP, your principal, interest, and MIP payments would be based on the rate of 8.25 percent.)

SMART TIP:

MMI and MIP usually are required only when a buyer puts less than 20 percent down. Often the costs can be cancelled when home owners can prove with an appraisal that they have (through payments and appreciation) accumulated at least 20 percent equity in their property. Home owners must file a written request with their lender when they wish to have the coverage cancelled.

Prepaid Interest

Most lenders require and collect a portion of a month's interest to be paid when the transaction is closed. (As an example, on a $150,000 loan at 8.75 percent, 15 days' interest would be $531.25.)

Remember, all closing costs are negotiable and buyers should not be afraid to ask for the charges to be reduced.

Chapter 20 includes many ways for borrowers to save money when they are purchasing a home, and while they own the home.

> **SMART TIP:**
> In the United States, interest is collected by lenders in arrears (and paid in arrears by borrowers). In other words, you are given a loan on the first of the month; at the end of that month, you owe one month's interest on the loan. Therefore, if your transaction closed on May 15 and your first payment was to be made July 1, the lender would require you to pay, up front, the 15 days' interest (May 15 to June 1). Your July 1 payment would include the interest owing in June. In Canada and many other countries, interest is paid in advance; therefore, a June 1 payment would include interest for June.

HOW TO AVOID THE MOST COMMON MISTAKES MADE BY BUYERS

Undoubtedly, the most common mistakes made by potential home buyers are:

- Failing to be prequalified before they begin looking for a home
- Being unrealistic about the properties they can afford and being willing only to accept their "dream home"
- Failing to spend enough time in a community or neighborhood to determine if the area is a:
    a. good place to invest both time and money
    b. place where they will be content for a substantial term of ownership
- Buying strictly on emotion and not basing their buying decision on a combination of factual data and personal desires
- Failing to negotiate effectively all of the factors involved in their home purchase

- Failing to inspect the property properly before making an offer

Now let's look at solution-oriented approaches to avoid these common mistakes.

Problem 1: Failing to be prequalified before looking for a home.
Solution: Before you ever start looking at homes or talking with real estate salespeople, spend the time to go through a formal qualification process with one to three reputable lenders in the area where you will be buying.

This will identify for you the amounts of loans you can obtain and will help you to understand the different methods you may have to employ to be able to purchase a property.

As an example, potential buyers may discover that their credit report has a number of derogatories (late payments, etc.) that cannot be explained to a lender's satisfaction. The buyers may be forced to use alternative purchasing methods, such as a seller carry-back loan or a short-term bridge loan, until they can correct the credit history.

Knowing this information before starting your home search can save all parties to the transaction a great amount of time when properties are viewed and offers are submitted. Also, if potential buyers know exactly how much home they can purchase, they will not make the mistake of looking at and desiring homes that they cannot afford to buy.

Problem 2: Being unrealistic about the homes you might accept and being willing only to accept your "dream home."
Solution: Determine what you "want" and what you "need" in a home. Many potential home buyers tend to start their home search by driving around neighborhoods, finding the area and the homes that they like before they ever determine in which areas they can actually afford to buy.

As indicated in the solution to the last problem, buyers who first go through a formal prequalification process will eliminate part of the "dream home" problem.

After potential home buyers have been prequalified, a good start in their home search is to simply make a list (nothing fancy, just a letter-size piece of paper with a line drawn down the center of the page). At the top left should be written: What we "need" in a home. And the top right should read: What we "want" to have in a home.

The illustration below shows one potential home buyer's "needs" and "wants" list.

FIGURE 2.2
NEEDS AND WANTS CHECKLIST

WHAT WE **NEED** IN A HOME.	WHAT WE **WANT** IN A HOME.
☐ ~~Two bedrooms~~	☐ Quiet street
☐ Walk to elementary school	☐ Two-car garage
☐ Walk to grocery shopping	☐ Large master bedroom
☐ 15 minutes to town	☐ Dining room
☐ Fenced back yard	☐ Nice front yard
☐ One-car garage	☐ Boat parking
☐ Bright; not dark	☐ Room to add on
☐ Lots of closet space	☐ ~~Three bedrooms~~
☐ Three bedrooms	☐ ~~Two baths~~
☐ Two baths	☐ _____
☐ _____	☐ _____
☐ _____	☐ _____
☐ _____	☐ _____

The information from this list should be transferred to the Home Search Checklist when you begin looking at specific properties. (A Home Search Checklist can be found in the Appendix.)

As you can see, these home buyers were realistic with regard to what they needed in the home, as opposed to what they would like to have.

Note that during this hypothetical couple's home search, they made one change: moving the third bedroom and second bath from the "want" side to the "need" side. This change occurred during their home-buying process when it was discovered that the couple was expecting another child. Therefore, they felt the third bedroom and second bathroom became a necessity rather that just a desired item. Also note that the family has only one car, so the wife wanted to be within walking distance of shopping and elementary schools.

Remember, even during your buying process, your needs and wants can change. For this reason, it is critical that you maintain good communication with your real estate professional.

Most home purchasers are not nearly as realistic as our example couple. Buyers who are caught up in the "dream home" syndrome almost never find the home for which they are searching.

Problem 3: Failing to spend enough time in a community or neighborhood to determine if the area is a place to invest both your time and your money and where you will be happy for a substantial period of time.

Solution: First, buyers should be very positive about the neighborhood in which the home that they are interested in is located. Then they should be completely satisfied with the home they are considering before an offer is prepared.

Buyers often make the mistake of viewing a home only once or twice before making an offer. A community or neighborhood may change dramatically, seeming very quiet and appealing during the day, but becoming a very troubled area at night. Buyers need to make sure that they get an around-the-clock, twenty-four-hour view of a neighborhood.

In my seminars, I get quite a laugh when I suggest that buyers should stay up until midnight at least one Friday and Saturday night and drive through the neighborhood where they are considering purchasing a home. However, many times buyers have written to me months later to thank me for that suggestion. Streets that were empty during the day turned into race-tracks for teenage cruisers at night, and silent homes had been transformed into party locations.

As a potential home buyer, make sure that you see the home and the neighborhood a minimum of five to six times before making an offer. Remember, get the "twenty-four-hour view!"

Problem 4: Buying strictly on emotion and not basing your buying decision on a combination of factual data and personal desires.

Solution: Buyers need to go back to their original "needs and wants" list and attempt to find some factual justification for that particular home purchase. Buyers will sometimes see a home and it will be "love at first sight." The home may be overpriced, in a questionable neighborhood, and may not have the amenities and features that the buyers want and need, but, for some unknown reason, buyers become unrealistic and feel they must purchase that home.

When this happens, buyers also must learn to trust the professionals who are assisting with the purchase. These individuals have experience and can give buyers insight into transactions where other buyers have made the same mistake.

Problem 5: Failing to negotiate effectively all of the factors involved in your home purchase.

Solution: Often novice home buyers contact only For Sale by Owner (FSBO) property owners, thinking that they will get a better deal if real estate brokers are not involved. Unfortunately, most buyers do not have the experience or the ability to effectively negotiate the many factors that must be considered in a real property purchase. Make sure you have the capability to negotiate effectively or utilize the services of a real estate professional.

Buyers who negotiate their own transactions often find that they have forgotten many important items after the deal has already closed. Buyers must remember that because they are a party to the transaction, their emotions will play a great part in their dealings with the sellers.

An old adage from the legal field is very appropriate in home buying: "An attorney who represents himself often has a fool for a client."

Problem 6: Failing to inspect a property properly before making an offer.

Solution: Buyers can alleviate many problem situations by utilizing the information and forms in this book to inspect a home properly. Then, when they make an offer, it will contain a clause indicating that it is conditional upon the home passing certain professional inspections, such as termite, roof, and formal home inspection.

Unfortunately, most buyers and many real estate salespeople do not know how to inspect a home properly. Buyers must examine homes completely and systematically before making an offer.

Buyers should also request a complete Seller Disclosure Statement prior to making an offer on a property. Figure 1.1 is a sample statement. (Almost every state has its own Seller Disclosure Forms. Use the form that is customary for your area. Most real estate brokers have these forms available.)

> **SMART TIP:**
> By utilizing the services of an experienced professional real estate agent or broker, buyers dramatically minimize their chances of making any of the six most common mistakes.

DO YOU NEED A REAL ESTATE AGENT?

No . . . you don't need *just* a real estate agent. What you need is an experienced, honest, ethical, and well-qualified real estate professional who has the ability and expertise to help you obtain the home that you desire at the very best possible price.

As I say throughout this book: In the real estate field (just as in every other field), some salespeople are very good, some are fair, and

> **SMART TIP:**
> In most cases, buyers are better off using the services of a real estate agent or broker. In most purchases, the seller of a property will pay the commission.

some are not so good. You must take the time to choose an agent or broker who will do the best job for your individual needs.

DO YOU NEED AN ATTORNEY?

In most states, you are not required to have an attorney participate in a standard real property transaction. However, if the transaction is abnormal in any way, an attorney should examine the paperwork to make sure that all parties are protected.

Some examples of situations where it might be wise to seek approval of the transaction by an attorney might be on:

Seller carry-back purchases
Subordination clause transactions
Title problems on the property
Special liens against the seller
Any transactions out of the ordinary

If you do use the services of an attorney, make sure that he or she is well versed in real estate transactions. Lawyers tend to avoid saying "I don't know." Contact another attorney if you have any indication that one isn't experienced in this area.

CHAPTER THREE

Where Do You Start?

Serious potential home buyers should start their home search not by looking at homes but by examining their own financial position. They should look at their gross income, their net income, their discretionary income, their expenses . . . and ultimately their net worth.

Over 99 percent of home buyers and 99.6 percent of first-time home buyers obtain a home loan. Therefore, it is imperative that home buyers evaluate their overall financial position before they take any action toward purchasing a home. Also, buyers need to be aware of exactly how much down payment is required for their loan for lenders to consider them as a good lending risk.

CALCULATING YOUR FINANCIAL POSITION

The personal Net Worth Calculation Sheet in Figure 3.1 will help you evaluate your overall financial position. If you want help in working with the calculations, your agent or loan officer can help you prepare your financial evaluation.

Remember, it is important to show financial stability when you apply for a home loan. In some cases, if you have a high-debt ratio, your net worth may be a negative figure. Don't panic! You may still be able to buy a home, but you may have to be a little more creative in your financing.

FIGURE 3.1

NET WORTH CALCULATION SHEET

Assets	Value	Debts	Amount owing
1. _____ _____		1. _____ _____	
2. _____ _____		2. _____ _____	
3. _____ _____		3. _____ _____	
4. _____ _____		4. _____ _____	
5. _____ _____		5. _____ _____	
6. _____ _____		6. _____ _____	
7. _____ _____		7. _____ _____	
8. _____ _____		8. _____ _____	
9. _____ _____		9. _____ _____	
10. _____ _____		10. _____ _____	
Total $ _____		Total $ _____	

Subtract *Debts* from *Assets* to determine **Net Worth**   **Net Worth** $ _____

FIGURING YOUR INCOME AND EXPENSES

Income

Most lenders will ask for your last two years' tax returns to verify the income that you have claimed. Lenders also may ask for current paycheck stubs to verify that your income has remained stable.

The first question many buyers ask is: For qualification purposes, can I count all of my income, including alimony, child support, second-job income, bonuses, commissions, money I make at the racetrack (what?), interest income, returns from stocks and bonds, income from trusts set up for you by your long deceased aunt . . . in other words, can I count it all?

Basically, all income that is consistent and can be verified and/or shows on your tax returns will be counted for qualification purposes. Some important points to remember when considering income claimed for qualification are:

- All of the borrowers' income may be included. (If two unmarried people are purchasing a property, the borrowers may have to show some stability or history as codwellers.)
- Lenders are looking for consistent verifiable income. For example, if you are a self-employed book writer, lenders will want to see at least two years (maybe more) of consistent income from royalties to consider those monies.
- If you have changed jobs in the past two years, but you have remained in the same industry, most lenders will consider that a stable employment history.
- If you are recently out of college, lenders will probably qualify you on your current income; however, they will consider your future earning potential when they look at

> **SMART TIP:**
> You can't have it both ways! If your work involves any activity in which you are paid cash (tips, sales of crafts, etc.) or you earn money from activities such as gambling and you *do not* claim the income on your taxes, lenders will not consider any of your nontaxed income for qualification. (Not to mention the fact that you are committing fraud on your tax returns, which could alleviate your need for a place to live if you get caught.)

your overall financial picture. Professionals such as doctors and lawyers may sometimes use their future anticipated income increases for a larger loan (if those income increases are verifiable).

- If you are self-employed, lenders may require more than two years' tax returns to verify consistent income. Self-employed income (for qualification purposes) is only that income on which you paid taxes. In other words, if your business grossed $1,000,000, but with all of your deductions you paid taxes only on $50,000, the lender would base your loan qualification on the $50,000.

- Commission or bonus incomes must be consistent to be included. If your commission or bonuses have continually increased over a two-year period, the lender may average the income for qualification.

> **SMART TIP:**
> Some deductions, such as depreciation on real or personal property, may be included in borrowers' income for qualification. These deductions are allowable but are only paper write-offs, not actual money out of pocket.

- If you claim alimony or child support as part of your income, you will need to provide a divorce or separation decree or statement that shows the income you receive and for what period of time you will receive it. Lenders may require that this income, if not shown on your tax returns, be verified with copies of your bank deposit records, a letter from the ex-spouse, or, in some cases, even copies of the actual canceled checks. (If this is required, it helps to be on good terms with the ex-spouse.) Child support does not have to be claimed as income by the recipient, because the person paying the child support is responsible for the tax liability.

- Income from part-time or seasonal jobs can be counted for qualification, again, if that income is consistent and is included on your tax returns.

Expenses

Generally, lenders are as interested in the borrowers' debts as they are in the borrowers' income. Debts include payments the borrowers must make consistently for cars, department store charge purchases, credit cards, child support, other college or education loans, boat payments . . . in other words, anything the borrowers must pay each month as a contracted or semicontracted obligation. Some lenders even include monthly expenses for utilities as part of the debt calculation (mostly on government-insured or guaranteed loans, such as Federal Housing Administration).

> **SMART TIP:**
>
> Most lenders do not count in your debt calculation any debts with payments of ten months or less left to retire the debt. An example might be a borrower who has a car payment of $200 per month and a loan balance of only $1,000. Only five monthly payments are left on the loan. If the same borrower had a loan balance of $2,400 or twelve months left to pay, it might be a good idea for him or her to pay an extra $600 toward the principal of the debt, thereby reducing the amount owed to $1,800 and shortening the term of the loan to nine months. In most cases, a potential lender would not count that debt for qualification purposes.

UNDERSTANDING THE HOUSING EXPENSE AND DEBT-TO-INCOME RATIOS

Lenders use two corresponding calculations: the *housing expense ratio* and the *debt-to-income ratio* to determine the loan amount that a home buyer may obtain.

The housing expense ratio is determined by dividing the monthly house payment (principal, interest, taxes, and insurance) by the borrowers' gross monthly income.

As an example, if borrowers have a monthly payment of $1,162 and their gross monthly income is $4,150 (1,162 ÷ 4,150 = .28 or 28 percent), the borrowers' housing expense ratio would be 28 percent, which is exactly the ratio that most lenders like to see.

An example of debt-to-income ratio is if the borrowers had monthly debts, including credit cards, car payments, alimony, and a house payment of $1,660 (1,660 ÷ 4,150 = 40 percent), the borrowers' debt-to-income ratio of 40 percent would be slightly higher than the 38 percent that most conventional lenders prefer.

With a ratio of 28 percent housing expense, a 40 percent debt-to-income ratio, a good credit report, and an acceptable property and appraisal, a lender probably would be willing to make this loan.

For the most part, conventional lenders like to see ratios of no more than 28 percent housing expense and 38 percent debt-to-income. With Federal Housing Administration (FHA) and the Department of Veteran's Affairs (VA) loans (government-guaranteed or insured loans), lenders usually allow ratios to be slightly higher. Their suggested ratios are 29 percent housing expense and 41 percent debt-to-income.

Lenders often refer to the expense ratio as the "front" or "front end" ratio; the debt-to-income ratio is referred to as the "back" or "back end" ratio.

WHAT FACTORS
CAN CAUSE LENDERS
TO VARY RATIOS?

A substantial down payment is probably the strongest factor in the variance of ratios by lenders. A borrower who has 20 percent or more of the purchase price as a down payment on a property would have a much better chance of a loan approval (with 30 percent/40 percent ratios) as opposed to a borrower with 5 percent of the purchase price down and the same ratios.

Another factor that can cause lenders to be more lenient with regard to ratios is a borrower's proven track record of substantial savings. For instance, suppose a borrower had a gross monthly income of $3,500, a housing expense ratio of 30 percent, a debt-to-income ratio of 42 percent, and a 10 percent down payment; this borrower's financial position would appear weak. However, if we factor in that the borrower has consistently saved $1,000 per month for over fifteen months, the picture changes considerably. Lenders want to see a consistent record of a borrower's ability to repay the loan.

Another factor that causes lenders to vary their ratios is the exorbitant cost of property in some areas. Potential buyers in New York City or San Francisco would have little or no chance of ever qualifying at the 28%/38% ratios unless they had a six-figure income and a 30 percent down payment.

CALCULATING YOUR OWN RATIOS AND BORROWING POWER

Calculating Income

Use the form in Figure 3.2 to calculate your gross monthly income and your gross annual income. Please note that the form starts off using *annual income* figures. An example is followed by a blank form for your use.

FIGURE 3.2

GROSS MONTHLY INCOME

TYPE OF INCOME	BORROWER	CO-BORROWER
Base Salary *(Monthly Salary x 12)*	$44,000	$29,000
Commission (Monthly Commission x 12)	$4,000	0
Bonuses	0	$1,000
Interest and Dividends	$320	$320
Child Support *(Monthly x 12)*	0	0
Alimony *(Monthly x 12)*	0	0
Tips/Extra Income *(Monthly x 12)*	0	0
Trust *(Other Income)*	0	$1,000
Other Income	0	0
TOTAL	$48,320	$31,320

Borrower Total ($48,320) + Co-Borrower Total ($31,320) = $ 79,640
Gross Annual Income = $ 79,640
Gross Monthly Income = $79,640 ÷ 12 = $ 6,637

(rounded to the nearest dollar)

FIGURE 3.2a
GROSS MONTHLY INCOME

Type of Income	Borrower	Co-Borrower
Base Salary *(Monthly Salary x 12)*	$_____	$_____
Commission (Monthly Commission x 12)	$_____	$_____
Bonuses	$_____	$_____
Interest and Dividends	$_____	$_____
Child Support *(Monthly x 12)*	$_____	$_____
Alimony *(Monthly x 12)*	$_____	$_____
Tips/Extra Income *(Monthly x 12)*	$_____	$_____
Trust *(Other Income)*	$_____	$_____
Other Income	$_____	$_____
TOTAL	$_____	$_____

Borrower Total ($) + Co-Borrower Total ($) = $_____

Gross Annual Income   = $_____

Gross Monthly Income = $ ÷ 12   = $_____

(rounded to the nearest dollar)

Next use the following forms to calculate your debts and expenses. Figure 3.3 provides an example; Figure 3.4 is for your use.

FIGURE 3.3
MONTHLY DEBTS AND EXPENSES
(all Debts with 10 months or more to pay)

DEBTS & EXPENSES	BORROWER	CO-BORROWER
1. Cars	$338	$185
2. Furniture	0	0
3. Credit Card	$80	0
4. Credit Card	0	0
5. Credit Card	0	0
6. Credit Card	0	0
7. Credit Card	0	0
8. Personal Loans	0	0
9. Student Loans	$125	$100
10. Alimony	0	0
11. Child Support	0	0
12. Boat	$140	0
TOTAL	$683	$ 285
Borrower Total ($683) + Co-Borrower Total ($285) =		$968
Total Monthly Debts	=	$968

FIGURE 3.4
MONTHLY DEBTS AND EXPENSES
(all Debts with 10 months or more to pay)

DEBTS & EXPENSES	BORROWER	CO-BORROWER
1.	$_____	$_____
2.	$_____	$_____
3.	$_____	$_____
4.	$_____	$_____
5.	$_____	$_____
6.	$_____	$_____
7.	$_____	$_____
8.	$_____	$_____
9.	$_____	$_____
10.	$_____	$_____
11.	$_____	$_____
12.	$_____	$_____
TOTAL	$_____	$_____

Borrower Total ($_____) + Co-Borrower Total ($_____) = $_____

Total Monthly Debts = $_____

Next check your borrowing ratios by using the acceptable figures of 28 percent for housing expenses and 38 percent for debt-to-income. Figure 3.5 is an example using the figures for the previous borrowers; Figure 3.6 is a blank form for your own use.

FIGURE 3.5

HOUSING EXPENSES AND DEBT-TO-INCOME RATIO CALCULATION CHART

FRONT END CALCULATION

1.	**$6,637** Gross Monthly Income	x	**.28 or 28%** Suggested Housing Expense Percentage	=	**$1,858** Suggested Monthly House Payment (PITI)
2.	**$6,637** Gross Monthly Income	–	**$968** Monthly Debt Payments	=	**$5,669** Gross Monthly Income Less Debts

DEBT-TO-INCOME RATIO

BACK END CALCULATION

3.	**$1,858** Suggested Monthly House Payment (PITI)	÷	**$5,669** Gross Monthly Income Less Debts	=	**.33 or 33%** Debt-to-Income Ratio

Now, what does all of this mean with regard to your own personal borrowing power? First, you must realize that the more debt you have, the less loan you will qualify for with commercial lenders. Second, there are so many ways to buy a home that even if you are over the recommended debt-to-income ratios, most probably you will still be able to buy in some way. You may need to use some other type of alternative financing. (See Chapter 11 for alternative financing methods.)

FIGURE 3.6

HOUSING EXPENSES AND DEBT-TO-INCOME RATIO CALCULATION CHART

FRONT END CALCULATION

1. $_____$ x   .28 or 28%   = $_____$
    Gross   Suggested   Suggested
    Monthly   Housing Expense   Monthly House
    Income   Percentage   Payment (PITI)

2. $_____$ – $_____$ = $_____$
    Gross   Monthly   Gross Monthly
    Monthly   Debt   Income
    Income   Payments   Less Debts

DEBT-TO-INCOME RATIO
BACK END CALCULATION

3. $_____$ ÷ $_____$ =   ._____ or ____%
    Suggested   Gross Monthly   Debt-to-Income
    Monthly House Income   Ratio
    Payment (PITI) Less Debts

IN WHAT PRICE RANGES SHOULD YOU BE LOOKING?

Before you begin looking at specific homes, it is best to be prequal-ified (which is covered in the next section of this chapter). Howev-er, a good method to determine the average price of homes at which you should be looking is as follows:

Home Price Estimate
Calculation

1. Calculate your gross monthly income.
2. Subtract your monthly debt payments that will run ten months or more.
3. Calculate your gross annual income less expenses (the answer to #2) x 12.
4. Multiply your annual income less expenses (answer to #3) x 3.
5. Determine your down payment. Add the amount that you have decided will be used as a down payment.
6. Add your down payment to your answer to #4.

This figure gives you the approximate price of homes for which you should qualify, assuming you obtain a fixed-rate loan at 8.5 percent amortized for 30 years.

For each ½ percent upward variance in interest rates, you can deduct 4 percent from the estimated purchase price. For each ½ percent downward variance in interest rates, you can add 4 percent to the estimated purchase price.

Next is an example of the home price estimate using a gross monthly income of $6,637 and monthly debts of $968.

Home Price Estimate
Calculation

1. Gross monthly income = $6,637
2. $6,637 – $968 = $5,669 Gross monthly income less debts
3. $5,669 x 12 = $68,028 Gross annual income less debts
4. $68,028 x 3 = $204,080 Approximate amount of loan available
5. $204,084 ÷ .90 (90%) = $226,760 x 10% down = $23,000 down payment
6. $204,084 + $23,000 (approximately 10%) = $227,084

In this example, the buyers should limit their search to homes costing approximately $227,084.

CALCULATING MONTHLY PAYMENTS

The amortization chart in Table 3.1 will help you determine monthly payments required to fully *amortize* a loan (i.e., to pay off the loan in incremental payments). To use the chart, multiply the payment amount per thousand times the number of thousands in the loan.

TABLE 3.1

PAYMENT AMORTIZATION TABLE

Payment Amount Per Thousand[a]

INTEREST RATE[b]	30-YEAR	25-YEAR	20-YEAR	15-YEAR
7	6.65	7.07	7.75	8.99
7.5	6.99	7.39	8.06	9.27
8	7.34	7.72	8.36	9.56
8.5	7.69	8.05	8.68	9.85
9	8.05	8.39	9.00	10.14
9.5	8.41	8.74	9.32	10.44
10	8.78	9.09	9.65	10.75
10.5	9.15	9.44	9.98	11.05
11	9.52	9.80	10.32	11.37
11.5	9.90	10.16	10.66	11.68
12	10.29	10.53	11.01	12.00

[a] Payment amounts per thousand are rounded to two decimals to save space; therefore, your actual payment may vary by a few cents when it is calculated by your lender.
[b] Interest rates are shown only in ½% increments. If your actual is an odd figure, your lender or your real estate agent can calculate the exact payment for you.

For example:

$125,500, 30-year amortization, 8% interest
Read across the top of the table to 30 years.
Slide down the left side of the table to 8%.
Find where the two meet at 7.34.
Multiply 125.5 (number of thousands) by 7.34 (amount per thousand) = $921.17
    amortized monthly payment.

SHOULD YOU
FORMALLY PREQUALIFY?

In a word . . . absolutely!

Buyers should be formally prequalified before they ever begin to look at properties. Unfortunately, many potential buyers begin their home search process by allowing a real estate salesperson to "guesstimate" their purchasing power. The buyers then find the home in which they are interested and make an offer, then the offer is accepted. The purchase is conditioned on the buyers qualifying for and obtaining a loan. The sellers are overjoyed. The agent thinks he or she has earned a nice commission, and the buyers are ecstatic because they think they have fulfilled a lifelong dream of home ownership. However, in too many cases, all of this exuberance soon turns to dismay when the buyers are told that they do not qualify for a loan amount large enough to purchase the home.

PREAPPROVED vs. PREQUALIFIED

Many lenders offer some type of prequalification written certificate that shows the loan amount for which the buyers have been preapproved. Buyers with a written preapproval are in a much better bargaining position with sellers and agents than buyers who are guessing at their buying power.

HOW DOES THE PREAPPROVAL
PROCESS WORK?

Potential buyers who wish to be formally prequalified and obtain a written preapproval certificate must go through almost the entire loan application process just as if they were obtaining a loan for a specific home. This process includes the application, the credit report, bank statements, deposit and employment verifications, examination of tax returns by the lender, and so on. In other words, once the written preapproval is complete, the potential borrowers practically have a check waiting for them. (This, of course, is subject to the lender's appraisal and approval of the subject property.)

Some lenders have a phone service whereby potential buyers can call to qualify for "loan-by-telephone" approval. Buyers can learn a great deal about the products and services offered by their local lenders simply by spending a couple of hours on the phone calling several lenders. (The proper questions to ask these lenders is covered in detail in Chapter 12.)

HOW CAN YOU CHECK YOUR OWN CREDIT?

Credit reports are available to all consumers who request a copy and pay the required fee (usually less than $25). You must make your request in writing and must include your name, present and past addresses, date of birth, and social security number. You also may be asked to provide a copy of other types of identification, such as your birth certificate, driver's license, immigration certificate, or passport.

UNDERSTANDING A CREDIT REPORT

SMART TIP:

Credit reports are accessible to consumers under federal law. If you have been refused credit based on information obtained from a credit report, the reporting agency must provide a copy for you upon your request at no charge. Local credit reporting agencies are usually affiliated with major national companies, such as:

TRW	Equifax
P.O. Box 2350	P.O. Box 740241
Chatsworth, CA	Atlanta, GA
91313	30374
1-800-682-7654	1-800-685-1111

Either of these companies will provide a copy of your credit report, sometimes at no charge.

You must examine your credit report carefully when you receive it from the reporting agency. Check the report for the proper information and be sure that there are no mistakes that could preclude you from receiving a loan. Figure 3.7 is a simplified credit report. Take a few minutes to acquaint yourself with the information contained in it.

FIGURE 3.7 **CREDIT REPORT**

TERRY EILERS

Allreport Credit Corporation
275 South Street
Anywhere, USA 26161
(800)123-4567

Report #: 0037161   Date: 02/01/97

Report Requested By: Easy Loan and Mortagage
1217 Overland Street
Anywhere, USA 26161
(800)789-8998

Applicant #1:	John Jones	SS#:	573-32-6113	DOB:	2/16/61
Applicant #2:	Mary Jones	SS#:	514-37-8616	DOB:	5/14/62
Address:	1246 Almond	Marital Status:	M	Dependents:	2
Term: 2	Anywhere, USA 26161	Housing Status:	R		
Previous Address:	806 Flower Street				
Term: 1	Anywhere, USA 26161				

Applicant #1		Applicant #2	
Employer:	GTE	Employer:	Alta Guides
Position:	Lineman	Position:	Dog Trainer
Term:	4	Term:	5
Verified By:	Patty Olivier	Verified By:	John Key
Income:	Refused	Income:	Refused
Previous Position:	Line Asst.	Previous Position:	N/A
Term:	3	Term:	N/A

Creditor	Report Date	Open Date	Type	Balance	High Balance	Payment Amount	Times Past Due	Payment Status
Macy's	3/1	2/88	CH 6	455	2762	Revolving	001	As Agreed
Killians	3/1	2/92	CH 6	210	640	Revolving	000	As Agreed
Charge Card	3/1	1/89	CH 6	964	3480	Revolving	000	As Agreed
Arco	3/1	2/90	I	340	6680	340	000	As Agreed
Charge Card II	3/1	3/92	CH 6	190	600	Revolving	000	As Agreed

Collections:	Date Filed	Amount	Status
TRI-AP Medical Corp	2/90	4,700	Paid 5/90

Inquiries Past 90 days:	Date:
Eastern Bank	1/96
End	

As you can see, even this simplified version of a credit report contains a great deal of information. The following is a brief description of each section of the report.

Report #: This is an assigned number that is used to refer to your information.

Report Requested By: This is the name of company or individual requesting report.

Income (under application section): Often, on credit reports, the income will be indicated as "refused." Due to the Right to Privacy Act, many employers will not supply income unless a separate verification of income, signed by the applicant, is submitted.

Creditor: The entity that has given the credit to the applicant. The sample report contains five creditors, which appear to be two department stores, two credit cards, and a bank loan that was probably a personal or car loan.

Report Date: The date the credit bureau obtained the information.

Open Date: The date the account was opened.

Type: The type of account. "CHG" usually means a revolving charge account, such as credit cards or department store accounts. "I" means an installment debt. In many states, real estate loans do not show on credit reports unless they have gone to collection or foreclosure.

Balance: The current balance of the debt.

High Balance: The amount of the debt at its highest balance.

Payment Amount: The set amount of the monthly payment or "Revolving" if the payment amount changes based on the balance.

Times Past Due: The number of times the payment on the debt has been late. As you can see by the example, these applicants have been late only once on any of the debts.

Payment Status: What the current payment status of the debt is.

Collections: Any debt that has been referred to a collection agency. Often collections by a hospital or medical agency indicate the applicant had a large medical expense and possibly no health insurance. On the sample report it is noted that payment of the debt was made in full; however, this could still reflect badly on the applicant's credit history.

Inquiries: This section indicates who has requested the applicant's credit report in the last ninety days. If the applicant had applied for credit, it would show in this section. Multiple inquiries might indicate that the applicant has applied for credit numerous times.

HOW TO WORK AROUND OR CORRECT PAST CREDIT PROBLEMS

If you have what are referred to as "derogatories"—slow payments, collections, and the like—on your credit report, you should explain or correct those problems as quickly as possible.

Sometimes a letter of explanation will give your lender reason enough to overlook a minor problem. Make sure the letter details and explains fully why the situation occurred and, most important, why it will not occur again.

If you have a poor payment record because you are constantly struggling to pay your bills, it might be a good idea to get some professional help. Consumer Credit Counseling Services is a nationwide, nonprofit organization that provides excellent credit counseling either free or at a reasonable cost. To contact this organization call 1-800-388-2227. Other organizations in your city may provide credit counseling services. Look in your local yellow pages under "Credit Counseling."

Lenders may have problems with borrowers who have little or no credit. If this is your case, you may have to use your payment history on rent, utility bills, or unrecorded credit accounts. You should supply the lender with canceled checks and letters from creditors indicating the consistency of payments.

MISTAKES ON YOUR CREDIT REPORT

If you discover mistakes on your credit report (this is not uncommon), take action to correct them as soon as possible. Contact the credit reporting agency and obtain the information on the creditor who has filed the credit discrepancy. Contact the creditor directly and fix the problem immediately.

SOME TIPS ON CREDIT

- Avoid making large credit purchases, such as cars or boats, until *after* you have purchased a home. The large payment obligations may preclude you from qualifying for your home loan.
- Always be aware of your credit balances, specific charges, and payment records.
- Avoid skipping payments. If you cannot make payments consistently, get some help and get back on track.
- Contact creditors immediately if you have a problem. Do not wait!
- Start saving money on a regular basis. Try to put away at least three months' income in case you have a financial emergency.

SPECIAL CREDIT PROBLEMS

If you have numerous credit problems, late payments, and generally a bad credit report, this derogatory information will stay on your credit report for seven years. If you file bankruptcy, it will be reported on your record for ten years. After the specified periods, the derogatory information should drop off your record automatically. However, sometimes consumers must contact the credit bureau and see that the adverse information has been deleted.

CHAPTER FOUR

Finding the Right Home for You

As mentioned briefly in the last chapter, buyers who want to obtain the right home for the right price and the right terms should begin with a specific and exact plan. In this chapter I help you identify and analyze many of the aspects that should be included in that strategy.

WHAT ARE YOUR MOTIVATIONS FOR BUYING?

Do you need more space? Are you buying primarily for the financial rewards? Are you just tired of paying for and taking care of someone else's property? Is this a forced move due to a transfer?

After you have established your motivations for buying, you must identify how quickly you need to accomplish your home purchase. Keep in mind that your motivations for moving will play a major role in your decisions about the homes you will consider and the home you will ultimately purchase.

Buyers who are transferred to a new locale and given a week to find a home and a month to move may not be able to take the time to search for the perfect home. Urgency can play a great part in your home purchase.

PLANNING FOR NOW AND TOMORROW

If you are like most buyers, you will make your purchase based on the thought of owning and living in this home for a long period of time. However, the average term of the home ownership nationwide is only approximately seven years. When you are preparing to purchase a home, you must do your best to identify what your needs and wants will be during the home ownership period. Keep in mind that your family may grow or shrink in size, and your requirements for a home may change dramatically. In other words, what is your plan for the next two, five, seven, or ten years, and will the home you are considering fit with that plan?

Some buyers will purchase with the idea of possibly remodeling a home in the future and will accept a home that barely meets their needs. More times than not, these buyers never complete the remodeling plans and end up selling and then purchasing another property more suited to their family's changing needs. This purchase and the move is often more costly than if they'd bought a more appropriate property to begin with. Buyers who purchase a home hoping to remodel in the future often discover that the cost of the remodel is more than was anticipated, and it is almost impossible to recover the expense when the home is sold.

Figure 4.1 shows how much you can expect to recover of the total cost of each type of remodeling once you sell your home.

FIGURE 4.1
THE VALUE VS. THE COST OF REMODELING

Types of Change	% Estimates of Cost Added to Value of Home	$ Estimate Cost to Make the Change
Bathroom Addition	65	6,900
Bedroom Addition	65	7,400
Swimming Pool	30	26,000
Hot Tub/Jacuzzi	20	5,600
Major 2nd-Story Addition	50	35,000
Kitchen Remodel	75	16,000
New Carpet	80	4,200
New Paint	100	950
Professional Improvement		
Exterior Landscaping	30	7,000
Extensive Decking	35	2,500
Garage Addition (if no garage exists)	40	6,500

I have heard it said that a contractor can improve the looks and livability of a house simply by discussing with the owner the cost of remodeling that home! Always purchase your home from the point of view of both a buyer and a future home seller.

SMART TIP:

I strongly recommend that all potential home buyers read *How to Sell Your Home Fast, for the Highest Price, in Any Market.* It will give you a better understanding of the sellers' viewpoint and provide you with the information you will need to know when you ultimately sell your home.

ALWAYS THINK OF THE FUTURE SALE

Always buy . . . thinking of selling!

As the potential buyer of a property, ask yourself these questions:

- Will the home that you are considering remain competitive on the market? (If not, what will need to be done to the home to make it competitive should you decide to sell the home in three to five years?)
- Are you paying reasonable market value for the property and not overpaying out of emotional desire?

Remember, as a seller, you must consider what the home is worth to other buyers in a competitive market. Is there a reasonable expectation that the home will increase in value at the same rate as other homes of comparable value? If the home is in an area of digression, will you suffer the financial loss when the value of the property remains stable or even declines? (Digression is discussed in more detail later in this chapter.) Again, you will be able to obtain from real estate professionals information regarding appreciation rates that will help you evaluate the financial future of an area.

Although no one can guarantee the future, the history and the current market trends of an area can give you a sound foundation on which to base your decision to purchase a particular property.

NEW HOME OR RESALE?

There are advantages and disadvantages for both new home and resale property purchases. For the most part, the decision will be purely your preference. However, it is important that you examine carefully all aspects of both types of home purchases before making a final decision.

New Homes

New homes are pristine and very appealing in that they are fresh like a new car—even the smell is appealing. In most cases, homes in new subdivisions require fewer major repairs and come with contractor warranties for at least the first year of ownership. Also, in many areas throughout the country, new homes are simply the best deal on the market. Many new home tracts have special financing terms available that can save a buyer thousands of dollars in interest. Many subdivision homes can be obtained with small down payment options and in certain cases, buyers will not have a payment for 90 days after they move in. Further, some of the homes have long-term warranties (three to five years) included at no extra cost to the buyer.

In areas that are not strong sellers' markets and where there is a large inventory of well-priced homes, developers or contractors sometimes offer other special incentives, such as landscaping, fencing, upgraded floor coverings, special appliances, or window coverings at no extra cost.

Another factor that you should consider about new home areas is that most tracts have a very unfinished look and feel about them for the first few years. Usually the individual homes do not have a great deal of landscaping around them,

SMART TIP:

Remember that in new home areas, especially subdivisions, these subdivisions only seem to be self-contained, almost islands unto themselves. In some cases, the surrounding areas may have high crime rates and declining economic conditions, and may even cause the new homes to appreciate more slowly than comparable homes in other areas. Again, no one can tell the future. However, through information provided by an experienced real estate agent or broker and other professionals involved in the industry, you can prepare an excellent evaluation of an area's future financial stability and growth direction.

there are few mature trees or shrubs, and the neighborhood feels less established.

Resale Homes

Previously owned homes (resale homes) usually have a much more completed or established look and feel (both the homes and the neighborhoods). However, in many areas, buyers are forced to sacrifice some of the amenities offered in new homes to be able to obtain the neighborhood atmosphere they desire in an older, more established area.

It is important, especially with previously owned homes, that you thoroughly inspect the properties using the information in this book and the services of professionals when appropriate. Also, you should always ask that a home warranty be included with the sale of the home. (See Chapter 14 for more information on home warranties.)

You also should ask to see all of the available records on repairs and maintenance for a property. As previously mentioned, obtain a complete Seller Disclosure Statement on the property before you make an offer. (See Figure 1.1 for a sample Seller Disclosure Statement.)

> **SMART TIP:**
> If you want to make an offer on a property prior to receiving information on certain repairs, maintenance records, or a Seller Disclosure Statement, the offer can be written to read: "This offer is conditioned upon buyer receiving and approving home repair and maintenance records as well as a completed Seller Disclosure Statement." (*See Chapter 13 for more on contract preparations.*)

HOW OLD WILL YOU GO?

Again, you will have to decide how old a property you are willing to purchase, based on your own desires and resources. Most knowledgeable, professional real estate salespeople will have information on problems that have occurred in homes in certain neighborhoods.

Sometimes homes that have been built during a certain period or by a certain builder will have consistent problems. Some examples include electrical, plumbing, roof, cement work, and foundation problems. You will need to ask the real estate agents, sellers, neighbors, home inspectors, lenders, appraisers, and whomever else may know if there has been anything consistently wrong with homes in an area.

If properties in a neighborhood have the same consistent problems but they have not shown up in the particular home you are interested in, hire a professional inspector to examine the home for the potential problems (as a condition of any offer made on the property).

Bill Bartel of Complete Home Inspections has been a Realtor® for over twenty-three years and states: "Without exception, any offer made on a property that is five years or older should include a request for a complete home inspection by a professional home inspector. Again, a Seller Disclosure Statement should also be obtained before an offer is made."

Buyers of very old structures, such as Victorians or homes of historical significance, need to be aware that repairs or reconstruction on these types of properties always seem to cost considerably more than the estimates originally obtained.

Not long ago, a couple of home buyers told me of their experience with the purchase and restoration of a circa 1850 Victorian home in the Boston area. Prior to purchasing the home, they had complete and extensive professional inspections and contractor estimates. Unfortunately, the buyers experienced the two unforgiving laws of old-home restoration: Things always cost more than you expect, and things always take longer than you think.

When the restoration on their property was finally complete, the expenses had skyrocketed from an anticipated $230,000 to almost $400,000. Also, the time for completion (estimated to be approximately six months) grew to just over 18 months.

Also, if you have young children and you are considering buying a very old home, you should think about how well your family will adapt to the neighborhood. Often people who live in areas of older homes do not have young children. Consequently, in some

SMART TIP:
Older-home restoration is not necessarily a good idea for any buyers with limited resources or any urgency to move into and occupy a home.

cases, schools are not accessible, and children must travel great distances to attend classes and to be with their friends.

In our previous example, not only did the restoration of the Victorian become a financial burden, but the buyers discovered after they moved into their home that most of the people living in the area were elderly and there were few children for the buyers' children to play with.

HOW IMPORTANT
IS LOCATION?

An overused saying in the real estate industry states: The three most important things to consider when purchasing a home are *location, location, and location!*

As overused as this old cliché is, no truer words have ever been spoken. In interviews with potential buyers nationwide, over 90 percent said that their first consideration with regard to a home purchase was location. Location of a property is paramount when it comes to establishing the value of property, and location directly predicates the number of buyers who will be interested in the home.

WHAT ARE THE TRANSITIONAL
PHASES OF A NEIGHBORHOOD?

Potential buyers need to be aware that areas, neighborhoods, and even entire communities go through four distinct transitional periods over thirty to one hundred years: the development/building and improvement phase, the stability phase, the digression phase, and the restoration or redevelopment phase.

Development/Building and Improvement Phase

This development phase occurs when construction takes place and neighborhoods are developed and improved. Ultimately, property values increase and open land is developed into residences, shops, schools, and commercial properties.

The term of this phase is usually three to ten years.

Stability Phase

The transitional stability phase is recognizable by: the continued increase in values of property, mature landscaping throughout the area, the stability and growth of the area population, stability or slight increase in local school enrollment, and the physical appearance of a mature and well-established neighborhood.

The term of stability is usually fifteen to forty years.

Digression Phase

In the digression phase, a neighborhood begins to show definite signs of age and deterioration. More of the properties become non–owner occupied (rentals) or possibly commercial units. Toward the end of this phase, some properties will be vacant and even boarded up. Foreclosures sometimes will become common in this type of area, and the governing agencies (cities, counties, etc.) are forced to condemn or even destroy buildings that are no longer habitable. Also, in this phase, school populations often continue to decline until the schools are closed.

Often streets and sidewalks fall into disrepair and mature trees and shrubberies reach their life span and are removed for aesthetic or safety reasons. Also, crime rates have a tendency to increase in this phase. At best, the value of the properties remains static; at worst, they decrease.

Many investment buyers will purchase properties during the phase of digression, especially if it is apparent that the area is primed to begin to move into the redevelopment phase. In most cases, investment buyers who purchase properties in the digression phase simply rent and retain the real estate until the area begins to improve. At that time, they make whatever improvements are necessary on the properties either to increase rent on the homes or commercial units or to sell the properties when the area improves and the values have increased.

The digression phase usually lasts ten to twenty years.

Restoration or Redevelopment Phase

The restoration phase is simply the rebirth of an area. Dilapidated structures are reconstructed and new homes or commercial units are built. Old properties that are structurally sound but are run down are restored. Roads, highways, and sidewalks are repaired or replaced. If it is a residential or residential/commercial mix area, properties begin to increase in owner occupancy and children once again become a factor in the population. In some cases, schools reopen or new schools are built.

This restoration or redevelopment phase most often occurs in cities or suburban areas and usually lasts five to fifteen years before returning to another stability phase.

Many cities offer special home purchase programs that encourage redevelopment of certain areas. If you are interested in obtaining information about programs that might be available in your area, contact your local city or county housing authority or one of the HUD offices. (See "Resources" for HUD information.)

CITY, SUBURBAN, OR RURAL—WHAT DO YOU REALLY WANT?

You must ask yourself two important questions with regard to the type of area (city, suburban, or rural) you want to live in:

- What kind of lifestyle do you really want?
- What kind of lifestyle can you afford?

Many people think that they really want to move to the country: buy a little land, grow a few veggies, and raise some farm animals. And, in most cases, buyers who finally achieve that goal are fairly happy with the country atmosphere and their resulting lifestyle. However, in some cases, people are quite surprised at how difficult it is to adapt to the much slower pace and to the major change in the availability of services such as restaurants, shopping, and car repair.

Some of you may remember the television comedy *Green Acres* starring Eddie Albert and Eva Gabor. In that portrayal of country life, Eddie was living out his lifelong dream of country living: pitching hay, milking cows, and shoveling . . . (well, you know what they shovel on a farm). Eva, on the other hand, could think of nothing but moving back to the city.

In the opening of each episode, Eddie Albert would sing, "Green Acres is the place for me . . . " and Eva would sing, "New York is where I want to be . . . "

As you might imagine, Eddie and Eva were in complete contradiction when it came to their living preferences.

It is hoped that you and your family are in some agreement about where and how you want to live, and most important, what you are going to do when you get there. In other words, are you going to be willing to travel into the city or surrounding areas for the things you need and want to do?

Many families dream for years of living in the country, then discover after they have made their move that their new lifestyle is more difficult than they anticipated. The complaint mentioned most often is how far new country property owners have to drive to shop, for children's activities, and for general daily functions. Also, cost is a consideration when a family moves to a rural area. Buyers may save a considerable amount of money on a property located far outside of the city, only to find that their everyday living expenses have increased dramatically. Staples such as gas, food, and clothing can be more costly in small rural areas. Generally, it takes better planning and structure for a family to live in a rural area than in a suburban or city area.

Before you decide where to live, consider schools, churches, organizations, sporting activities that you like to attend and/or participate in . . . generally, all of the activities that make up your everyday life.

On the other hand, for many people, the positive aspects of living in a rural area far outweigh the negatives: the solitude, the lack of noise and pollution, the star-filled skies, the difference in attitudes of neighbors, the lower crime rates . . . the list is endless.

Suburban areas seem to meet the needs and desires of the majority of home buyers. Offering many conveniences and easy access to the cities, suburban areas are the "happy medium" for many property owners. Often commutes to cities are relatively short, and

> **SMART TIP:**
> Always consider the convenience of your home to your lifestyle activities. Unless you are absolutely (100 percent) convinced, you should not buy a property that will precipitate a total change in lifestyle. It may be better to rent for a while to try out the new life before you purchase a property.

sometimes very effective and comfortable public transportation is available.

Although there has been an enormous increase in the number of home buyers moving back into city areas, suburban communities remain the highest growth area and the most popular for buyers ages twenty-five to fifty.

As I asked at the beginning of this section: What kind of lifestyle do you really want? And what kind of lifestyle can you really afford?

Buyers need to be aware that many styles of homes often predicate the area's feeling and prices of properties. As an example, Victorian homes are found most often in city areas, possibly surrounded by many other Victorians.

Buyers who limit their home search to only one or two styles of homes have a tendency to fall into the "dream home" syndrome. Unless they have unlimited resources, they often suffer a great deal of frustration when trying to match their other needs with only one or two styles of homes.

SIZE, FEATURES, AND AMENITIES

As I mentioned earlier, when you prepare your list of features and amenities that you want in a home, it is important that you divide your list into absolute "needs" and other things that you would "want" to have in a property, but that are not absolute necessities. This information should be transferred to your Home Search Checklist, which you should keep close at hand when you make your second viewing of a property to help you decide which homes are the ones you are interested in purchasing. (See the Appendix for a Home Search Checklist.)

Inspect the property very thoroughly and make notes in the comments section regarding specialty items and amenities that you like and dislike about the home. If you have special needs, such as a workshop or RV parking, and a home you like does not possess those amenities, you may consider adding them. However, before you make an offer to purchase the home, make sure you receive several written estimates of how much adding the improvements will cost. Remember, you may not fully recover the cost of these changes or improvements if you sell the home in the first few years of ownership.

YARD REQUIREMENTS

If a property in which you are interested does not possess all of the yard features that you desire, you may want to add certain items, such as fencing, patios, or outbuildings. Again, research and obtain estimates on the cost to make the improvements before you make an offer.

It is also important to check out the adjoining properties, even if it means doing a little peeking over the fence. If the three adjoining backyards contain a pack of barking Rottweilers, a pool filled with every child in the neighborhood under twelve, and a cemented area where seven race cars are parked, maybe you should consider another home.

> **SMART TIP:**
> It is not uncommon for buyers to ask sellers to build, replace, or repair fencing, outbuildings, or make other exterior improvements as part of the purchase contract. Sellers, especially in a strong "buyers' market," may make large concessions to generate an offer.

Also determine how much time and expense will be necessary to maintain a yard. For example, an owner of a property may pay for a yard service to maintain the exterior of a property and make the home the neighborhood showplace. However, you may not be able to afford the yard services. Consequently, you may be forced to expend many hours of work each week to keep up with a high-maintenance exterior, or you could decide to relandscape so the yard will be less time consuming.

A few items that could increase the time required to keep a yard in perfect condition include: odd-shape yards or large grass areas, specialty plants such as Bonsai trees or certain types of rosebushes, cement-bordered walkways or trails, steep terrain or rolling topography, ponds, large trees that drop their leaves each year, and prolific growth hedges.

AVOIDING COMMON PROBLEMS

When I talked earlier about the age of homes you might consider, I touched on some of the problem areas that you need to be aware of.

Again, the most costly repairs are the roof, electrical, plumbing, water seepage or leakage into the home or basement, and the overall disrepair of the home. Another costly repair can be problems with pools or spas, such as plumbing problems, electrical problems, drainage or cleaning systems, pumps, refinishing, or cement work.

With the proper professional inspections and a complete home warranty, buyers can feel fairly assured that they will not be faced with major repair bills in the first few years of ownership. (See Chapter 7 for avoiding certain potential problem areas in a home and Chapter 14 for details on home warranties.)

CHAPTER FIVE

Choosing a Real Estate Agent

According to a survey conducted by an independent research company, approximately 98 percent of home buyers nationwide indicated that they used the services of a real estate agent or broker to find a property and to guide them through the many facets of the home-buying process.

Although licensed real estate agents and brokers are extremely plentiful, finding a true real estate professional takes some effort on the buyer's part. Remember, you want someone whom you can trust and believe in, who will be there to guide you when things are difficult. Also, you want someone who has the expertise to help you find the best home for your needs and desires at the best possible price and terms available.

Whew . . . that sounds almost like someone you'd want to marry! Well, not quite, but pretty darn close. This person is going to guide and help you make one of the biggest commitments and investments you may make in your entire life.

This chapter will lead you step-by-step through the task of choosing an agent or broker and will ensure that your choice is based on the proper considerations.

WHAT SHOULD AN AGENT DO FOR YOU?

A professional, experienced, and well-qualified real estate agent or broker can guide you through the rather complex and often confusing maze that collectively makes up the home-purchase process.

The following list will give you some idea of the responsibilities that your real estate professional should take on your behalf.

1. Educate you through the entire home-buying process.
2. Help you to understand all of the paperwork.

3. Handle any problems that might arise during the entire transaction.
4. Properly prepare any forms, contracts, and disclosures that are required and see that those items are legally correct.
5. Help you find the right home in the right neighborhood.
6. Screen homes before your inspection to make sure the property meets your needs.
7. Show homes to you in an effective and professional manner.
8. Guide you with regard to repairs that should be made.
9. Provide comparable sales data to help assure that you are paying the proper price for the home.
10. Guide you in your selection of competent escrow/closing and title people.
11. See that all required disclosures are made.
12. Suggest which professional inspections should or must be made on the property.
13. Help you to spot sellers who are attempting to take advantage of you.
14. Help you to understand the use and limitations of good-faith deposits.
15. Advise you as to when you should seek the advice of an attorney.
16. Make sure that the appraisal process is handled properly.
17. Help you to understand the complete loan, escrow/closing, and title process.
18. Advise you on any books or publications that you should read before, during, and after the transaction has closed.
19. Help you to negotiate the best price available for all costs and fees related to the transaction.
20. Negotiate and deal effectively in your behalf with the seller, other agents, escrow/closing, title people, and attorneys.
21. Advise you as to how homes should be prepared to show and sell.
22. Advise you as to any inspections such as septic, well, or soil, that might be applicable to the specific property in which you are interested.
23. Help you recover any overages that are paid during the closing process.

24. Guide you as to how the escrow/closing instructions should be prepared.
25. Properly handle the walk-through process with you prior to the final closing.
26. See that any repairs or requirements are met prior to the closing.
27. Advise you of any contractual changes that might be necessary prior to the closing.
28. Advise you as to what course of action to take if the seller refuses to close the transaction.
29. Oversee the entire closing process.
30. See that the completion of the transaction is smooth right through to things such as obtaining the keys and possession of the property.
31. See that each and every facet of the buying process is handled effectively and professionally, in your best interest.

> **SMART TIP:**
> If you decide to attempt to purchase a property without using the services of a real estate professional, make sure that you are well versed in real estate and contract law. Also, before you make or accept a final offer, have the entire transaction reviewed by a real estate attorney.

AGENT, BROKER, SALESPERSON— WHAT'S THE DIFFERENCE?

From the day you tell anyone that you are thinking of buying a home, you will be besieged by real estate licensees who want to represent you in the purchase of your home. If you start collecting these salespeople's business cards, you will be confused as to just who is who in this real estate profession.

Understand, there are over a million licensees and former licensees floating around the nation, so it goes without saying that there are a lot of opinions as to how you should go about purchasing a home.

Keep in mind, for the most part, that a person of average intelligence who knows little about real estate can read a book or two, memorize a few sample test questions, take and pass a state exam, send in the required fee, and . . . whamo, become licensed to guide buyers and sellers on probably the largest and most important investment they will ever make. Oh, and also collect substantial fees for doing so.

If that thought is a little scary . . . it is meant to be! There is a great deal of incompetence in the real estate sales field primarily because it is just too easy to obtain and maintain a license.

This is not to demean the entire profession, because there are also many excellent, well-trained, and experienced true professionals who are credits to the industry. However, it is incumbent upon you as a buyer or seller to choose very carefully the agent or broker with whom you will work.

Some of the titles used by real estate salespeople include agent, broker, sales associate, broker associate, salesperson, sales consultant, buyer's agent, buyer's broker, Realtor®, and Realtor® Associate (yes, Realtor® is spelled with a capital R and has a registered trademark).

Keep in mind that regardless of a person's title, his or her basic job is to sell a property to you and earn a commission. Most real estate salespeople do not earn a dime until you have made that property purchase and closed the transaction.

To make it simple, there are only three titles that you need to understand as a buyer: broker, agent, and Realtor®.

The principal broker in a company is the big boss. He or she is licensed by the state to operate a real estate brokerage. All brokers are licensed to independently operate a real estate brokerage (Some states have some special requirements.). Some brokers, however, choose to operate as an associate under the license of another principal broker and usually take the title of broker associate.

The next title of which you should be aware is agent (sometimes referred to as sales agent or sales associate). Agents are associated with and work under the license of a real estate broker. As mentioned earlier, most licensees operate as independent contractors, which means that they have no salary and no expense account, and they are paid strictly on the commission (based on a percentage of the brokerage fees that they bring into the company when a property is sold).

When a home is listed for sale, that listing is taken by the principal broker or by an associate agent or broker under the license of the principal broker. Therefore, the listing is actually the principal broker's listing, and the agent or broker who actually deals with the client is the agent of record.

The next title of interest is Realtor®. Agents or brokers who are members of a local Board of Realtors®, which is affiliated with the National Association of Realtors® (NAR), are entitled to use the designation Realtor®. These agents and brokers (Realtors®) have agreed to follow the Code of Ethics, which, in some cases, is more stringent than state laws. When the term Realtor® is used, it must be capitalized and the ® (registered trademark designation) must be shown after the word.

WHO PAYS THE COMMISSION TO BROKERS AND AGENTS?

In most cases, the sellers' broker/agent and the buyers' broker/agent are paid commission by the sellers, based on the sale price of the property. This commission usually varies somewhere between 5 and 10 percent, depending on the type of property, the overall market condition, and what commission has become customary in an area.

Most commonly, commissions are split between the selling principal broker and the listing principal broker. If agents or associate brokers who represent these principal brokers are the ones actually dealing with the buyers and sellers, these associates are in turn given a percentage of the commission.

SMART TIP:
Commissions are always negotiable, and buyers and sellers need to be aware that commissions are never set by Boards of Realtors® or multiple listing service organizations.

Because the sellers pay the commission, in the past a Latin phrase, "*caveat emptor*," was associated with real estate transactions. In English this phrase means "buyer beware." It became widely accepted that because the seller was the only party paying the sales commission, the seller was the only party actually represented by the agents/brokers. Even if an agent/broker was working with a buyer, that agent/broker actually represented the seller and was acting as a subagent of the listing broker.

However, in the past few years, laws have changed to recognize designations such as buyer's agent, dual agent, or subagent acting on behalf of the buyer.

A seller's agent has what is known as a fiduciary relationship with that seller. This means that the agent must do everything in his or her power to obtain for that seller the highest possible price for the property, maintaining complete and total confidentiality and loyalty with and for that seller.

> **SMART TIP:**
> Regardless of how agents are affiliated with the seller, they are required by law to deal honestly and fairly with all parties to the transaction.

In most states, if buyers choose to work with a buyers' agent, they can do so. The buyers' agent will negotiate strictly on the behalf of the buyer and with only the buyer's interest in mind. Most buyers' agents receive a flat fee or a commission based on the sale price of the property. Some buyers' agents require a deposit or retainer fee to obtain their services, and some will negotiate their fee or commission to be paid as a percentage of the sale price of the property.

Often a buyers' agent will ask you to sign an agreement that specifies that you will work exclusively with him or her for a period of time (usually 60 to 180 days).

In some cases, the selling agent/broker and the buyers' agent/broker actually will work for the same principal broker. This may create what is known as a dual agency. In many states, when this occurs, both buyers and sellers

> **SMART TIP:**
> Real estate agents, brokers, and lenders are precluded from providing any information with regard to race, color, creed, sex, religion, or any other factor that could be construed as discriminatory. Also, the services provided by these professionals must be equal to all persons with no regard to the buyer's race, color, creed, sex, or religion.

must sign a Dual Agency Disclosure Statement. This statement discloses that a dual agency exists and makes all parties to the transaction aware that one broker is actually representing all parties and is collecting the entire commission fee.

FRANCHISE OR INDEPENDENT BROKERAGES

Many brokers who open their own brokerage will choose to join a franchise, such as Century 21, Prudential, Coldwell Banker, ERA, Realty Executives, or REMAX. Although franchise brokers have the advantage of being affiliated with a large company, these brokers still operate as an independent brokerage. The franchise companies provide a referral system, national advertising, agent training, and some other advantages. However, because every brokerage operates independently, there is no guarantee that a buyer or seller will always have a competent agent/broker to assist them.

Independent brokerages (not affiliated with franchises) often have training programs and referral networks. Buyers and sellers should choose a company and an agent/broker based solely on the reputation of that company or individual.

SPECIAL TRAINING DESIGNATIONS

Many agents/brokers, after completing certain training programs, will indicate the achievement by placing the designation after their name. An example might read:

John A. Jones, CRS, GRI
Broker Associate

This would indicate that John A. Jones, a broker associate, has completed the required courses and testing to be named as a Certified Residential Specialist and a Graduate of the Realtors® Institute. Both of these designations are issued by the National Association of Realtors®, and both titles require extensive classroom training as well as a substantial experience.

Again, these designations do not guarantee that the agent/broker will provide the service and expertise that you need. However, they do indicate that the person has made an effort to improve his or her knowledge and capabilities.

HOW DO YOU FIND THE RIGHT AGENT?

The best way to find the right agent is to look around and ask questions. Ask your neighbors, friends, and everyone you know: Whom did they use to help them buy their home? Was it a good transaction? Did the agent do what he or she said they would do?

At the very least, you will find out which agents you may not want to use!

One of the biggest mistakes you can make when choosing an agent/broker is to choose a friend

> **SMART TIP:**
> Buyers and sellers should always ask what the designations mean after an agent's/broker's name. Some sales trainers give out their own designations to salespeople who have attended even a daylong sales program. If initials mean only that an agent/broker showed up for a seminar, ate a doughnut or two, bought a set of tapes, and went on his or her way, that designation doesn't mean much.

> **SMART TIP:**
> Do not choose an agent just because you are acquainted with the person from your country club. Check the person out. Ask for a reference list of former buyers, then call the previous customers and see how their experiences were with that agent/broker.

or relative just to help them "get going" in the business. You never want to be the guinea pig for trial-and-error techniques. How would you feel about flying with a pilot, if it was his or her first flight after getting a license to fly? Okay, how about investing your money with a financial planner that had no experience in financial planning but had been a cab driver for twenty years?

Remember, taking the time to choose the right agent can make all the difference in how comfortably and effectively your home purchase will progress.

The guide in Figure 5.1 will help you in choosing the proper agent for your needs.

FIGURE 5.1

BUYERS' GUIDE TO CHOOSING AN AGENT

WHAT SHOULD YOU ASK THE AGENT?	EXPLANATION AND INTERPRETATIONS OF ANSWERS
1. Do you work as a full-time salesperson?	1. This is critical only if the agent is not a serious professional. There are a number of agents in the business whom we call "Perpetual Participants" and who are mainly in the business to close a deal once in a while and socialize with other agents. Some part-time people are very good agents and producers.
2. How long have you been a real estate agent?	2. Again, some people prove themselves very quickly; however, you do want some experience. Consider this with the next seven questions for a better overall picture.
3. What special training have you had?	3. Find out if the agent has continued learning and improving him-/herself since becoming licensed.
4. Are you a Realtor® or a Realtor® Associate (a member of the National Association of Realtors®, NAR)?	4. The Realtor® designation signifies that the agent is a member in good standing with the NAR and, further, that agent has agreed to abide by the ethics and professional standards established by that organization. Membership in this organization is voluntary. If the agent you are interviewing is not a Realtor® or a Realtor® Associate, ask why.
5. What special designations do you possess (for example, GRI [Graduate Realtors® Institute] or CRS [Certified Residential Specialist])?	5. Certain designations indicate that the agent has completed certain training and/or has completed training and a specified number of closed transactions. Both GRI and CRS are excellent designations but do not in themselves ensure that you are picking the right agent.

FIGURE 5.1

BUYERS' GUIDE TO CHOOSING AN AGENT *(continued)*

WHAT SHOULD YOU ASK THE AGENT?	EXPLANATION AND INTERPRETATIONS OF ANSWERS
6. How many homes have you sold and closed over the past six months? How many were your listings that sold by other agents, and how many have you actually sold yourself?	6. Good production agents should have a minimum of two to four sales per month (including their listings that have sold). Some agents will have as many as ten to 12 per month. Some agents are primarily listing agents. You need a good buyers' agent. They may take and sell lots of listings, but seldom work directly with a buyer.
7. Do you have a full-time team of affiliates with whom you work consistently who will see that no details are missed?	7. Can the agent recommend a good escrow/closing person, a competent lender, etc.? Why are these people the best to work with?
8. How will we progress from today forward if we decide to work with you?	8. Competent agents will suggest that you be formally prequalified and spend a great deal of time identifying what you want and need in a home before they ever begin showing you properties. If they want to throw you in a car and start driving around immediately, forget it! Find another agent who knows what he or she should be doing.
9. Do you belong to the Multiple Listing Service (MLS)?	9. This is very important. Unless there is no MLS available in your area, walk away from an agent who does not belong. Almost all listings in the area are in the MLS.
10. Do you have suggestions as to how I might save money on fees and closing costs when I buy my home?	10. Pay close attention. If the agent has no suggestions, you will have a few for him or her. (Remember, Chapter 20 deals with ways to save money when buying a home.)
11. How much time each week can we expect that you will be able to spend finding and showing us homes?	11. Six to ten homes or more would not be unreasonable to expect an agent to show you. An honest agent may tell you truthfully that he or she doesn't have that much time. Thank the person and find another agent.

FIGURE 5.1

BUYERS' GUIDE TO CHOOSING AN AGENT *(continued)*

WHAT SHOULD YOU ASK THE AGENT?	EXPLANATION AND INTERPRETATIONS OF ANSWERS
12. Will you preview homes prior to our viewing the properties? If not, do you keep a record of the homes you have seen on caravans and broker open houses (brokers' opens)?	12. If an agent is too busy to preview homes, how will he or she know if you are looking at homes in which you will be interested? If an agent does not attend "brokers' opens" and "caravan tours" of homes each week, he or she probably does not see enough homes to serve your needs as a discerning buyer.
13. Why do you feel you and your company would be the best for us to work with in the purchase of our home?	13. Remember, whatever people are selling, they should be able to sell themselves first.
14. May I have a list of references of people with whom you have worked to purchase a home in the past three to six months, and may I contact a couple of those people if I choose to?	14. If agents won't give you references, get rid of them! If they will give you only a couple of names, ask why. If an agent is new and does not have many real estate references and you still would like to work with him or her, ask for personal references.

FIRING AN AGENT

For the most part, if an agent is not doing the job for you, simply tell him or her that you are going to find someone else to work with. You may or may not wish to explain your decision, but at least tell the person what you are doing. Never leave one agent hanging and looking for other properties for you while you are out with another agent buying a home.

If you have signed an Exclusive Buyer's Agreement in which you have agreed to work with only one particular agent for a period of time, simply ask to be released from the agreement (in writing, of course). If the agent refuses the release, go to the broker. If the broker refuses, go to the Board of Realtors®. If the board cannot get cooperation on your behalf, letters to the editor in the local newspaper often have an enormous impact. No agent wants bad publicity.

OTHER CONSIDERATIONS

When you choose an agent to work with throughout your home-buying process, remember that you will be spending a great deal of time with that agent: finding the home, writing an offer to purchase, negotiating the offer and counteroffers, doing all of the inspections and paperwork, getting through the title reports and appraisals, and closing the transaction. *Choose an agent you like to be with*. If an agent is extremely competent but you can't stand the person, you may have a very long and frustrating transaction.

Understanding Proper Resale Home Pricing

Proper pricing is one area of the home purchase that potential buyers often overlook when they begin to learn about home buying.

With few exceptions, buyers do not want to pay more than market value for a property. However, in some cases, buyers may choose to pay an inflated price to obtain a home of which they are especially fond. In these cases, the market truly becomes a willing seller-willing buyer scenario. Unfortunately, in other cases, buyers pay an inflated price for a property purely out of their ignorance of proper resale pricing.

In this chapter, you'll learn all of the aspects of resale pricing and how to be sure you're making an offer at the right price.

HOW PRICES EVOLVE

In the early and mid-1990s, Las Vegas, Nevada, became the fastest-growing major city in the nation. According to the chamber of commerce, approximately 6,000 people per month were moving into the area and approximately 1,000 per month were leaving. This type of transition into a community usually creates a terrifically strong sellers' market. However, because Las Vegas became a mecca for new home builders, the resale home market had to compete with new homes in every price range from $60,000 to multimillions. Consequently, sellers discovered that to sell their homes effectively, they had to compare their homes not only to other resale properties on the market but also to many new neighborhoods that offered more amenities plus new home appeal.

During this period, resale homes priced at or below market value stayed on the market an average of thirty days. However, homes that were overpriced between 10 and 19 percent averaged more than ninety days on the market. Also, of the homes that were overpriced 10 percent and above actual market value, over 98 percent ultimately sold at or below actual market value.

Now, what does this mean to you as a buyer? If over 5,000 people per month are moving into that area and only 2 percent are overpaying for a home, over 1,000 people *per year* are overpaying for their properties! And that is only one city in the nation. Multiply that figure by hundreds or thousands and you can see that many unknowing buyers are paying more than they should for their homes.

MISTAKES MADE IN HOME PRICING

To best understand proper pricing, it is important for buyers to know the most common pricing mistakes that sellers make when attempting to sell their properties.

THE "GOTTA GET" PRICE

Many sellers base their sales price not on factual comparable sales data but on how much they want to *net* out of the sale of the property. Most sellers do not stop to think that the amount of equity that has accumulated in their home should be a purely objective, market, fact-based figure. Also, emotion should play little or no part in the calculation of their home's value.

Unfortunately, most sellers figure out how much they want to net, add the remaining loan balance and sales cost figures, and that number becomes their "gotta get price," regardless of the home's true value. This price becomes the sellers' one and only concern, and they usually ignore the market value facts and say, "We *gotta get* this amount for the property or we won't sell."

Unfortunately, in many cases, a real estate agent will take the listing at that unrealistic price, put the property on the market, and hope and pray that an unsophisticated buyer will show up and pay the totally unrealistic price. Or the agent hopes that the sellers will become more realistic and maybe a little desperate and accept a reasonable price when an offer is received.

SMART TIP:

No experienced, qualified real estate professional should ever take a listing priced considerably above market value in the hopes that the sellers eventually will come down to a reasonable price. Many times these overpriced listings remain on the market for months or even years, pass from one brokerage to the next, and eventually sell at or below market value, or possibly are taken off the market by the sellers.

Overpriced listings are as much the fault of the real estate sales community as they are the sellers themselves. However, regardless of the reason or fault, overpriced listings do exist. Basically, buyers need to learn to ignore properties that are offered for sale by unrealistic sellers.

SMART TIP:

One basic rule to remember is that if a home seller is unreasonable about the price and does not base it on factual comparable data, walk away from the home. Until that seller becomes realistic, he or she will be nothing but trouble for everyone who tries to deal with him or her.

"I Can Always Come Down, But I Can't Go Up"

The second most common pricing mistake sellers make is thinking that they can start high on the price and wait for offers. These sellers usually believe that some buyer may come along and offer more than the home's actual market value.

This type of thinking and pricing usually creates the same result as with the "gotta get" price scenario.

Most buyers fix their sights and efforts on a certain price range of homes. As an example, if buyers have been prequalified for a home loan of $95,000 and they have $20,000 to put down, the price range of homes at which they will look will be somewhere between $115,000 and $130,000.

If the sellers have a home with a market value of approximately $120,000, but they choose to price their home at $160,000, they actually will price their home out of the true buyers' market. Most buyers who would be interested in and qualify to purchase the home at the actual true value will never see the property because it is too far above their price range. On the other hand, buyers who are looking for a home in the $150,000 to $160,000 range will not be interested in the property because they can receive so many more amenities for the same price in other homes on the market.

"We've Spent It, Now We Want It Back"

Another common reason for overpricing is sellers trying to recover all the money they have spent on improvements made to the home.

As mentioned earlier, in most cases, home owners seldom recover 100 percent of what they spend on improvements or remodeling. As an example, a seller may have installed a pool that cost $40,000. If comparable homes in the area that do not have a pool are selling for $100,000, it does not mean that the seller's home would be worth $140,000. Most likely, comparable homes in the area with pools would be selling for approximately $115,000 to $130,000, and this would be the most appropriate comparison that could be made for property valuation.

According to national averages, sellers usually recover about 60 percent of the cost of a pool.

Sellers who spend a great deal of money remodeling or improving their homes with expensive wallpaper or carpets, specialty lighting fixtures, extensive or elaborate window coverings, or personal taste items such as grow-box windows, rock gardens, fountains, or expensive exterior shutters should never expect to recover everything that they have spent on those improvements. This is particularly true when home owners choose to overimprove a home for the area in which it is located.

Old Appraisals

Some sellers will produce an old appraisal that indicates their property is worth more than the current market condition predicates. Volatile changes in market conditions have occurred recently, and in some

> **SMART TIP:**
> Buyers and sellers need to understand that in an area of comparably priced homes, the nicest property in the neighborhood will become a victim of *regression*, which means that its value will be pulled down by the lesser-value properties. The least cared for and least valuable home will become a product of *progression*, which means its value will be pushed up by the nicer, more valuable homes.

cases, home values have dropped for a period of time. In some areas, it takes several years for home values to regain the peak prices they achieve during hot sellers' markets. Appraisals three months or older may be completely outdated. Base your valuation of the home only on current market data.

UNDERSTANDING AND USING COMPARABLE SALES DATA

Although appraisers use many methods and factors to establish market values of properties, the most important component is comparable sales prices. If there are a number of comparable sales ("comps," as they are known) pinpointing a home's value is easy.

The three most critical elements with regard to finding acceptable comps are area or location, comparable amenities in homes, and sizes of homes. Just as appraisers use comparable sales to establish values of homes, real estate professionals and informed buyers will use exactly the same data to establish the market value on which they will base the purchase price for a property.

Most comparable sales data will be readily available to your real estate professional through their local Multiple Listing Service or real estate board. The information is maintained current within any thirty-day period; in some areas, the information is current on a daily basis.

Once a person understands how to read and understand comparable sales data, determining the proper market value of properties is a fairly simple process.

In a very "hot" or busy market, it is easy to find many like properties or comparable homes that have sold. However, as a market becomes less active, it becomes increasingly more difficult to find

> **SMART TIP:**
> Comparable home valuation is simply comparing like properties—homes with somewhat the same amenities in somewhat the same type of areas.

> **SMART TIP:**
> For most appraisers, to accept comparable sales data, it must be no older than six months. In some areas or for some lenders, appraisers will not accept comparables more than three months old.

like or comparable sales properties. Also, often it is difficult to find comparable sales for unique homes.

Many agents advise buyers and sellers that the only properties that can be used as comparables to establish market value are strictly within the same neighborhood as the home sale. This, of course, would be the best of all worlds, if three or four perfect comps existed for every property placed on the market for sale.

However, this is not always the case; many agents do not realize that an appraiser may go outside of a particular neighborhood and find another similar neighborhood for their valuation. By similar, I mean homes that were built at about the same time as the subject property. These homes probably will have similar amenities and sales prices as the subject property (equivalent homes with equivalent sales prices). This is why it is important for agents, sellers, and buyers to understand the entire sales market in an area, not just in a particular neighborhood when valuating home prices.

The Comparative Market Analysis (CMA) in Figure 6.1 shows the comparable sales data that was used to determine the market value of a particular home.

As you can see, once you learn to read and understand comparable sales data, determining the proper value of homes or properties is a fairly simple task.

If you are interested in a property that appears overpriced, it may be wise to make an offer and include pricing information of comparable homes in the area that have already sold. Doing so may help the sellers to see that they need to base the value of their home on factual data.

Table 6.1 shows a comparison between listing prices and selling prices in four states. Your agent should be able to provide you with the figures in your area.

SMART TIP:
Home values and offer prices must be based solely on sale/closing prices and never on listing prices. Sellers can list their home at whatever price they choose, but that doesn't mean it will ever sell at that price. The best pricing analogy for sellers to understand is simply: If you own stock and it is selling at about $80 per share, it does no good for you to offer your stock at $90 per share because no one will buy it at that price.

FIGURE 6.1

COMPARATIVE MARKET ANALYSIS

COMPARATIVE MARKET ANALYSIS

Date: _1/3/96_

For: _John and Mary Doe_

Address: _1217 Carbone Way_

Prepared By: _Bill Smith_

Competitive Market Value: $ _206,000_

Probable Sale Price: $ _205,000 – 207,000_

Seller's Acknowledgment: _Ed James_

Note: List prices and sale prices add - 000 to each price shown.
SQ. FT. is price per square foot. This figure is rounded to the nearest dollar.

ADDRESS/FEATURES	BED RMS	BATH	SQ.FT.	AGE	FAM. RM	DIN. RM	FIRE-PLACE	POOL	GAR.	LIST PR.	SALE PR.	SQ.FT	DAYS MKT.	TERMS	DATE SOLD	REMARKS
SUBJECT PROPERTY																
1217 Carbone	3	3	2720	8	X	X	X		2	210	205	76	–	–	–	
SOLD																
806 Smith	3	3	2800	9	X	X	X		2	220	210	75	64	–	12/1	
91 SOUTH	4	3	2750	8	X	X	2	X	2	225	219	80	78	OC 2nd	12/14	BEAUTIFUL POOL
230 ALTO	3	2	2600	6	X	X	X		2	220	193	74	29	–	12/30	
FOR SALE NOW																
1223 CARBONE	3	3	2840	8	X	X	X		2	212	–	75	41	–	–	VERY NICE
1380 CARBONE	4	3	2960	9	X	X	X		3	225	–	76	84	—	–	
8110 - 2ND	3	2	2500	8	X	X	X		2	185	–	74	74	—	–	WILL SELL QUICKLY
EXPIRED																
486 HOWARD	3	3	2900	8	X	X	X	X	2	232	–	80	180	–	–	RENTED
774 CAROL	3	3	2700	8	X	X	X		2	220	–	81	240	–	–	OFF MARKET

TABLE 6.1
LISTING/SALE PRICE DIFFERENTIAL

AREA	AVERAGE LIST PRICE*	AVERAGE SALE PRICE	PERCENTAGE OF DIFFERENCE BETWEEN LIST AND SALE PRICES	COMMENTS
Indiana	$162,000	$160,100	-1.0	Solid sellers' market
California	$259,600	$231,040	-11.0	Weak sellers' market
Arizona	$154,300	$148,050	-4.0	Fairly even sellers' and buyers' markets
Ohio	$110,000	$107,200	-3.0	Fairly even sellers' and buyers' markets

*These figures were provided from information supplied by Metroscan (a subsidiary of TRW Real Estate Information Services).

UNDERSTANDING HOW PRICES RISE AND FALL

Potential home buyers must understand the history of home pricing so they can better evaluate the market conditions that exist in their particular area.

In the late 1970s, when inflation was running in double digits, it was not uncommon in any area for sellers to list their home slightly above the current market value and receive four or five offers within a matter of days, all at or very close to the list price. In some cases, when buyers were adamant about purchasing a property, offers were presented that were written *above* the list price.

Only a few years later, in the early 1980s, home sales plummeted when mortgage interest rates rose to as high as 20 percent in some areas. Buyers who could qualify for these high-interest loans were scarce, and many properties sat on the market for six to eighteen months. When properties finally sold, the sellers seldom received their asking price, and many properties sold at or below market value.

Also, many of these sales included some type of owner carry-back or owner-assisted financing, special incentives provided by the seller, or even cash payments back to the buyer from the seller after the close of the transaction.

In many areas, it was not uncommon for sellers to receive 10 to 30 percent below the listed price for their property. That very difficult time in real estate history created a "willing buyer-willing seller market," and for the first and only time, comparable sales data had little value for the purpose of pricing.

Toward the mid- to late 1980s and on into the early 1990s, the market became somewhat more stabilized as interest rates dropped to the lowest rate in thirty years. However, while the real estate community—salespeople, lenders, title companies, and escrow people—readied itself for another dazzling, high-energy market like that of the 1970s, a surprising phenomenon occurred. Appreciation remained at only about 1 to 4 percent per year and the sales market was, at best, sluggish. In the past, when interest rates dropped, prices of properties rose quickly and dramatically due to the increase in qualified buyers and, ultimately, higher demand for homes. *(See Chapter 8 for the national mortgage interest rate averages.)*

In 1993, home sales rose only about 6 percent higher than in the prior two years. Several factors played a part in this unexpected improvement in the market, but the most prominent elements were a more stringent qualification process for potential buyers (it became much harder to obtain a loan) and insecurity on the part of buyers with regard to the overall economy. (People were afraid to buy or make a move.)

Early in 1995, after seven consecutive increases in the interest rates by the Federal Reserve Board (supposedly to curb inflation, which I might add, had risen only 2.7 percent in 1994), mortgage interest rates rose to over 10 percent in some areas, and housing sales again slumped dramatically.

Sale prices began to drop off and once again it became a buyers' market. Comparable sales data was scrutinized very carefully and comparable homes had to be exactly that, with little deviation. Buyers who could qualify at the higher interest rates were not afraid to make offers considerably below the listed prices because they recognized their strong bargaining position in the weak sellers' market.

Once again, the ultimate "willing buyer-willing seller" market came into play and more weight was placed on buyers' ability and willingness to repay a loan than on the property itself. Consequently, active and progressive real estate agents began listing properties at or just below market value and put a preprogrammed price reduction plan into place. This plan meant that the sellers would agree to reduce the list price of their home no less than every thirty days until the property sold. Also, the listing agents would ask the seller to reinstate the original listing period each time a price reduction occurred. For example, if the original listing period was six months, each time a price reduction occurred, that listing period would be extended to the original six-month term.

Although this type of listing strategy may seem somewhat radical, it became recognized as the most effective sales technique for a difficult market.

If a home has been prepared properly and marketed aggressively for thirty days and few, if any, potential buyers have viewed it, both agent and sellers should recognize that the price or lack of terms are probably the weak factors.

> **SMART TIP:**
> Buyers and sellers must realize that sellers who truly want to sell their home must be willing to match their sales strategy to the current sales market.

The significance of this history lesson to you as a buyer is simply this: Be aware that home sale prices can rise or fall considerably in just a few weeks or months due to the national economy, a local market condition, Federal Reserve intervention, a rise and fall in interest rates, or other world events that might cause instability in the housing market. Further, buyers must be able to properly analyze all of these factors when determining the price they will offer for a home.

Buyers also must be willing to recognize that homes comparable to the home in which they are interested actually have sold for more in the past than they are actually worth today. Buyers must understand the market and be able to recognize overpriced listings when they are viewing properties.

Buyers also need to try to determine how motivated sellers are and how urgently they want to sell their home. As an example, sellers who want to dispose of their home urgently (due to a job transfer or a pending foreclosure on the property) might be very motivated to negotiate with buyers. On the other hand, sellers who are planning to purchase a new property only after their existing home has sold might not have the need or urgency to negotiate a sale.

HOW OVERPRICING CREATES FINANCING PROBLEMS

Buyers and sellers also need to understand that a home actually must sell twice. The first sale is selling the home to the buyer, and the second sale is selling the sale price and the buyers' qualification to the lender.

If the lender's appraiser values a home at less than the purchase price that has been accepted by the buyers and sellers, a problem may arise. The lender may choose to base the loan amount on that appraisal and not on the agreed sale price.

As an example, if you were to make and have accepted an offer of $205,000, contingent upon obtaining a 90 percent loan of $184,500, the sale would be contingent upon the lender agreeing to the value of the property and the loan amount.

However, if the lender (lender's appraiser) valued the property at only $200,000 instead of the agreed-upon sale price of $205,000, you would have to make a choice as to whether you wish to pay more than the appraised value for the home. Also, if you decided to go through with the sale at the original sale price, the lender might ask you to come up with a larger down payment to keep the loan at the 90 percent loan to value (LTV). In other words, the lender would make only a $180,000 loan (90 percent of $200,000); you would have to put an additional $4,500 down.

In most cases, buyers will not agree to pay more than the appraised value for the property. If the lender will not reevaluate the appraisal and agree to lend the full $184,500, the buyers usually will ask the sellers to lower the sale price to match the appraisal.

Sometimes a lender will realize that its appraisal was low and agree to lend the amount that the buyers requested; however, those occasions are rare. That's why you need to be well versed in resale pricing procedures to be able to make proper and intelligent offers on real property.

How to View and Inspect Homes Properly

As a successful home buyer, you must learn how to view and inspect homes systematically, keeping in mind that some homes are truly "set up to show." If you have ever viewed an elaborate new model home, you know what I mean. The model homes view beautifully because they are professionally decorated and furnished; they don't just show, they show off!

You need to look deeper than just the surface appearance of the home.

WHAT ARE YOU LOOKING FOR?

There are three very important factors that you must always consider when viewing homes. These factors are:

- Location
- Overall condition
- Age

Location of the Home

First and foremost, you must remember that it will never matter how great a house is or how much you love it. If you don't like the neighborhood in which the home is located, you should not consider the property.

Buyers sometimes make the mistake of letting an agent talk them into viewing a home in a neighborhood that they have decided is not acceptable. The agent usually says, "The area is not exactly where you want to be, but this house is just perfect for you!" Unfortunately, the buyers usually love the house and either walk away feeling cheated because they never find another home they like as much, or they buy the home, live there for a short time, and end up selling (sometimes at a loss) because they hate the neighborhood. In either case, the buyers have set themselves up for failure.

Before you ever begin looking at specific homes, make sure the neighborhood is acceptable. If not, do not look at even one home there.

Overall Condition of the Home

As you view homes, you will be looking for the three Ds: dirt, discoloration, and damage. If a home is just dirty it can be cleaned, of course. However, oftentimes the cleanliness of the home will give you insight into the general upkeep a home has had. Compare the home you are viewing to the other homes in the area. Is it average, below average, or above average? How does it measure up?

If you see discoloration on the walls or ceilings, there is probably water leakage of some kind. It could be an old problem that has been repaired, but you better check it out.

Damage, of course, is anything that is in obvious need of repair. Some sellers will not make the repairs but will give a buyer a financial allowance for the work. However, the lender who will be making the loan on the property will have to approve an arrangement of that type.

Age of the Home

Age is of less concern than the condition of a home, in that older properties sometimes are so well built and maintained that they are actually better than new homes.

VIEWING AND INSPECTING HOMES

Viewing and inspecting a home should be a three-step process. Later in this chapter we detail each step, but for now you should know what the steps are:

1. Make a cursory view of a property and decide if the home is at all to your liking. Could you live there? Look only for shape, layout, size and general feeling. If it's a *maybe*, go to step 2.
2. Use your Home Search Checklist (located in the Appendix) and view the home again, checking to see just how much of what you want and need is in the home. Take note of what you like and dislike about the home. If after the second viewing you still

feel that the home is a consideration for purchase, make the third and most detailed inspection of the property.

3. Using the Home Inspection Form (located in the Appendix) go through the property carefully. Inspect every inch, nook, cranny, and crevice in the home. Take detailed notes, take pictures, make a video . . . anything and everything to help you know and remember as much as you possibly can about the property. Before you video or take photos in a home, make sure that you have the owner's or the owner's agent's permission to do so.

WHAT SHOULD YOU EXPECT?

Expect anything and everything!

As I indicated earlier, some homes will be set up, cleaned up, and prepared to show beautifully. It is always a joy to view these homes, even if you are not especially interested in them.

On the other hand, in many other homes you will swear that the total preparation for the sale amounted to running a dust mop over the wooden floors, mowing the grass, and sticking a "For Sale" sign in the front yard.

You must learn to be open-minded and look at the "potential" that the home has to meet your needs and desires.

AGENT PREVIEWING

In some cases, agents may preview homes before you actually see the properties, thereby "weeding out" the less than acceptable houses that, for any number of reasons, might not meet your requirements. If you have provided your agent with good, detailed information about your exact needs and desires, it will be quite simple for a competent agent to decide which homes you want to see.

Unfortunately, many agents are too busy to preview a dozen or more homes prior to the actual client showings. In that case, it is important that your agent takes the time to contact the listing agents and brokers and obtains as much information as possible about the homes.

Too often, potential buyers spend days riding around in a car with an agent viewing homes that do not come close to being acceptable. In these situations, the buyers probably have not given the agent enough information for the job to be done effectively; or maybe the agent is just not listening. In either situation, it is a waste of everyone's time.

Agents should be attending brokers' open houses and office caravan tours as often as possible to maintain an up-to-date working knowledge of the homes on the market. During those viewings, agents should take notes and really get to know the properties, thereby eliminating the need for previewing properties prior to buyer showings.

Step 1: Making the Cursory View

Begin your cursory view as you drive up to a property. An old real estate question is: How do you feel about the curb appeal? Try to think of coming home to this property every night; this is where emotion should play a part in your analysis of the home. What is your first impression and how do you feel about the property?

Throughout your first quick view of the home, simply look for your overall needs: the right number of bedrooms and bathrooms, kitchen requirements, layout, traffic flow through the house, yard requirements, and the general feeling of the property.

Don't be concerned now with room colors, wallpaper, specific decorating, drapes, window treatments, or floor coverings. Your only question should be: Could this home possibly meet our needs and desires, and is it worth making a more detailed inspection of the property?

If you think that there is just no way this home will meet your needs and wants, don't waste any more time and go to the next property.

If there is a possibility that this home could work, begin your second, more detailed viewing of the home.

Step 2: Using the Home Search Checklist

With your checklist in hand, go through the property again and take some basic notes with regard to how well the home and yard meet your wants and needs. Check every room and rate the amenities of the property as indicated on the checklist. (See the Appendix for a Home Search Checklist.)

When you have finished this second viewing, you will know if your interest in the property warrants the third and very detailed inspection process.

Step 3: Making the Real Home Inspection

Once you reach this step, you should have determined that this home could be where you will live in the near future. Now you need to complete a critical inspection.

As I said earlier, you are looking for the three Ds: dirt, discoloration or damage. Inspecting the home in parts rather than trying to make a complete inspection of each room is easier and more effective. To guide you through the inspection process, record your in-

SMART TIP:

One trick to use while making the third and most detailed inspection of a home is to carry a pad of Post-it® notes. Each time you discover a potential problem, make a note and "Post it" on the problem area. Some rooms may end up looking like a huge bulletin board, but you will know exactly what needs to be done without referring back to the inspection form. (If sellers are present during the showing, you may be better off *not* using this plan. Also, make sure you pick up all your notes before you leave the property.)

SMART TIP:

Sometimes buyers have a difficult time spotting problem areas when making an inspection. One great technique you can use to narrow your focus and see even the smallest of details is to create and use a "Buyer's Viewbox." Simply remove the top of a shoe box and cut a hole about four inches wide and two inches high in the bottom center. Hold the shoe box up to you about a foot from your face (like the viewing screen of a movie camera). Look at literally every inch of the house. As you move through a home using the viewbox, you will be amazed by how many small details will jump out at you. Using your viewbox, you will spot blemishes even the home inspectors sometimes miss. (Because it is very time consuming, do not use the viewbox until your third and most detailed inspection of the property.)

spection results on the inspection form provided in the Appendix. Also, save the garage and exterior inspection for last. (Perform the inspection in the order on the form.)

Floors and Baseboards

Start your physical inspection with the floors and baseboards. Go through each room noting each spot, tear, scuff, loose or broken tile, discoloration, or imperfection. Be very critical and take detailed notes of any tattered carpet or chipped and broken tile. Remember, record everything. You can decide later, if you make an offer on the property, what things are really of concern. If a home is full of furniture, you may need to ask that the furnishings be moved for inspection, or handle the question with a separate Seller Disclosure Form.

Look closely for discoloration of the carpet; this could indicate leaks and water damage. Check the floor underneath rugs or carpet.

Walls and Doors

Next check the walls and doors. As with the floors, go through each room and inspect the walls and doors for cracks, spots, dirt, fingerprints, holes, chipped or peeling paint. If any of the walls have wallpaper, check the seams (top, bottom, and sides) carefully.

Make sure that all doors operate smoothly, the doorknobs turn easily, the hinges are tight, there are no squeaks, all of the locks work, and the doors or door frames are not swollen or do not have cracks or missing pieces. Do all sliding glass doors operate and lock smoothly? Is there any sign of leakage around doors? Are exterior doors all solid core? Do special trapdoors to attic or the basement work properly?

> **SMART TIP:**
> If large areas of any walls are covered with paintings, posters, photographs, flags, animal heads, skins, or anything else, it may be wise to check behind them for damage. Get permission from the seller or the seller's agent if you are going to move anything. It would be much wiser to have the seller move the item for you.

Windows

Replacing windows can be very expensive, so it is important that you examine every window in the house carefully. Are all windows secure, and do they work smoothly and easily? Are all screens in place and secure? Are all latches, handles, and cranks in place, and do they operate correctly? Are all hinges in place, lubricated, and do they operate correctly?

If windows slide, do they move all the way up and down smoothly? Are any rope/pulley attachments in good shape and operating correctly? Is there any sign of leakage around the windows, frames, or sills?

If bars or security devices cover the windows, do they open properly from the inside for safety escape? Most important, do all locks work properly?

Window Coverings

In some cases, the window coverings will stay with the home. If so, unless you will replace them, see that the drapes are clean and in good repair. (Dry cleaning of drapes can cost hundreds of dollars; replacement, thousands of dollars.) Are all pull cords or opening and closing devices working well? Make sure all blinds and other coverings are in good shape and operate smoothly. Are all curtain rods straight, strong, and attached to the wall properly? Are there any stains or discoloration on the inside of the drapes or on the drapery linings? Stains could indicate leakage in the windows or walls, or just mean that the windows have been left open during bad weather. (Check it out.) Are the seams—top, bottom, and sides—secure and in good shape? Do all of the window coverings fit the windows properly?

Ceilings

Next check the ceilings. Room by room, look for cracking, chipping, discoloration, paint peeling, or blown acoustic falling off. Is all ceiling lighting working properly?

If blown acoustic ceilings are

> **SMART TIP:**
> Discoloration on the ceilings or walls may indicate a leak in the roof or the exterior walls. If this type of discoloration is apparent, make sure that you require a complete home and termite inspection. (This is also an inspection for water damage.)

discolored from smoke or grease, it may be better to have the ceilings reblown instead of trying to spray-paint them.

Kitchen

The kitchen comes next. Start with all of the cupboards and drawers. Are they the right height? Are there enough of them? Is there a pantry? Do all of the doors and drawers open or slide smoothly? Are all shelves secure and strong? Are all handles in good shape? Is there enough light in the kitchen? Are all light sockets working? Are the light fixtures clean and in good repair? Do the ventilation fans work properly?

Do the lights over the stove work? Is the stove top and front free of stains? Is the stove clock working? Are the stove drip pans and oven trays in good shape and free of stains? Are the interiors of all ovens free of stains? Are stove racks in place and in good shape? Turn on the stove and oven; do they work properly? Does the timer work? Do all burners operate smoothly? Are all stove and oven handles/buttons in good shape and working smoothly?

Are all sinks in good repair (any cracks, stains, scratches, or chips)? Are all faucets and handles in good shape? Do all handles turn or operate smoothly? Any leaks around faucets or handles? Is all caulking sealed and in good repair? Turn the water on and see if there are any leaks in or below the sinks? Do all drains work well? Does the garbage disposal work properly?

Do the dishwasher, trash compactor, microwave, refrigerator, and any other specialty appliances (that stay with the home) operate properly? Does the ice maker work (if there is one)? Are the countertops in good shape?

Check the floors to see if they are free of bubbles, swelling, or discoloration, especially in front or around sinks, drains, or the dishwasher.

Living Room and
Family Room (Bonus Room)

A home may have both a living room and a family room. Use a Home Inspection Checklist for each room. Does it have a good "feel" for a living or family room? Is it large enough? Will there be room for your furniture? Is there good traffic flow? Is it convenient to other rooms in the house? Will noise carry to or from this room?

Is it convenient to a bathroom? Where will you put your Christmas tree? Is there good heating, cooling, and ventilation? Is there good lighting? Are shelves or built-in cabinets secure? If there are any cabinet doors, do they work properly and are all handles in good shape?

If there is a wet bar of any kind in the home, it should be inspected using the bathroom inspection checklist plus the following questions: Is the bar itself secure and in good shape? Are upholstered items tattered, worn, peeling, or pulled loose from frames? Are all rails secure and undamaged? Are bar stools (if they stay with the home) in good shape? Is the specialty lighting operating properly?

Bathrooms

Each bathroom should be scrutinized carefully. Are the tubs in good shape (no cracks, discoloration, peeling, or chipping)? Is the tile and caulking secure and not discolored? Are the drains flowing well? Are the faucets in good shape with no leaks or drips? Are all handles working smoothly? Is there good water pressure? Are the plugs or stoppers accessible and operating correctly?

Do all ventilation fans or special wall heating units work properly and quietly? Are the countertops all in good shape (no chipping or loose edges)? Are there leaks under sinks or raised tubs? Is the ceiling in good condition (no peeling, mold, chipping, or soft spots)? Are the cabinets in good shape? Are the handles and doors operating smoothly (do they close and latch properly)? Are all the shelves in place and secure? Are the mirrors in good shape?

Does the toilet flush and refill properly? Are there leaks or seepage around toilet? Is the flooring in good shape (especially around toilet, tub, shower, and sinks)? Do the showers operate correctly and with good water pressure? Are the soap trays in place and in good shape? Are the shower heads the proper height? Are the shower doors or curtains in good shape (no stains or cracking)? If other devices, such as a spa tub, bidet, or steam room are included, do they work properly?

Bedrooms

People spend roughly 40 percent of their lives in their bedrooms. Make sure they are comfortable. Are they large enough for your furniture now and in the future? Are they the right shape? Are they or can they be lighted properly? Are the windows satisfactory? At what time of the day and does the sun hit the room?

Will there be comfortable traffic flow? Are they accessible to bathrooms? Are they situated in the home for convenience and/or privacy? Are the closets large and convenient enough? Is the view acceptable? Is there acceptable ventilation? Are there good heating and cooling vents or systems?

Closets

One of the biggest problem areas in many homes is the lack of closet space. Check the amount of closet space carefully and compare it to what you currently have as opposed to what you really need.

Are there enough closets, both for hanging clothes and for shelf storage? Are all hanging rods straight, in place, and secure? Are all hanging hooks and shelves in place and secure? Do any closets have a bad odor? Is the lighting in the closets adequate and does it work properly?

Laundry Areas

Laundry areas often are overlooked, but they are a very important part of a home. If the washer and dryer stay with the home, do they operate properly? Are there leaks at the washer connections? Is the dryer exhaust connected properly? If it is a gas dryer, are there leaks or any gas odor?

If the washer and dryer do not stay with the home, are there proper connections for your appliances (gas, electrical, etc.)? Any floor or wall damage (swelling around the dryer or washer from movement or leakage)?

If there is a sink, do the faucets work properly, the drains flow smoothly with no leaks, is the caulking secure, are all handles in good shape?

Is the laundry area well lit? Do all cabinet doors work smoothly? Are all handles in good shape? Are all shelves secure?

Staircases

Staircases also often are overlooked but are used extensively. Are the staircases comfortably wide enough and not too steep? Are there any sharp turns making it difficult to move furniture in or out? Are the stairs very solid or do they give with weight on them? Do the stairs squeak, groan, or make any other noises? Does sound reverberate through the house when someone goes up or down the stairs in a hurry? Are the handrails secure with no movement?

Is the covering on the stairs secure? If uncovered, is the finish of the stairs in good shape (no peeling or chipping)? Are there any nails protruding? Is each wooden railing piece or slide slat secure?

Are the posts at the top and bottom of the stairs and hand rail very secure and immovable? Are all decorative knobs or fixtures on rail or stairs secure and complete? Is the paint or finish on the exterior of the stairs and rails complete?

Are the staircases well lit? If a staircase goes to a basement or attic, is it safe? Is there a secure handrail? If the staircase is a movable, pull-down kind (usually to an attic), do all of the parts work properly and is it easy to operate?

Shelves, Bookcases, and Drawers

Next examine all shelves, bookcases, and drawers not already covered in other sections. Are all handles in good shape? Do the doors and drawers move smoothly? Is the finish on the inside and outside in good shape? Are all hinges moving smoothly? Are all shelves secure? All lighting adequate and working properly?

Fireplace or Wood Stoves

In some areas, nearly every home has a fireplace or wood stove. These units should be given close scrutiny.

Are there any cracks in the glass, frame, or actual stove/fireplace unit? Is all piping secure? Is there excessive burn or soot area around the fireplace pipes or the doors on the stove? Is the wood grate in place and does it appear to be the right size for the unit? Is there an adequate screen, glass, or covering to prevent sparks or cinders from escaping the unit? Do the screens, doors, or other entry to unit operate smoothly?

Do you like the size, shape, and style of the hearth and the mantel? If the fireplace tools stay with the home, are they in good shape? If there is a fan or forced-air unit, does it operate effectively and quietly? If there is a gas starter or if it is a gas unit, does it work properly? Is there any gas odor when the unit is off? Is there any sign of water leaks around the chimney or pipes where they exit the room into the ceiling or wall?

Electrical System

The basic items you will be concerned with are outlets, switches, and fixtures. Leave the extensive examination to the professional home inspector.

SMART TIP:
If a fireplace or wood stove has been used to burn a lot of paper, cardboard, pressed logs, or pitchy wood, have the chimney and flue professionally cleaned. At any rate, this service should be performed no less than every two years.

Are there an adequate number of outlets in every room? (Think of lights, appliances, and vacuums.) Are the switches and outlets located conveniently? Are all wall plates in good shape? Are all outlets and switches attached properly and secure? Do all specialty switches, such as dimmers, work properly?

Is there any apparent overusage in any electrical outlet? Any black or burned area around any outlet? If there is any specialty lighting (track lighting, spots, etc.), does the wiring appear to be done properly (no open cords, etc.)? If there are any pull switches, are the cords in good shape?

As you check the basement, attic, or other areas where some electrical wiring may be accessible, keep your eyes open for any potential problem areas, such as exposed, burned, broken or hanging wires, loose sockets, blackened face plates, or generally shoddy wiring. Never touch any exposed wiring or sockets!

SMART TIP:
It is a good idea to check every outlet in the home to see that it is working properly. This can be done by using a small night light. Also, inexpensive devices designed specifically for this purpose are available at any hardware store.

Also, if there have been any additions to or remodeling of the home, make sure that the electrical wiring was done to code. This may require an inspection by an electrician or a city or county inspector.

Heating and Cooling Units

Again, it is advisable to have heating and cooling units professionally inspected and serviced. Have these units been serviced recently? Do they operate properly? Is there a strong air flow? Do all vents open and close easily? Is there air flowing from every vent? Do units operate quietly?

If there are any window units, are they secure and are the frames sealed tightly? Are all of the exposed portions of the units properly covered and safe? Is all exposed ducting secure and insulated properly?

Do all thermostats work properly? Do all timing mechanisms on the units work properly? Do the pilot lights stay lit? Is there any gas smell around the gas furnace? If oil heating is used, are storage tanks easily accessible? If propane heating is used, is the tank accessible in all seasons? Do the units adequately heat and cool the home?

Basements and Attics

Basements and attics are of most concern if they are to be utilized as living or storage spaces. Are they dry (no leaks or dampness whatsoever)? Are there any stains or other evidence of prior water leakage? Is there enough headroom? Can the space be used adequately? Are there posts or dividers that break up the rooms or space uncomfortably? Are there appliances, such as a washer, dryer, heating unit, cooling unit, water softener, or water heater, that might make the areas less comfortable?

Is there adequate heating, cooling, and ventilation? Is there adequate lighting? Are all entryways and exits adequate? Are all stairways safe? Are all shelves, cabinets, and storage areas secure, accessible, and in good shape? Is there anything scary about these areas that might affect any of your family members? Are there any little critters running, crawling, or slithering around in these areas?

Noise Level

Some homes are just plain noisy! No matter where you are in the house, you can hear conversations in other rooms, the television playing, or water running in a tub. Check the home for noise by:

1. Turning on the showers or tubs and moving through the house while the water is running, especially the rooms adjoining bathrooms.
2. Standing downstairs and having someone walk heavily across the upstairs floors.

3. Having two or more people talking in the living room, kitchen, or family room while you wander through the rest of the house and listen.

4. Having someone move quickly up and down the staircase while you move from room to room throughout the house.

5. Having someone talk loudly in each of the bedrooms while you move into the other rooms.

6. Turning on the appliances, such as the washer, dryer, garbage disposal, dishwasher, or trash compactor, and walking through the house while they are operating.

7. Standing very quietly in the house and listening for traffic and outside noises.

Security Systems

If a home has a security system, make sure that it is operating properly and that the instruction manual is available when you take possession of the home.

Odors

That's right . . . smell! Walk outside, take a few breaths of fresh air, then enter the home and shut the door. How does the home smell? Nothing is worse than a home that has (for lack of another term) "house-a-tosis."

Surprisingly, the number-one complaint by buyers about homes is odor. The most frequently mentioned smells are animal odors, cigarette smoke, and mold. Unfortunately, if a home has been inundated with a bad odor for a long period of time, ridding it of that smell may be difficult.

Sometimes you will be greeted by the scrumptious smells of baking bread, simmering cinnamon, potpourri, or fragrance sprays when you enter a home. Be careful of these wonderful cover-ups. Sellers are taught to use these methods to improve the ambiance of a home. There is nothing wrong with these odor-enhancing techniques, as long as sellers are not trying to hide a severe problem. Lawsuits actually have resulted from sellers covering up smells that had permeated carpets, flooring, and walls and ultimately resurfaced weeks after the new buyers took possession of the property.

If the smell of the home is overwhelming in a good or bad way, be suspicious. If you are interested in the property but are legitimately concerned with the odor, ask that the home be aired out, then closed up tightly for a day just prior to viewing the property again.

This type of problem area can also be addressed on a separate Seller Disclosure Statement.

Porches, Decks, Patios, and Exterior Entryways

If a home has a deck, porch, patio, or entryway, make sure you check it out for looks, accessibility, and usability.

Are all stairs, guardrails, and handrails adequate and secure? Do the guardrails provide enough security (especially if you have children)? Is the deck, porch, or patio large enough for your uses? If the deck area has wooden flooring, is it finished and sealed properly (no nails sticking out) and is the surface smooth? Is the floor level? Does there appear to be any rotting or damage?

If the area is screened, is the screen fabric in good shape—no tears, rips, or pulling away at seams or edges? If the area is glassed, is the glass in good shape with no breakage or discoloration? Is the roof, awning, or other overhead covering in good shape?

Are any built-in barbecues in good working order? Is all built-in deck furniture in good shape? All locks, latches, doors, and cabinets in good working order? Does the doorbell work?

Garage

The garage has many areas that need to be examined. Is it large enough for your needs? Is it well lighted when the door(s) are open and closed? Is the floor in good shape and not discolored or stained? Are the walls in good shape (not marred, scratched, chipping, or peeling)? Are the doors and windows secure, working properly, locking adequately, and operating smoothly? Are all cabinets or drawers operating correctly? Are all benches and work shelves secure?

Are the fans or ventilation systems working properly? Does all overhead storage offer adequate access, and is the area secure (shelves, beams, etc.)? Is there adequate space for garden or power tools? If there is an animal door, is it installed properly, does it leak, does it work well, and is it small enough to not pose a security problem?

Do all electrical outlets and switches work properly? Do the main garage doors open and close easily? Are all hinges, springs, and mechanical parts in good shape? If there is an electric garage door opener, does it work properly? If the laundry area is in the garage, is it accessible even when cars are parked inside? If the water heater, water softener, or other appliances are located in the garage, are they out of the way, secure, and not posing a hazard?

Pools and Spas

This is another area where the services of a professional inspector or serviceperson is recommended.

Is the pool or spa professionally serviced or owner-maintained? Is it clean with no discoloration, mildew, or mold? Is the water clear and clean? Does the water appear to have the proper chemical balance? Are there any bugs in the water? Is there any algae near the waterline, on the sides or the bottom of the pool or spa? Any chipping or peeling of paint, stucco, or fiberglass in and around pool areas?

Are all of the pumps, heating units, cleaners, skimmers, hoses, and drains working properly? Are all ladders, steps, slides, diving boards, nets, and ropes in good shape? Does the water spray on water slides work properly?

Is all safety equipment accessible and in good working order? Are all gates, fences, and locks around the pool in good shape? Are all safety signs visible? Does the lighting work properly?

Is the pool or deck furniture that stays with the home in good shape? Is the decking in good shape with no cracking, chipping, or peeling? Are walkways to and from the pool in good shape?

Saunas and Steam Rooms

Do all heating units work properly? Are the benches in good shape (no splinters or nails sticking up)? Does the unit seal tightly? Does the timer work? Does the unit steam as it should (if it is a steam room)?

Home Exterior

The exterior of a home should be inspected as closely as the interior. Many problem areas will be visible even to the untrained eye.

Check the exterior walls—any cracks or holes in the stucco, wood, or other finish? Is the overall paint or finish in good shape? Any peeling, chipping, or major discoloration from the middle portion of the walls upward, which might indicate leaking? Any excessive water splash discoloration near the ground?

Are all gutters and down spouts in good repair and cleaned out? (Running a water hose into gutters is usually an adequate test method.) Are any of the eaves peeling, chipping, or molding? Are any of the corners of the building chipped or broken away? Are all of the window frames caulked and sealed well?

Are there any cracks in the foundation? Is the foundation painted or sealed properly? If there is a crawl space under the house, is it accessible? (Crawl spaces should never be used for storage!) Is the crawl space access screened or closed? Are ventilation openings both under the eves and beneath the house open and screened?

Are there any wooden structures attached or leaning against the house that might promote termites or other infestation? Are bushes, hedges, trees, or plants all situated so as not to rub or push against the exterior of the house? For security purposes, is all shrubbery trimmed back from windows and doors? Are all exterior doors (including the garage door) painted or finished properly?

Roof

The roof is a very important area to check. However, because it is not safely accessible, have a professional roof inspection if you or your agent think that it is necessary. If the roof is pitched (not flat), you will be able to see most of it simply by standing back and using binoculars.

Are any tiles, shakes, or pieces missing or out of place? Are there any holes or worn places? Is all caulking in good shape at the edges of the tile or composition and around any pipes or fireplaces? Are there any trees, limbs, or bushes scraping against the roof?

Are there any major areas of stain or discoloration possibly left by standing water? Are there any low areas or sections that appear to be sagging? Are the any antennas/satellites that appear to be causing damage to the roof? Are there any other wires connected to eaves or roof that could create leakage or other damage?

Yards

To many buyers, the yard is almost as important as the home itself.

Is it the right size and shape for your particular use? Are the bushes, trees, and hedges to your liking? If there is a sprinkler system, does it work properly (every sprinkler)? Are the sprinklers set low enough to allow easy mowing of the lawn? Is the lawn healthy? Are all of the plants and trees healthy? Do all of the plants stay with the property?

Is the yard set up for easy upkeep? Are all fences in good repair, well painted, and secure? Do all gates operate properly, latches work well, and locks secure? Is there any chipping, peeling, or major discoloration on fences? Are all driveways in good shape and free of major stains? Are all walkways in good repair? Are RV or special parking areas well maintained and in good shape? Are any special play or animal areas in good shape?

> **SMART TIP:**
> Make sure that you clarify whether all of the plants stay with the home. Sellers have been known to take bonsai trees, rosebushes, and other plants, thinking that these items are personal property.

CHECK THE UTILITY BILLS AND MAINTENANCE RECORDS

Always obtain a copy of utility bills for a least one year on any property in which you are interested. If sellers do not have the receipts or copies of the bills, they can get a printout from their utility companies.

Most home owners have records and receipts for any work that they have done on their property. Ask to see all of the maintenance and repair records for at least the past two years.

If you suspect that the home has suffered severe damage, such as from an earthquake, flood, hurricane, or other natural disaster, insist on receiving all repair and maintenance records relating to that damage and subsequent repairs.

WARRANTIES AND GUARANTEES

Always ask to see and obtain copies of any warranties or guarantees on any appliance, work (such as a roof), or repair that will remain in effect and pass with the sale of the home. For example, some roofs are guaranteed for as long as fifty years.

> **SMART TIP:**
> Remember, in most states, sellers are legally responsible to disclose to you any known problems with the home. If they fail to do so, they could be liable if something goes wrong after you purchase the home.

WHAT REPAIRS MUST BE MADE?

When the appraisal is completed, the appraiser may list certain repairs that must be made before the transaction can close. Also, he or she may request that certain professional inspections be made before the loan is approved. These inspections might include roof, termite, or even a complete home inspection.

If potential buyers have discovered problems (on their own), they have several choices as to how they might address the repairs. The best way is simply to include the repair as part of the offer to the sellers. As an example, if buyers want the sellers to install new carpet in a home prior to the close of the transaction, the written offer to purchase might include a stipulation along the lines of: This offer is conditioned upon the seller paying for and having installed new carpet throughout the home. Color, grade, and style of carpet shall be the buyer's choice. The cost shall not exceed $25 per square yard installed or a total cost of $4,500.

The second way for buyers to handle this example is to ask the sellers for a $4,500 allowance for new carpet, either off of the sale price of the home or to be returned in the escrow/closing. This option allows the buyers to choose and install the carpet on their own, with no time constraints.

The third option is to leave the decision as to the necessity for the repair or improvement to the appraiser or inspector. The buyers or buyers' agent should mention to the appraiser/inspector that they feel the carpet needs to be replaced and would like that area to receive special attention during the inspection. Likely the appraiser/inspector will note the area of complaint and the request itself on the written inspection form. In some cases, the appraiser/inspector may decide that the repair is not necessary and will decline to call the requested repair on the inspection.

If buyers have decided that a certain repair is necessary, they always should include the request for the improvement as part of the written offer to purchase. Remember, the key to a successful real estate transaction is negotiation up front when the offer is made.

SWEAT EQUITY

Sometimes buyers will have the expertise and will want to make necessary repairs themselves. In these cases, with the lender's permission, the sellers will take a specific dollar allowance off the home's sale price. The transaction will close and the buyers will be given time to complete the repair. At that time, the lender will have the opportunity to inspect and approve the work.

For example, an appraiser calls the replacement of exterior decking as a condition for lending the amount for which the buyers have applied. The sellers obtain a quote of $2,000 to have the work done. The buyers can complete the work and ask the lender for permission to do so after the close of the transaction. The lender approves the sweat equity request and agrees to a $2,000 credit toward the buyers' down payment for the repair. The transaction closes, the buyers make the repair (saving a considerable amount on labor), and sixty days after the close, the lender inspects and approves the work that the buyers completed.

The buyers save about $1,500 because they did the work themselves. This type of arrangement is an option in some cases, both with conventional and government loans.

LEGALITIES OF SELLER DISCLOSURE

Some defects in a home may not show up or be able to be detected even by a professional inspector. An example is an interior wall that was damaged by a leak in the roof or exterior wall. Some sellers make a severe mistake and try to cover up a problem that exists in a home. In this case, sellers might repair and repaint the wall, but not make the necessary repair in the roof or exterior wall to stop the leak. Sellers who think that buyers will not take action will be in for a rude awakening when the leak reappears six months later.

Another common mistake sellers make is not advising potential buyers that there may be ongoing, recurring problems with the property. An example might be plumbing problems that recur due to tree roots growing into underground pipes. Completely solving this problem might require tree removal or pipe replacement. (Either case could be very costly.)

Sometimes sellers will be advised that a heating or cooling system will need to be replaced in the near future. Again, if they fail to advise the buyers of the potential problem, those sellers could be liable under the laws of required seller disclosure.

WHAT MUST BE DISCLOSED?

Since the mid-1980s, many states have made it mandatory that sellers disclose to buyers any existing problems or defects of which they are aware. As of July 1, 1996, only four states—Alabama, Arizona, Kansas, and Tennessee—do not require disclosure in the form of a Seller Disclosure Statement. All other states require that sellers disclose any substantial problems or defects that could affect the value of the home. No longer does the Latin phrase *caveat emptor* (buyer beware) apply. Sellers can choose to sell a home with many problems and defects in an "as-is condition," but in most states those sellers must disclose every problem area that affects the value of the home.

HOW SHOULD DISCLOSURE BE DONE?

In many states (about twenty-eight as of July 1, 1996), sellers are required to complete a written Seller Disclosure Form or Statement. These forms cover everything from appliances to roofs, plumbing, flooring, and termites. In some cases they even require disclosure with regard to zoning changes or new bonds or assessments that might affect the cost of living in the home or the area.

Other areas of disclosure that have become critical recently are environmental hazards such as lead, asbestos, and radon. Certain states require special testing for these hazards.

Even in states where seller disclosure is voluntary (not required), it is recommended that every seller disclose all problem areas. Losing a potential buyer might be better than making the sale and ending up with years of litigation and expense.

Here is a question that arises periodically: Are sellers required to disclose strange, bizarre, or possibly offensive occurrences that have been related to or happened in the house? Some examples might be a home where a rape or murder occurred, someone died in one of the bedrooms from a highly contagious disease, or the home is reputed to be haunted. Each state has different rules that affect the required seller disclosure. In some states, court cases have determined that sellers do not have to disclose these bizarre incidents; in fact, if the disclosure is made, it may violate certain civil rights.

To understand required seller disclosure in your particular area, check with your real estate professional. If the agent cannot provide adequate information, call your State Department of Real Estate; it will be able to direct you to the proper source.

THE SELLER DISCLOSURE STATEMENT

The Seller Disclosure Statement in Figure 7.1 is an example of the form required or used in many states.

When completing this form, sellers should be very specific about any problem areas. As an example, if sellers indicate that a leak exists, they should include where exactly

SMART TIP:
With regard to seller disclosure, remember that sellers are not warranting anything and they are not agreeing to fix the problem, they are merely disclosing the problem area. How the problem will be addressed will be up to you as the buyer.

FIGURE 7.1 **REAL ESTATE SELLER DISCLOSURE STATEMENT**

REAL ESTATE SELLER DISCLOSURE STATEMENT

Property Address:_____ Inspection Date:_____

The following aspects of the above-referenced property have been personally inspected by the undersigned buyers and their condition noted accordingly on this form.

The disclosure statement concerns the real property situated in the city of _____ , county of _____ , State of California, described as _____ . This statement is a disclosure of the condition of the above described property in compliance with section 1102 of the Civil Code as of _____ , 19_____ . It is not a warranty of any kind by the seller(s) or any agent(s) representing any principal(s) in this transaction, and is not a substitute for any inspections of warranties the principal(s) may wish to obtain.

Coordinate with Other Disclosure Forms: This Real Estate Transfer Statement is made pursuant to Section 1102 of the Civil Code. Other statutes require disclosures, depending upon the details of the particular real estate transaction (for example: special study zone and purchase-money liens on residential property).

Substituted Disclosures: The Seller disclosures have or will be in connection with this real estate transfer, and are intended to satisfy the disclosure obligations on this form, where the subject matter is the same: _____
_____
_____

Seller's Information: The Seller discloses the following information with the knowledge that even though this is not a warranty, prospective Buyers may rely on this information in deciding whether and on what terms to purchase the subject property. Seller hereby authorizes any agent(s) representing any principal(s) in this transaction to provide a copy of this statement to any person or entity in connection with any actual or anticipated sale of the property.

The following are representations made by the Seller(s) and are not the representations of the agent(s), if any. This information is a disclosure and is not intended to be part of any contract between the Buyer and Seller. Seller ❏ is ❏ is not occupying the property.

A. The subject property has the items checked below:

❏ Range	❏ Oven	❏ Microwave	❏ Dishwasher	❏ Trash Compactor
❏ Garbage Disposal	❏ W/D Hookups	❏ Window Screens	❏ Rain Gutters	❏ Burglar Alarm
❏ Smoke Detector(s)	❏ Fire Alarm	❏ TV Antenna	❏ Satellite Dish	❏ Intercom
❏ Central Heating	❏ Central Air Conditioning	❏ Evaporators Cooler(s)	❏ Wall/Wind Air Cond.	❏ Sprinklers
❏ Public Sewer System	❏ Septic Tank	❏ Sump Pump	❏ Water Softener	❏ Patio/Decking
❏ Built-in Barbecue	❏ Gazebo	❏ Sauna	❏ Pool	❏ Spa/Hot Tub
❏ Security Gate(s)	❏ Garage Door Opener(s)	❏ Attached Garage	❏ Not Attached Garage	❏ Carport
❏ Pool/Spa Heater—Gas	❏ Pool/Spa Heater—Solar	❏ Pool/Spa Heater—Electric	❏ Water Heater—Gas	❏ Water Heater—Solar
❏ Water Heater—Electric	❏ Water Supply—City	❏ Roof—Age_____	❏ Fireplace	

B. Are you (SELLER) aware of any significant defects/malfunctions: If yes, list/describe:
_____
_____
_____
_____

C. Are you (SELLER) aware of the following:

1. Substances, materials, or products that may be an environmental hazard such as, but not limited to, asbestos, formaldehyde, radon gas, lead-based paint, fuel or chemical storage tanks, and contaminated soil or water on the subject property.	❏ Yes	❏ No
2. Features of the property shared in common with adjoining landowners, such as walls, fences, and driveways, whose use or responsibility for maintenance may have an effect on the subject property.	❏ Yes	❏ No
3. Any encroachments, easements, or similar matters that may affect your interest in the subject.	❏ Yes	❏ No
4. Room additions, structural modifications, or other alterations or repairs made without necessary permits.	❏ Yes	❏ No
5. Room additions, structural modifications, or other alterations or repairs not in compliance with building codes.	❏ Yes	❏ No
6. Landfill (compacted or otherwise) on the property or any portion thereof.	❏ Yes	❏ No
7. Any settling from any cause, or slippage, sliding, or other spoil problems.	❏ Yes	❏ No
8. Flooding, drainage, or grading problems.	❏ Yes	❏ No
9. Major damage to the property or any of the structures from fire, earthquake, floods, or landslides.	❏ Yes	❏ No
10. Any zoning violations, nonconforming uses, violations of "setback" requirements.	❏ Yes	❏ No
11. Neighborhood noise problems or other nuisances.	❏ Yes	❏ No
12. CC&R's or other deed restrictions or obligations.	❏ Yes	❏ No
13. Homeowners' Association that has any authority over the subject property.	❏ Yes	❏ No
14. Any "common area" (facilities such as pools, tennis courts, walkways, or other areas co-owned in undivided interest with others).	❏ Yes	❏ No
15. Any notice of abatement or citations against the property.	❏ Yes	❏ No
16. Any lawsuits against the seller threatening to or affecting this real property.	❏ Yes	❏ No

Seller certifies that the information herein is true and correct to the best of the Seller's knowledge as of the date signed by the Seller.

Seller:_____   Date:_____

it exists, how extensive it is, when it occurs, and what damage has been caused as a result.

As you get closer to the actual offer and transaction process, you will need to develop a basic understanding of financing, terms, and the guidelines lenders use to decide which applicants are given loans and on what conditions.

The next four chapters will give you an in-depth look into the actual lending process.

CHAPTER EIGHT

Understanding Financing and Terms

AN OVERALL VIEW OF LENDING

Lenders use a process called "underwriting" to approve loans. During this underwriting process, lenders look at many factors to determine who will receive a loan and on what properties that lender is willing to loan. Most important, lenders will decide exactly how much they are willing to loan to a particular borrower on a particular property.

Four principles are used as the basis for making lending decisions. These are commonly known as the four Cs: capacity, credit, character, and collateral.

It is important for buyers to understand these four terms, how they relate to the loan process, and how they play a critical role in the underwriting and the ultimate decision-making process for the lender.

Capacity

This means that you should have the capacity to repay the debt. Here your employment is evaluated, including your actual occupation and how long you have been doing that type of work. How long have you been on your current job? How much do you earn, and what is the likelihood of your continuing in your position?

Included in the capacity is the evaluation of your expenses. For example, how do you live? After deducting your expenses, will you have the capacity to repay the loan?

Credit

This term actually should be called credit history, because lenders are very interested in how much you owe, how often you borrow, if you pay your bills on time, and generally speaking, whether you live within your means.

Lenders are looking for signs of stability; they will examine how long you have lived at your current and past addresses and how long you have worked at your current and past job(s).

Character

Character is rather esoteric in that lenders are looking at how truthful you are in your business dealings and how you handle your obligations. Lenders will look at the existence of past or present lawsuits and bankruptcies or liens that might appear on a borrower's credit history.

Collateral

Collateral refers to the property on which the lender will make the loan. Lenders' analyses of property include more than the borrower's willingness and ability to repay the loan. They also look at the value of the property itself. (A borrower might be less likely to repay a loan if the property decreases in value).

Lenders want a solid source of collateral for any money that they loan.

In general, lenders can't wait to loan money, but once the loan has been made, they can't wait to get the money back.

DOWN PAYMENTS

For many buyers/borrowers, the most difficult part of the home-buying process is saving enough money to make a down payment. If buyers qualify, mortgages are available in most areas for as little as 3 percent down.

VA loans insured by the Department of Veteran's Affairs are available to qualified veterans with no money down. However, in some areas (particularly in major cities), prices have risen so high that the maximum no-money-down, VA guaranteed loan of $203,000 is not enough to purchase a property.

Buyers must understand that even though they can secure a low or no-money-down loan, often they will not qualify for the substantial monthly payments that result.

Down payment requirements for different loans vary from

lender to lender and from area to area. However, as a rule, your down payment will be predicated by the price of the home and the amount of the payment for which you can qualify.

As mentioned previously, the standard down payments on loans range upward from about 10 to 20 percent for conventional loans and 3 percent for government loans. Bear in mind, however, that the larger down payment you can provide, the better chance you will have of your loan being approved. Lenders much prefer buyers who have made a substantial up-front investment on a home, thereby reducing the loan-to-value ratio and the risk for that lender.

THE LOAN PROCESS

Figure 8.1, on the next page, will give you a visual breakdown of what actually occurs in the loan process. A more in-depth explanation of the entire process follows.

INTEREST RATES

Interest rates can vary dramatically from lender to lender in any area or specific market. Also, certain lenders may vary their interest rates from borrower to borrower based on the borrower's overall credit and the property being purchased.

Most probably, a large company will be able to borrow at a lower rate of interest than average home buyers who are buying their first home. Lenders often base their interest rates on the risk involved in making the loan. Usually, borrowers who are considered low risk will get a lower interest rate; high-risk borrowers get a higher interest rate.

On a smaller scale and with less variance in the rates, borrowers with a substantial down payment, a solid credit history, and a good employment record probably could obtain a loan at a lower interest rate than borrowers with a small down payment and just mediocre credit and employment.

Interest rates can greatly affect the amount that borrowers ultimately pay for a property. Table 8.1 shows the total amount of

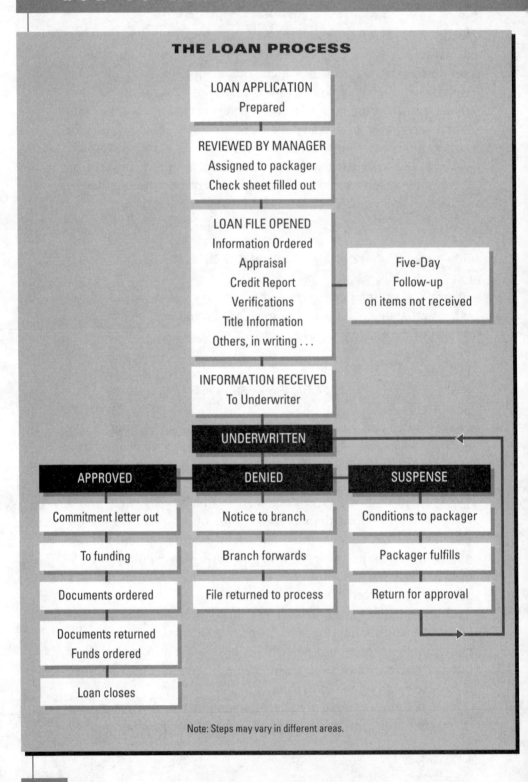

THE LOAN PROCESS

LOAN APPLICATION
Prepared

REVIEWED BY MANAGER
Assigned to packager
Check sheet filled out

LOAN FILE OPENED
Information Ordered
Appraisal
Credit Report
Verifications
Title Information
Others, in writing . . .

Five-Day
Follow-up
on items not received

INFORMATION RECEIVED
To Underwriter

UNDERWRITTEN

APPROVED

DENIED

SUSPENSE

Commitment letter out

Notice to branch

Conditions to packager

To funding

Branch forwards

Packager fulfills

Documents ordered

File returned to process

Return for approval

Documents returned
Funds ordered

Loan closes

Note: Steps may vary in different areas.

< FIGURE 8.1 **THE LOAN PROCESS**

principal and interest that borrowers would pay for a property if the loan was repaid over a thirty-year period at interest rates of 8, 9, 10, and 11 percent. The original loan amount was $125,000.

TABLE 8.1

LOAN REPAYMENT INTEREST RATE COMPARISON

ANNUAL INTERST RATE

	8%	9%	10%	11%
Monthly Payment	$917.21	$1005.78	$1096.96	$1190.40
Total Amount Paid in 30 years	$330,194.06	$362,080.18	$394,907.21	$428,545.53

As you can see, over thirty years, the total amount paid varies by over $98,000 in interest between 8 percent per annum and 11 percent per annum.

Over the past thirty years, interest rates have varied considerably,

SMART TIP:
Keep in mind that all interest paid is considered a write-off for tax purposes, making home ownership one of the best deductions.

reaching the highest point in 1981 and the lowest point in 1993. Table 8.2 shows the national average home loan interest rates from 1965 to 1995.

Payments can vary considerably depending on the interest rate charged. Using our previous example of a loan amount of $125,000, amortized over thirty years, Table 8.3 indicates the monthly payments on the loan at interest rates ranging from 7 to 12 percent.

TABLE 8.2
NATIONAL MORTGAGE
INTEREST RATE AVERAGES

Year	Average Rate (%)	Year	Average Rate (%)
1965	6.80	1981	16.66
1966	6.85	1982	15.32
1967	6.96	1983	13.24
1968	7.53	1984	12.69
1969	7.27	1985	11.70
1970	7.46	1986	9.64
1971	7.52	1987	9.64
1972	7.71	1988	10.12
1973	8.71	1989	9.86
1974	9.55	1990	11.66
1975	9.40	1991	8.85
1976	9.02	1992	8.27
1977	9.00	1993	6.83
1978	9.93	1994	8.21
1979	11.41	1995	8.93
1980	14.07	1996	8.37

TABLE 8.3
PAYMENT COMPARISON CHART

Annual Interest Rate (%)	Monthly Payment
7.0	$ 831.63
7.5	$ 874.02
8.0	$ 917.21
8.5	$ 961.14
9.0	$1,005.78
9.5	$1,051.07
10.0	$1,096.96
10.5	$1,143.42
11.0	$1,190.40
11.5	$1,237.86
12.0	$1,285.77

You will note at 7 percent interest, the monthly payment is $831.63, but at 12 percent, the monthly payment is $1,285.77. That is a difference of over $450 per month, *for the same loan amount.*

ANNUAL INTEREST RATE vs. ANNUAL PERCENTAGE RATE (APR)

What's the difference between the annual interest rate and the annual percentage rate?

The term "Annual Percentage Rate" (APR) is often confusing to borrowers in that the APR can differ slightly from the annual interest rate which the borrower was quoted and charged on their loan.

The APR is simply the actual cost to the borrower for the loan, including the annual interest rate charged plus any costs that were charged to obtain that loan.

The following example shows the calculation of a borrower's APR charged on a loan.

Loan Amount = $125,000
Annual Interest Rate = 8.5%
Points paid to obtain a loan = 1.5
(Each point represents 1 percent of the loan amount. Points are explained further later in this chapter.)

APR = 8.66%

Understand, borrowers will repay a loan amount of $125,000. However, the truth-in-lending laws view the points paid to obtain the loan as prepaid interest. Therefore, when the APR is calculated, the amount of the points is deducted from the actual loan amount because the points were paid up front to obtain the loan. I know this seems confusing, but the next example should clear it up for you.

Loan Amount = $125,000
(borrowers will repay this amount)

Points paid to obtain a loan = $1,875
Actual Amount Received = $123,125
(by borrowers after points were deducted)

APR = 8.66%

Because the borrowers had to pay 1.5 points ($1,875) to obtain the loan, the APR is actually 8.66 instead of the 8.5, which is the annual interest rate charged. If the borrower paid nothing up front in fees or points to obtain the loan, the annual interest rate and the APR would be the same.

POINTS

Lenders may ask borrowers to pay the points at the inception of the loan. In some cases, these points may be added to the loan amount and financed over the term of the loan. Again, each point represents 1 percent of the loan amount.

Lenders sometimes use points to make their interest rates appear more appealing. As an example, a lender may offer 8 percent interest with 6 points or 9 percent interest with no points. Buyers/borrowers must learn to recognize that the actual interest rate charged on either of these loans would be approximately the same over a thirty-year period. However, the APR would be considerably higher (if the borrower plans to keep the home for a short period of time) on the 8 percent loan with 6 points if the loan was paid off in the first ten years (if the home was sold or possibly refinanced).

BUY DOWNS

Some lenders will offer borrowers "buy-down" options when the loan is originated. This means that the borrowers will have the option of paying points up front (prepaid interest), which will in turn reduce the annual interest rate they will pay for the term of the loan and ultimately lower their monthly payments.

Buy-down programs usually become very popular when interest rates are high. The following example shows one option offered by a lender to reduce a borrower's annual interest rate and monthly payments.

Loans available up to $500,000 on special buy-down programs
Amortized for 30 years
Due in 15 with no prepayment penalty
9% with 0 points
8% with 8 points
7% with 16 points

Using a loan of $125,000, note that the payments vary from $831.63 on the 7 percent loan to $1,005.78 on the 9 percent loan.

Also, note that the APR varied only 0.18 percent because of the points charged to obtain the loan at 8 and 7 percent.

Buy-downs are used most often in cases where a borrower has substantial cash reserves but has limited income and wants or needs to reduce the monthly payments on the loan.

Buy-down programs should be used only by borrowers who are planning to retain the home for a long period of time. (Any shortening of the term can substantially increase the APR.)

As an example, sometimes retirees who have substantial cash reserves, are planning to remain in the home forever, and want to reduce their monthly payments use buy-downs.

> **SMART TIP:**
> Prior to applying for a loan, borrowers should obtain a list from the lender of all fees charged to obtain a loan. Costs and fees can vary considerably from lender to lender.

OTHER LOAN FEES

Lenders also may charge other fees when you obtain a loan. These include loan origination fees, document preparation fees, and notary fees. Borrowers must question each additional fee and make sure that they are absolutely required.

TERM CHOICES

Lenders often give borrowers numerous choices on the terms of their loans; however, the most common choices are thirty-year and fifteen-year terms.

As with the interest rate, the term of the loan can dramatically change the amount borrowers ultimately pay for the loan.

The following two examples demonstrate the variance in the total interest cost to borrowers on a $125,000 loan at an interest rate of 8.0 percent for the terms of fifteen years and thirty years.

	15-YEAR TERM	30-YEAR TERM
Monthly Payment	$1,194.57	$917.21
Total Repayment Cost	$215,021.72	$330,194.06
Interest (paid over term)	$90,021.72	$205,194.06

As you can see, by increasing the monthly payment by $277.36, the borrowers reduce the term of their loan from thirty years to fifteen years and save over $115,000 in interest over the term of the note.

Using the example of a $125,000 loan, interest of 8 percent, an original term of thirty years, and an original monthly payment of $917.21, Table 8.4 shows how the

> **SMART TIP:**
> Borrowers who obtain a thirty-year loan can make additional principal payments each month and reduce their term and the amount of interest they will pay for the loan.

TABLE 8.4
TERM CHANGES AND INTEREST SAVINGS WITH EXTRA PRINCIPAL PAYMENTS

Extra Payment made each month	New Term	Total Interest over Term	Amount Saved over 30-Year Term Loan
$25 ($942.21)	27 Years, 1 month	$181,218.25	$23,977.35
$50 ($967.21)	24 Years, 10 months	$163,228.58	$41,967.02
$100 ($1017.21)	21 Years, 6 months	$137,440.18	$67,755.42
$200 ($1117.21)	17 Years, 3 months	$106,262.47	$98,933.13

> **SMART TIP:**
> Most lenders allow a borrower to pay as much as 20 percent per year of a loan balance for the first five years of the loan with no prepayment penalty. After five years, usually there are no prepayment penalties on a loan, regardless of how much extra you pay. Most government-guaranteed or insured loans, such as FHA or VA, have no prepayment penalties throughout the term of the loan.

> **SMART TIP:**
> Borrowers need to be aware that principal reduction payments are not deductible for tax purposes. Only interest can be used as a tax write-off.

term of a loan is reduced by

making additional principal payments of $25, $50, $100, and $200 per month.

WHO LOANS THE MONEY?

In today's market, there are literally hundreds of ways for buyers/borrowers to finance real estate.

Most retail lenders who make home loans directly to borrowers utilize the guidelines established by Federal National Mortgage Association (FNMA, also referred to as Fannie Mae).

Several government agencies have been set up to purchase loans that were made to individual borrowers. These agencies include: FNMA (Fannie Mae), the Federal Home Loan Mortgage Corporation (Freddie Mac), and the Government National Mortgage Association (Ginnie Mae). Although other private investors, as well as some large companies and pension funds, buy mortgage loans, these three government agencies purchase over 80 percent of the home loans made in the United States.

When a loan is made that follows FNMA guidelines, that loan is referred to as a "conforming loan." If a loan is made outside of these guidelines, it is referred to as a "nonconforming loan."

Government agencies and private investors usually buy loans in blocks (several loans at a time) rather than buying individual loans as they are made. As an example, an individual lender may make ten conforming loans of $200,000 each to home buyers. FNMA will then purchase that $2 million worth of loans from the lender, which in turn frees up $2 million of the lender's money, which can then be used to make other home loans.

Many times lenders will retain the "servicing" on the loans that they sell to investors. This means that the lenders will continue to be responsible for the collection of the loan payments. The investors pay the lenders a small percentage of the interest (usually ¼ to ½ percent) for the servicing.

Often individual borrowers do not know of their loan being sold to an investor; in most cases, borrowers never know or should have any concern as to who actually "holds the paper." If the company servicing the loan changes, borrowers will be notified as to the new entity to which the payments should be made; otherwise, as far as the borrowers are concerned, nothing will change with regard to the terms of the loan.

WHO'S WHO IN
THE LENDING ARENA?

Borrowers will obtain their home loan from four main sources: savings and loan associations, commercial banks, mortgage bankers, and mortgage brokers.

Savings and Loan
Associations

Historically savings and loans (S&Ls) have concentrated their lending activities toward the home loan business. However, in recent years, with major deregulation by the government, savings and loan organizations have expanded their services to virtually match the activities of banks. The S&Ls offer checking accounts, savings accounts, personal, commercial and business loans, safe deposits, and home loans. Although S&Ls offer all these services, their primary lending concentration is still on housing.

Commercial Banks

Generally speaking, commercial banks are the most diverse and active of all finance institutions or entities. These banks offer all types of services, including savings accounts, many specific investment options, charge cards, as well as commercial, personal, residential, agricultural and business loans, plus all other banking-related services. Commercial banks are definitely the "Big Daddys" of lending.

Mortgage Bankers

Mortgage bankers usually use their own money to fund mortgages; however, they ultimately sell the loans to another entity, such as a bank, a savings and loan association, pension or retirement funds, private investors, or a government agency.

When mortgage bankers sell a block of mortgages to an

investor, they often retain the servicing of these loans; they will continue to be responsible for the collection of the payments from individual borrowers. Mortgage bankers are paid a small percentage of the interest (usually ¼ to ½ percent) for this servicing agreement.

Mortgage Broker

Unlike mortgage bankers, mortgage brokers do not actually loan their own money. For a fee, mortgage brokers actually arrange financing for a borrower from a lender. This lender could be a bank, a savings and loan, a private individual, or another entity, such as a credit union or pension fund.

Mortgage brokers act as a middleman between the borrower and the lender. They are paid a commission or a fee, paid by the borrower, the seller, or even the lender, for arranging the financing.

TYPES OF FINANCING

In most cases, buyers/borrowers will obtain an FHA (Federal Housing Administration) government-insured, a VA (Department of Veteran's Affairs) government-guaranteed, or a conventional conforming loan when they purchase their home.

FHA and VA Loans

Commonly referred to as government loans, FHA and VA loans are advantageous for some buyers primarily because they offer low down payments.

Some disadvantages of government loans are that often they require more paperwork and take longer to close. In some cases, sellers are reluctant to accept an offer that is conditioned on buyers obtaining a government loan because they are aware of the delays that occur with such loans.

Numerous types of government loans are available. FHA loans offer as little as 3 percent down, and qualified veterans can obtain a VA loan with no money down.

Conventional
Loans

Conventional loans offer borrowers much more flexibility than government loans because they can be tailored to fit specific borrowers' needs.

Conventional loan products include fixed rates, adjustable rates, graduated payments, low down, seller-carry participation, equity sharing, biweekly loans . . . the list is virtually endless.

A borrower with as little as 5 percent down can obtain a conventional loan, usually in a much shorter processing time and at an interest rate comparable to or even lower than an FHA or VA loan.

In the next three chapters, we cover the specifics of the different types of loans.

Fixed-
Rate
Loans

Most buyers/borrowers and many real estate salespeople believe that fixed-rate loans are the best loans available for almost any buyer, regardless of the circumstances of the purchase or the personal financial position of the buyer. However, adjustable-rate mortgages often outperform fixed-rate loans over the period that buyers actually have the loan.

In the United States, the average term of a loan is somewhere between three and four years. Previously I explained that the average term of home ownership was between seven and eight years, so you can see that the average term of a loan is considerably less than the average term of home ownership. With this information, it should be apparent that home owners are refinancing to reduce their interest rate when lower rates are offered.

Buyers need to recognize that they can save money not just on the actual cost of the home but also on financing.

WHAT ARE THE ADVANTAGES?

Fixed-rate loans have two main advantages:

- They offer borrowers the security and peace of mind that comes with knowing their interest rate and payment will remain the same for the entire life of the loan.
- Their terms are fixed as well, so the loan and the loan process are easy to understand.

WHAT ARE THE DISADVANTAGES?

Buyers/borrowers need to be aware that if they obtain a fixed-rate loan when rates are very low, the rate and terms are fixed for the entire term of the loan. The buyers can feel confident that they are in a financially acceptable position for as long as they own their home.

However, if buyers/borrowers obtain a fixed-rate loan in a time when rates are not extremely low, the fact that the terms and rate of the loan are fixed for the entire term may not be an advantage.

As discussed in Chapter 8, mortgage interest rates recently reached their lowest rate in 1993. Many borrowers who had obtained higher-interest fixed-rate loans refinanced and were forced to pay refinancing charges, just as if they were purchasing the home for a second time.

On the other hand, borrowers/home owners who had adjustable-rate loans simply enjoyed the advantage of their loan rate moving down to a lower rate automatically, without paying any refinancing costs.

Another disadvantage of fixed-rate loans is that often the initial interest rate is higher than adjustable rates, and, consequently, the initial payments will be higher, which can make it more difficult for the borrowers to qualify for the loan.

And last, fixed-rate loans sometimes have more stringent qualification procedures and requirements than ARMs.

SMART TIP:
Adjustable-rate mortgage (ARM) loans often have a lower beginning interest rate primarily because when these loans are sold to investors, the investors can feel confident that if rates edge up, the return on their investment will also move up, keeping pace with other financial placements.

SELECTING THE PROPER TERM

Traditionally, buyers/borrowers have obtained thirty-year terms on their loans; however, in some cases, a shorter-term loan will have a slightly lower interest rate. In the last chapter, I discussed the enormous amount of interest savings that occurs when borrowers make a larger monthly payment and shorten the term of their loan.

Some lenders offer a variation of the thirty-year fixed-rate loan, which is amortized (payments of the amount necessary to pay off the loan in thirty years) for thirty years but due in ten or fifteen years. That means that a balloon payment will become due and payable at the ten- or fifteen-year due date. If borrowers still own the home, they can pay off the loan by refinancing at the current interest rate. Again, this type of loan gives lenders some security by knowing that they will not be stuck with an extremely low-interest-rate loan for thirty years.

Borrowers need to be aware that when they make a home loan payment (especially in the initial years of the loan), only a very small part is actually principal. The majority of each payment is interest. Table 9.1 will give you some idea of the amount of interest and principal in payments at different times during a thirty-year amortized loan. In the example, the loan amount we are beginning with is $125,000, with interest of 8.5 percent amortized for thirty years. The fixed-monthly payment, principal, and interest is $961.14.

TABLE 9.1

SAMPLE LOAN AMORTIZATION CHART

	AMOUNT OF INTEREST	AMOUNT OF PRINCIPAL REDUCTION	REMAINING BALANCE
1st Payment	$885.42	$75.72	$124,924.28
36th Payment (3 years of payments)	$863.51	$97.63	$121,907.26
60th Payment (5 years of payments)	$845.49	$115.65	$119,362.97
120th Payment (10 years of payments)	$784.50	$176.64	$110,753.53
180th Payment (15 years of payments)	$691.36	$269.78	$97,604.33
276th Payment (23 years of payments)	$429.91	$531.23	$60,693.19

As you can see, even after fifteen years of payments, the remaining balance on the loan was still over $97,000. Therefore, if a borrower did choose to take a loan with payments amortized over thirty years but the balance due in fifteen years, there would be a substantial amount left to refinance after the first fifteen years of payments.

The bottom line is, borrowers who can afford to make a higher payment and shorten their mortgage term will save a great deal of money in interest. (However, as I have said several times, all mortgage interest is a write-off for tax purposes; additional principal reductions are not.)

Another way to save money and not reduce the term of the loan is to make a payment equal to one-half of a normal monthly payment every two weeks instead of once per month. This type of biweekly payment schedule is discussed further in Chapter 11.

The following loans were offered by different lenders in 1996. As you can see, the loans with shorter terms offered borrowers a considerably better interest rate and lower payments than traditional thirty-year fixed-rate loans.

Length	Amount of Interest (%)	Loan Origination Fee
30-Year	9.5	1.5 points
20-Year	8.9	1 point
15-Year	8.75	1 point
15-Year	8.675	½ point
15-Year Due in 30-Year Amortization	9	½ point
5-Year Due in 30-Year Amortization	8.75	0 points

Unless borrowers are sure that they are going to keep their home and their loan for a long time (fifteen years or more), adjustable-rate mortgages probably will prove to be the best deal.

Adjustable-Rate Mortgages

Since their introduction in 1981, adjustable-rate mortgages (ARMs) have grown in popularity with lenders and investors as well as with many well-informed buyers.

Unfortunately, most borrowers and many real estate agents and brokers do not thoroughly understand the many advantages of ARMs and hesitate to use this progressive and useful loan option.

ARMs have become more popular, primarily due to their lower starting rates, which allow more buyers to qualify and, in many cases, allow them the opportunity to purchase a more expensive and nicer home. ARMs have lower starting rates primarily because borrowers are assuming some of the risk with regard to interest rates rising.

As mentioned earlier, most lenders sell a good portion of their loans to investors, and almost every investor who purchases home loans prefers ARMs because the rate on these loans varies with the current market rates.

WHAT ARE THE ADVANTAGES?

The advantages of ARMs are numerous; however, borrowers seem to find the following four main points most appealing:

- Lower beginning or starting interest rates (often called "teaser rates") mean lower payments at the beginning of the loan and more borrowers can qualify.
- Because the interest rates and the payments are lower, borrowers often can qualify for a larger loan amount and a more expensive home.
- Many times, the cost (in points) to obtain an ARM is less than a fixed-rate mortgage.

- In general, due to less stringent qualification requirements, it is easier for borrowers to qualify for an ARM.

Another possible advantage of an ARM is that if market interest rates decrease, the rate and payment on the borrower's loan will automatically decrease.

WHAT ARE THE DISADVANTAGES?

The main disadvantage of an ARM is that the interest rate and payment could increase during the term of the loan, if market interest rates increase.

Another disadvantage is that ARMs generally are more difficult to understand. With a standard thirty-year fixed-rate mortgage, borrowers can pretty much keep track of and understand amortization on an ongoing basis. Because the rate on an ARM may change more often than the payments (usually payments change no more often than every six months or year), the amortization is more difficult to track. Borrowers are less apt to accept a loan that is more difficult to comprehend.

> **SMART TIP:**
> Lenders usually provide ARM borrowers with a complete amortization breakdown of their loan no less than once each year. If your lender does not provide a yearly statement, request one. You will need the information for tax purposes.

HOW DO ADJUSTABLE-RATE LOANS WORK?

It is easier to understand an ARM if you think of the loan as being similar to a savings account. A T-bill (Treasury Bill) account that pays 5 percent for ten years would be similar to a fixed-rate loan. On the other hand, an ARM would be more like a passbook account that pays whatever the going market rate is at any particular time. You may be paid more or less than the opening rate.

Table 10.1 details the interest rate and payment changes that occurred in a five-year period on an ARM. Note that the beginning or teaser rate was 2.25 percent below the fixed rates at the time of origination.

TABLE 10.1
PAYMENT AND RATE COMPARISON CHART
FIXED VS. ARM
Original Loan Amount $100,000

MONTH	YEAR	ARM INTEREST RATE (%)	MONTHLY PAYMENT	INCREASE OR DECREASE IN MONTHLY PAYMENT	30-YEAR FIXED-RATE AT THIS TIME (%)
July	1990	9.50	$840.85	N/A	11.75
January	1991	9.92	$871.44	+$30.59	9.90
July	1991	8.80	$793.54	-$77.90	8.75
January	1992	8.67	$785.18	-$ 8.36	8.50
July	1992	8.67	$785.18	0	8.25
January	1993	7.91	$733.69	-$51.49	8.00
July	1993	7.02	$671.65	-$62.04	6.75
January	1994	7.88	$727.26	+$55.61	7.75
July	1994	8.24	$750.81	+$23.55	8.25
January	1995	8.66	$778.35	+$27.54	8.50

Note the following from the table:

1. The beginning rate of 9.5 percent allowed the borrowers to qualify for the loan, which they would not have done at the thirty-year fixed-rate of 11.75 percent.
2. The beginning payment of $840.85 was $168.56 less than the thirty-year fixed payment of $1,009.41.
3. The average thirty-year fixed rate for the five-year period was 8.64 percent. The average ARM rate for the same period was 8.53 percent.
4. The average monthly payment on the ARM loan was $773.80. If the borrowers had received the average of the thirty-year fixed rates for the entire five years, their payment would have been $778.86.

As you can see, the ARM loan outperformed the thirty-year fixed-rate loan. Also, borrowers who pay attention to the market could have refinanced their ARM in July of 1993 and obtained a thirty-year fixed loan at a rate as low as 6.5 percent. Another consideration should be that the ARM loan averaged $750 to $1,000 less to originate, once again bringing down the overall cost of the loan.

COMMON TERMS

As you begin to examine ARM loans in more detail, you will be exposed to many new terms. The next few sections will help you understand the terminology of ARMs.

Index

The interest rate charged on an ARM loan is based on the movement of an index, which is specified at the time of the loan origination. These indexes measure borrowing and lending costs throughout the United States.

All indexes used to establish ARM rates are independent of the lender and can be verified at any time by borrowers.

Some examples of the most commonly used indexes are the 11th District Cost of Funds, the six-month and one-year Treasury Bill indexes, the six-month Certificate of Deposit (quoted by the New York Reserve), and the London Interbank Rate (LIBOR).

Margin

To establish an interest rate on an ARM loan, a lender begins with one of the indexes, taking the index figure and adding a percentage (usually 1 to 3 percent), which is called a margin. This margin is the lender's profit.

In the following example of an ARM rate calculation, the current index rate of the 11th District Cost of Funds is 5.7 percent and lender's margin is 2 percent.

11th District Cost of Funds:

5.7% Index + 2.0% Lender's Margin = ARM Quoted Interest Rate 7.7%

The margin usually remains constant for the term of the loan; however, the interest rate charged to borrowers may rise or fall depending on the movement of the index.

Table 10.1 detailed the actual charges in interest that the hypothetical borrowers were paying. At the beginning of the loan, their rate was 9.5 percent. If the lender's margin was 2 percent, the rate of the index being used was 7.5 percent. By January 1995, the index rate had dropped to 6.66 percent, thereby reducing the interest rate charged to 8.66 percent, after the same 2 percent margin was added.

Note Rate

The note rate (sometimes referred to as the fully indexed rate) is the rate at which the note or mortgage is actually written. In some cases the beginning or teaser rate is lower than the note rate.

Beginning
or Teaser Rate

Most lenders offer beginning or teaser rates for ARM loans during the first three to twelve months of the loan. This initial rate can vary considerably from lender to lender, but also may vary from loan to loan with any one lender.

The teaser rate is sometimes called a discounted rate. In some cases, the actual note rate is higher than the teaser rate, which means that a borrower's interest and payment would rise at the first incremental interest change period, even if the index remained stable.

For example, a loan could be originated at a teaser or discounted rate of 7.75 percent, but the actual rate on the note or mortgage would be 8.25 percent. After six months, even though the index on which the rate is established stayed at the same rate, the borrowers' interest would increase to 8.25 percent and their payments also would rise to accommodate the .5 percent increase in interest. On a $100,000 loan that is amortized for thirty years, the increase in monthly payments would be about $35.

Beginning or teaser rates are used to attract borrowers and, in some cases, to help them qualify.

WHEN CAN RATE AND PAYMENT ADJUSTMENTS OCCUR?

With most ARM loans, rate and payment adjustments will occur at six-month or one-year intervals, depending on how the original loan or mortgage contract is written.

Some lenders have loan contracts that allow rate and payment adjustments to occur every month. Unless borrowers have no other choice, monthly rate and payment deviations are not recommended.

Also, some lenders have contracts that allow interest rate changes to occur every month but payment changes to occur only every six months or year. Borrowers need to know that this type of loan can create a negative amortization—or an increase in the loan balance—if the interest change in any one month is substantial. Again, this type of loan is not recommended.

> **SMART TIP:**
> Borrowers should be sure that if they do obtain an ARM loan, interest rate and payment adjustments occur at the same time. Also, these adjustments should occur no more than every six months.

WHAT IS AN ADJUSTMENT CAP OR CAP RATE?

The most common question asked by borrowers who are considering an ARM loan is: If interest rates skyrocket, will I be faced with a huge increase in my payment?

To provide borrowers with some security and to reduce the risk of enormous payment increases, most lenders have incremental caps on the amount that a rate and payment can rise. Also, a final maximum cap rate is established at usually 5 to 6 percent above the note rate.

An example of the caps established on a particular loan might be as follows: a six-month rate and payment adjustment with a maximum of 1 percent increase per adjustment period or a total increase cap of 2 percent per year. The cap rate cannot increase more than 5 percent throughout the term of the loan.

Now, let's suppose that rates did skyrocket and remain high for a long time. (Keep in mind that historically, this has not happened, and it is unlikely ever to occur in the future.) What is the worst scenario that could happen if home loan rates went to 15 percent in the first six months of a loan?

Let's consider a borrower who had obtained an ARM loan in the amount of $100,000 with a beginning note rate of 7.0 percent, payable at $665.30 per month and amortized for 30 years. The incremental caps were 1 percent maximum increase each six months with a maximum of 5 percent total increase. How would the borrower's payments increase?

1st 6 months	$665.30
2nd 6 months	$732.59 (rate 8.0%)
3rd 6 months	$802.21 (rate 9.0%)
4th 6 months	$873.34 (rate 10.0%)
5th 6 months	$934. 30 (rate 11.0%)
6th 6 months	$1,017.10 (rate 12.0%)

As you can see over the two and one-half years, the borrower's payments increased by $351.80 with a 5 percent increase in the interest rate. Now, what is the chance of this happening? The best way to see the future is to understand the past.

If you refer to Table 8.2 and Table 10.1, you should feel fairly confident that interest probably will never increase substantially nor remain at high rates for a long time.

Could it happen? Yes. Will it happen? Probably not.

Borrowers need to be aware of and look closely at the cap features that are available from different lenders and on particular loans with those lenders.

IS AN ARM FOR YOU?

As indicated throughout this chapter, ARM loans offer numerous advantages:

- Borrowers can qualify when they might not do so with a fixed-rate mortgage.
- Buyers might obtain a larger loan and a more expensive home.
- Rates may go down without refinancing.
- Often, ARMs are less costly to obtain.

However, with an ARM, there is a better than average chance that your rate and payment will increase sometime during the life of the loan.

Now that you have a basic understanding of the difference between fixed-rate loans and adjustable-rate mortgages, the choice is yours.

CHAPTER ELEVEN
Other Types of Financing

In some cases, borrowers may be forced to use alternative methods of financing. If they have had credit problems or have not yet established a credit history, conventional and government lenders may hesitate to risk a substantial amount of money on a home loan. However, buyers may utilize numerous terms and financing options to purchase real estate property.

In other situations, buyers simply may find it more advantageous to use some type of creative financing methods rather than the services of a commercial lender. This chapter will give you an overview of less conventional financing and purchase options.

OWNER FINANCING
OR OWNER CARRY-BACKS

Owner financing or owner carry-backs are especially popular during times of high interest rates or very weak sellers' markets. Market conditions can be adversely affected by a weak local or national economy, a natural disaster such as a hurricane or earthquake, or simply by business slowing down in an area for whatever reason. During these difficult economic periods, sellers often assist buyers by carrying all or a portion of the loan or mortgage.

In other situations, sellers may *want* to carry their own paper to be able to collect the interest that normally would be paid to a commercial lender. A 9 percent return on a mortgage is certainly better return than what sellers would receive if they were to place their money in a passbook savings account.

Also, sellers may be forced to carry their own paper because of the type or condition of the property. Often commercial lenders will not lend money on open land or on property that needs a great deal of work to bring the structure up to an acceptable standard. Fixer-uppers are often owner-financed, at least until the buyers/borrowers have completed enough work on the property to be able to obtain more conventional financing.

When sellers want to receive a premium price for their property and the market condition or the property is not necessarily the best, good seller financing options might help them sell at a price close to market value.

In some cases, desperate sellers may even offer the property at or below market value and include seller financing options that make the purchase an outstanding value. An example might be when sellers have purchased and moved into another home and are making two monthly loan payments. Most people cannot handle two mortgage payments for too long without becoming desperate.

In these cases, sellers may offer a property for little or no down payment, a lower interest rate than the market predicates, and payments as low as interest only.

Most times owner carry-back financing situations are combined with an assumption, taking a loan "subject to," a *land contract* or *contract of sale*, a *seller-carry subordinate loan* or a *wrap-around* or *all inclusive*. All of these options are explained later in this chapter.

HOW DOES AN OWNER CARRY-BACK WORK?

As mentioned, owners who consider financing or assisting with the financing on a property can use many options. Very simply, owner financing means that sellers become the bank and completely finance the property for the buyers or carry a portion of the loan on the property.

In most cases, a seller carry-back financing contract will be a mortgage or deed of trust situation whereby title actually passes to the new buyers/borrowers. However, in some cases, a seller carry-back will be set up with a land contract or contract of sale and the title to the property will remain in the sellers' name until the entire loan or obligation has been paid.

One example of a common owner carry-back situation might be if buyers were to "assume" an existing loan on a property and carry a second. Here's how it might work.

SALE PRICE $145,000

Buyer puts 5% down	$7,250
Buyer assumes existing loan with a balance of	$64,000
(with an interest of 8.5% and payments of $580 per month)	
Buyer carries second loan	$73,750
(at 8% interest, interest-only payments, all due in 10 years)	
Total Sale Price	**$145,000**

Now let's compare this to the standard conventional thirty-year financing first from the buyers' point of view. If the buyers had obtained a thirty-year fixed-rate mortgage for $137,750 (5 percent down deducted from the sale price) at the going rate of 9 percent, the monthly payment would have been $1,108.37. After ten years, the buyers/borrowers would owe $123,189.47.

As the contract was written with the sellers carrying a second and the buyers assuming the original first mortgage, the terms will be:

Buyers' monthly payment on 1st mortgage:	$580
Buyers' monthly payment on 2nd mortgage:	$492
Buyers' total monthly payment:	$1,072

After ten years the buyers/borrowers would owe:

1st mortgage:	$58,875
2nd mortgage:	$73,750
Total:	**$132,625**

After ten years, the buyers/borrowers would owe $9,436 more on the seller carry-back contract; however, they paid $4,364 less in monthly payments. Also, because the remaining balance or payoff is made ten years in the future, the payoff dollars will be worth considerably less due to inflation. Even at only 3 percent per year inflation, the $4,364 difference will have a spending power of about $2,950.

As you can see, both buyers and sellers are winners in that they each got what they wanted. The buyers obtained their home at a good market price with reasonable interest and payments. The sellers received an excellent rate of return on their money and ultimately were paid (over the ten-year period) $198,915 for the home. (This figure includes all interest and payoff of first mortgage.)

Some lenders are willing to make a first mortgage loan to borrowers and allow the sellers to carry a second note as well. One loan is called an 80-10-10. This means that the lender loans 80 percent of the sale price, the sellers carry a 10 percent second, and the borrowers put 10 percent down. As an example, if the sale price on a property was $150,000, the buyers/borrowers would put $15,000 down, the sellers would carry a sec-

ond loan of $15,000, and the lender would loan $120,000 as a first mortgage.

Many lenders find this type of financing acceptable because the sellers actually share in the risk of the loan.

WHAT IS AN ASSUMPTION?

An assumption means that new borrowers assume the responsibility of a loan that was made to another borrower.

As mentioned in the last section, in a weak sellers' market, assumptions will become more prevalent and often will be combined with some type of seller carry-back. Some loans cannot be assumed; buyers who want to assume a loan should obtain a copy of the note to determine if that particular loan is assumable.

In some cases, an original note will indicate the terms by which a loan can be assumed. As an example, the note may state: This note is fully assumable upon full qualification of the buyer(s) at the current thirty-year interest rate. In this case, an assumption would not be much good since the buyers must qualify just as if they were obtaining a new loan, and the interest would go up to the current rate.

TAKING OVER
A "SUBJECT TO" LOAN

Taking a loan "subject to" is similar to an assumption in that borrowers assume the responsibility for repayment of a loan. However, in the "subject to" loan, the original borrowers actually remain in the first position of responsibility. Should the new buyers default on repaying the loan, the original borrowers again become responsible for repayment.

Government loans such as FHA or VA are most often taken "subject to" rather than actually being assumed. However, if new buyers/borrowers do have VA eligibility, they actually can assume a VA loan and the original borrowers can be allowed to remove their name and responsibility from the note. This allows the original borrowers to reuse their eligibility to purchase another property.

CONTRACT OF SALE
OR LAND CONTRACT

In some areas of the country, all types of owner carry-backs are referred to as *land contracts*. However, in most cases, the term "land contracts" or "contracts of sale" refers to a sale and financing situation whereby sellers carry back all or part of the financing on a property. The title of the property actually remains in the name of the sellers until the entire obligation has been paid, at which time the title passes to the buyers. This type of financing is similar to that used for major personal property purchases, such as cars or furniture.

Sometimes commercial or private individual lenders will make loans using a contract of sale to reduce their risk. Should the borrower default on the loan, it is easier for that lender to foreclose or take back the property when the title is already in their name.

In some states, special loans are available to qualified veterans from the state government. An example is a Cal-Vet loan, which is available to qualified California veterans at an interest rate considerably below the market rate. The money for these loans is made available from the sale of special bonds that are offered to the public. Most of these special "vet" loans are contracts of sale. The title to the property remains in the name of the state until the entire obligation has been repaid.

Land contracts or contracts of sale become more popular during times of high interest or generally weak real estate markets.

Unfortunately, these types of creative financing often create legal problems if the paperwork and disclosures are not prepared and explained properly and completely.

Again, buyers who have a limited or less-than-perfect credit history may be inclined to use a contract of sale to purchase a property.

From sellers' points of view, a contract of sale feels less risky since the title to the property does not change until the buyers have repaid the entire obligation.

SMART TIP:

Anytime creative or alternative financing is used in a real estate transaction, all parties to the transaction should seek the counsel of an attorney who is well versed in real estate and contract law.

SMART TIP:

With a contract of sale, although the title to the property remains in the lenders' names until the entire obligation is paid, lenders in many states must go through a process very similar to a foreclosure action if they are forced to reclaim the property. These required legal actions are primarily for the buyers' protection.

WRAP-AROUND OR ALL-INCLUSIVE LOANS

In special situations, buyers may ask sellers to participate in a wrap-around or all-inclusive type of lending arrangement. These types of financing are a little more difficult to understand and should not be undertaken without the guidance or approval of a real estate attorney.

Wrap-around or all-inclusive loans involve sellers carrying back an entire loan amount that includes at least one other loan balance for which the sellers will retain the responsibility for repayment. (I know this sounds very confusing, but it's really very simple.)

For example: The buyers purchase a property for $135,000, agreeing to a down payment of $15,000. The sellers will carry the loan of $120,000 at an interest rate of 9 percent, payable at $1,000 per month principal and interest. The note will be due and payable after ten years. After the ten years of payments, the remaining balance will be $100,649. The sellers agree to continue making payments of $319 per month on the first mortgage, which has an interest rate of 8 percent, and $86 per month on the second mortgage, which has an interest rate of 8.5 percent. At the end of the ten-year term, when the current buyers refinance the loan, resell the property, or in some way pay off the remaining balances due, the original sellers agree to pay the balances, if any, that are remaining on the first and second mortgages. The sellers agree to sign the title over to the buyers when the entire $120,000 obligation is paid. Figure 11.1 depicts the wrap-around/all-inclusive loan.

FIGURE 11.1

WRAP-AROUND OR ALL-INCLUSIVE LOAN

$135,000 SALE PRICE			
$15,000 DOWN PAYMENT			
Buyer pays $1,000 per month.	$120,000 note carried by the seller at 9% interest, payable at $1,000 per month, all due in 10 years	Seller's own equity $74,500	Seller pays $319 and $86 per month. Seller's net per month is:
		2nd mortagage $13,000 Seller pays (8.5% interest)	$1,000
			− 319
	Buyer pays	1st mortgage $32,500 Seller pays (8% interest)	− 86
			$ 595

Now, your question may be: Why would sellers choose to carry a wrap-around or all-inclusive loan? Very simple . . . money!

If on the last example, the sellers' first mortgage included interest of 8 percent and the second mortgage included interest of 8.5 percent, the sellers are actually being paid interest on someone else's money because the buyers are paying 9 percent on the entire obligation. Consequently, although the buyers are only paying 9 percent interest, the sellers' rate of return on their actual equity of $74,500 is 9.52 percent. The return amounts to over $6,700 the first year and over $60,000 in ten years.

BIWEEKLY
MORTGAGE/LOAN

Another type of loan offered by some lenders that is somewhat creative is the biweekly loan or biweekly mortgage.

This type of loan was created in the mid-1980s and was referred to as a "Yuppie loan." It was thought that since most working couples received a paycheck every other week, they could make a loan payment of approximately one-half the normal monthly payment every two weeks instead of the standard monthly payments.

This payment method creates a faster payoff because there are principal reductions more often and, by paying every two weeks, a borrower actually makes twenty-six biweekly payments in a year, which adds the equivalent of an extra month's principal reduction each year. The result is a substantial reduction in interest paid primarily due to the shortening of the term.

Table 11.1 shows the interest savings on a biweekly payment compared to a thirty-year standard monthly payment loan.

This type of incremental payment arrangement is most acceptable to borrowers who are paid either a weekly or an hourly wage. If borrowers are paid a monthly salary and receive their check once or twice per month, an extra biweekly payment can become a burden.

TABLE 11.1

INTEREST SAVING ON BIWEEKLY LOAN

Term	Loan Amount	Payment	Term	Total Interest Paid Over Term
30-Year Monthly Payment Loan	$125,000	$961.14	30 Years	$221,011.07
Biweekly Payment Loan	$125,000	$480.57 Paid every two weeks	23 Years	$136,735.76
			Interest Savings	$84,275.31

OTHER TYPES OF SPECIALTY LOANS

Many lenders offer numerous specialty loans for particular borrowers' needs. Some examples of these loans are 5/25 convertible, amortized for thirty years, due in five or seven, shared equity, no down payment or delayed down payment, lease option, and personal property as a down payment.

5/25 Convertible

In this loan, borrowers pay a specified rate or an adjustable rate for the first five years and then the loan converts to a fixed-rate for the last twenty-five years. After five years, borrowers can either convert at the market rate of interest or pay off the loan by refinancing or selling the property.

Amortized for 30 Due in 5 or 7

Usually this is a fixed-rate loan in which the payments are amortized for thirty years with a balloon payment in five or seven years. Remember, there is a very good chance that you will either sell the home or refinance within five to seven years.

Shared Equity Loans

A lender makes a loan, usually at a lower-than-market interest rate and usually for no more than five years. The borrower agrees to sell or refinance the home at the end of the term, at which time the lender will share in the equity appreciation that has occurred over the term of ownership.

As an example, a home sells for $125,000 and the borrower obtains a loan for $110,000. The lender charges 6 percent interest. (Market interest rate is 7.5 percent, giving the borrower a 1.5 percent interest break.) The home is refinanced after five years and it is determined that the market value of the property is $145,000. The lender receives 40 percent of equity gain, or $8,000.

$$\begin{array}{r} \$\ 145,000 \\ -\ \$\ 125,000 \\ \hline 20,000 \\ \times\ \ 40\% \\ \hline \$\ \ \ \ 8,000 \end{array}$$

The lender's actual return on investment including interest and equity share is over 8.5 percent. Many private and some commercial lenders will consider equity-sharing loans when appreciation is very high in an area and demand for homes is exceptional.

No Down Payment
or Delayed Down Payment

This type of financing will, in most cases, be a seller carry-back arrangement. (However, as discussed earlier, VA-guaranteed loans are available to qualified veterans with no money down.)

Most no-money-down financing situations involve desperate sellers who have not been able to sell their home any other way. Sometimes a no-money-down, seller carry-back arrangement also involves a property that cannot be financed any other way by a commercial lender. This may occur due to building code violations or possibly a property that is obsolete. Many fixer-upper or dilapidated properties can be purchased with little or no money down. However, as mentioned earlier, buyers who purchase any type of fixer-upper need to be aware of the time and expense necessary to bring the property to an acceptable condition.

Delayed down payments or incremental down payments (balloon payments) are often used with open land purchases. However, at times sellers will accept a small initial down payment and additional balloon payments. An example might be:

Sale price of the home:	$225,000
Initial down payment:	$5,000
Seller carry loan:	$220,000
Monthly payments of:	$1,770 (including interest of 9%)
Balloon payments:	$5,000 (due at the beginning of each year for 4 years, $20,000)
Loan balance:	$185,784 (due and payable after 5 years)

You might consider a purchase scenario involving balloon payments when there is an expectancy of endowments, sizable tax returns, or if you are planning on future income increases. Again, buyers and sellers should not enter into any type of creative financing arrangement without the counsel of a real estate attorney.

Lease Option

If sellers are unable to sell their property and become somewhat desperate or if they are in no hurry to sell, they may consider selling with a lease option. For buyers with little or no down payment, a lease option may be the only way they can buy a home.

A lease option involves buyers leasing a property for a period of time. At the end of the lease period, the potential buyers have the option to purchase the property, usually at a price predetermined at the time the lease portion of the contract was written.

Often a small portion of the lease payment is applied to the down payment for purchase, if or when the leasees exercise their option to purchase the property. In some cases, leasees may make a small down payment at the inception of the lease option as a good-faith deposit, especially if the lease has been written to include lease payments that are less than the rental market predicates.

Personal Property
as a Down Payment

Sometimes sellers may accept personal property as a portion of or all of a down or incremental balloon payment. The property could be a boat, car, jewelry, precious metals, stocks or bonds, animals, antiques, or any other assets that would be valuable.

If buyers are planning to use personal property as a down payment, they should receive preapproval from their specific lender of choice. In some cases, lenders are hesitant to make a loan when the only investment the buyers are making is something other than liquid assets.

CHAPTER TWELVE
Choosing a Lender

As I have said, choosing the right lender and the right loan is almost as important as choosing the right home.

Lenders, in a sense, are very much like car dealerships in that they offer a product for almost every buyer. These lenders (like dealers) try to meet the needs, desires, and financial requirements for as many customers as possible. To receive the very best deal on a loan, borrowers may have to search for that loan just as they would to obtain the best car for their money. Also, borrowers sometimes must negotiate with a lender to get the best interest rate and the lowest cost to obtain the loan.

BEGINNING YOUR SEARCH

Many types of lenders—ranging from major commercial lenders to private investors—are willing to make real estate loans. The very best way to find the right lender for you is just to shop around. Talk to people you know who have gotten a loan, talk to your real estate professional, talk to the lenders themselves. In other words, find out who is doing the best job at the best rates.

In some cases, real estate brokers may own their own mortgage brokerage and pay their agents a higher sales commission if the

SMART TIP:
Don't just shop for rates. Sometimes lenders may quote a very low interest rate but also may charge exorbitant fees or points to obtain the loans. Look at the entire loan package before making a decision.

SMART TIP:
If your real estate professional recommends a lender, always ask if he or she is being compensated in any way by that lender. If agents are getting paid to make recommendations or steer borrowers to specific lenders, borrowers should be very cautious to see that the recommended company does, in fact, offer the best loan at the best price for their needs.

agents can direct their buyers to the "in-house" lender. The practice has become quite prevalent in Southern California, New York, and Florida and sometimes creates a less-than-acceptable situation for unknowing buyers.

WHAT ARE YOU LOOKING FOR?

When you are shopping for a lender and a loan, you need to be aware that you are not shopping just for the best interest rate. Instead, you are looking for an overall loan package that best

SMART TIP:
Unfortunately, buyers are sometimes directed to a particular lender or title company because those companies provide "perks" (not all of them are legal) for the agents or brokers. Sometimes the brokers actually own or participate in the ownership of these affiliate companies. Buyers need to check the recommendations and shop around on their own.

meets your needs, including the best interest rate, the best cost to obtain the loan, the proper term, and the best complete service from a lender.

MAKING RATE COMPARISONS

You must learn to compare interest rates and costs to obtain a loan. Table 12.1 shows the same type of conventional loans offered by four different lenders at the same time and in the same market area.

Although each of these loans is for a fixed-rate mortgage, the rates and costs to obtain the loans vary considerably.

Using a loan example of $125,000, Table 12.2 details the cost in fees and points to obtain each loan; the overall APR (the rate the borrower is actually paying for the money, including the costs to obtain the loan); the APR for a five-year term; and the total cost of the loan to the borrower for the first five years.

As you can see, Lender 1 offers the best interest rate; however, the fees to obtain the loan are considerably higher than the other lenders' fees. Also, Lender 1 requires a twenty-year amortization, which increases the payments on the loan.

TABLE 12.1
RATE COMPARISON CHART

	Lender 1	Lender 2	Lender 3	Lender 4
Annual Interest Rate	7.5%	8.5%	8%	9
Loan Fee	1%	1%	0	0
Points	6	1	2	0
Term	20	30	30	30
Monthly Payments	$1,006.99	$961.14	$917.21	$1,005.78

TABLE 12.2
LENDER COMPARISON CHART

	Lender 1	Lender 2	Lender 3	Lender 4
Cost to Obtain a Loan	$8,750	$2,500	$2,500	0
Long-term APR	8.47%	8.72%	8.21%	9%
5-Year APR	9.36%	9.01%	8.50%	9%
Total Cost of the Loan for the first 5 years (including interest, points and loan fees)	$52,797	$54,531.34	$51,369.66	$55,1996.87

Lenders 2 and 3 both offer the same cost to obtain the loan: 1 percent loan fee and 1 point, or no loan fee and 2 points respectively. However, Lender 3, because of the lower interest rate, has the lowest long-term APR and five-year APR as well as the lowest overall cost of the loan over a five-year period.

Although Lender 4 doesn't charge buyers to obtain the loan, it is actually the most expensive overall loan for a five-year period.

Of these loans, the third appears to be the best overall loan. Borrowers could save over $3,800 during the first five years of the loan by choosing Lender 3 over Lender 4. This amounts to a savings of almost $64 per month.

HOW TO USE THE MORTGAGE COMPARISON CHECKLIST

SMART TIP:
Most lenders are willing to assist you in determining the cost to obtain a loan and to compare loans and costs from them and from other companies. Also, many real estate professionals have computer programs that can calculate the costs to obtain a loan.

The following Mortgage Comparison Checklist (Figure 12.1) should be used when you are shopping for a loan. (Refer to Chapter 9 or to the Glossary if you have forgotten any of the terminology used in the checklist.)

Once you have chosen a house and a lender, it's time to make an offer.

FIGURE 12.1

MORTGAGE COMPARISON CHECKLIST

Name of Lender	ABC Mortgage	Lender 2	Lender 3
Name of Contact/Phone Number	Jerry 111-000		
Loan Amount	$125,000		
Types of Mortgage Offered	ARM		
Interest Rates	8.5%		
Points	1		
APR	8.67%		
Loan Term	30		
Down Payment			
with PMI	Less than 20%		
without PMI	20% or more		
Lock-ins			
upon application	Yes		
upon approval	Yes		
written agreement	Yes		
Effective how long?	60 days		
Cost of Lock-in	$400		
Lower Lock-in Rate (if rates drop)?	Yes, additional charge		
Prepayment			
Is there a penalty?	Yes		
How long?	5 years		
How much?	6 months interest		
Extra principal payments allowed	Yes, up to 20% of the balance - 1st five no penalty		
Assumable?	Yes		
At what cost?	2 Points		
Need to qualify?	No		
At what rate?	11th District Cost of Funds + 2		
Impound account required?	Yes		
For Taxes?	Yes		
Comments	Have numerous other loan products available		
For Insurance?	Yes		

FIGURE 12.1 MORTGAGE COMPARISON CHECKLIST *(continued)*

NAME OF LENDER	ABC MORTGAGE	LENDER 2	LENDER 3
Estimated Loan Process Time	60 Days		
Closing Cost Estimates	$300+down		
Application Fee	$50		
Origination Fee	$625		
Credit Report	$25		
Appraisal Fee	$300		
Survey Fee	$0		
Attorney Fee	$0		
Title Search			
Title Insurance	$740		
Lender's Title Policy	$185		
Document Preparation Fee	$0		
Points	$1250		
Payment Schedule			
Monthly	X		
Biweekly			
Adjustable Rate Mortgages only			
Interest rate	7.5%		
Initial rate			
Index used	11th District Cost of Funds		
Adjustable Intervals	6 months		
Rate caps			
Periodic	1%		
Lifetime	5%		
Payment cap	Yes		
Margin	2%		
Can negative amortization occur?	No		
If convertible, when do you convert?	After 2 years		
Fees	2 Points		
Rate	11th District Cost of Funds +2		

Making an Offer to Purchase

The time has finally come. You've searched out the right neighborhood, found the right home, and now you are ready to make an offer. As they say at the opening of the Olympics, "Let the games begin!"

UNDERSTANDING THE OFFER PROCESS

In every state in the U.S., as well as in every province in Canada, all real estate contracts must be in writing. This includes the offer to purchase or deposit receipt that will be used to make an offer on a property.

Even if you have given your agent permission to bargain for a property on your behalf, that agent must have a signed purchase contract before he or she actually can present your offer. (Only if an agent has a signed power of attorney to act for you can written offers be made in your name.)

When you have found a home for which you wish to make an offer, the offer process will go something like this.

1. Your agent will prepare an Estimated Closing Cost Worksheet, which will give you an estimate of what it will cost you to purchase the home. This will include all closing costs and your down payment (based on the amount you have decided to offer for the home).
2. You and your agent will prepare the actual purchase contract or deposit receipt, which will become your offer to purchase and will be presented to the sellers. This form can be as few as one page or as many as ten pages, depending on what is customary in your area.
3. Your agent will then contact the sellers' agent and set an appointment to present the offer. In some areas, it is customary

for buyers' agents to present the offer (in the presence of the sellers' agent, of course).

4. The sellers then will take a short time to evaluate the offer, discuss the information, and decide if they wish to accept what you have offered. The sellers' agent will also prepare a Net Proceeds Statement for the sellers, which will detail the estimated costs to sell the home and how much they actually will receive under the terms of your offer.

5. The sellers then will either accept the offer or prepare a counteroffer.

6. If the sellers accept your offer, you begin the closing process. If the sellers give you a counteroffer, the ball is back in your court and you must decide if you will accept, reject, or counter the counteroffer.

Estimating Closing Costs

Before an offer is prepared, your agent should complete an Estimated Closing Costs Worksheet for you. This will show you approximately how much money you will need to close the transaction when that time arrives. Table 13.1 is an example of an Estimated Closing Costs Worksheet.

The Deposit Receipt or Purchase Contract

Your offer will be prepared on a deposit receipt or purchase contract, which is a legal and binding document. These forms may contain numerous sections and subsections and appear quite complicated; however, you probably will have an agent or broker guide you through the complexities.

A copy of an eight-page deposit receipt/purchase contract is shown in the Appendix. *This form is copyrighted and cannot be reprinted.* For information on how to obtain the forms used in your area, contact your local agent or broker or your local Board of Realtors®.

In some areas, other addendum forms will be used in conjunction with the purchase contract to clarify certain things such as required geological surveys, inspections, or floodplain explanations. Your agent should know exactly what forms are used in your area.

TABLE 13.1

BUYERS' ESTIMATED CLOSING COSTS WORKSHEET

Sale Price $220,000

ITEM	CLOSING COSTS
Brokerage Fee	$0 (paid by the seller)
Title Insurance	$425 (½ paid by the buyer)
Points (if any)	$1800 (1 point)
Escrow/Closing Fee	$340 (½ paid by the buyer)
Document Preparation	$0
Fees Paid For Seller	$0
Recording	$30
Bonds & Assessments	$0
Appraisal	$200
Inspections	$140
Other Lender Fees	$200
Tax Services	$0
Repairs	$0
Home Warranty	$200 (½ paid by the sellers)
Attorney Fees	$0
Miscellaneous	$200
Down Payment	$40,000

Estimated total necessary to close transaction = $43,395

WHAT ARE THE TERMS OF THE PURCHASE?

If you looked through the purchase contract in the Appendix, you probably noticed that almost every possible term or condition is addressed. In most sections, it is simply a matter of filling in the blanks.

A purchase contract should include:

• Date
• Location contract is written
• Buyer's name
• Amount of deposit
• Purchase price

- Property address and/or legal description
- Financing terms
- Condition of property upon transfer
- Special property disclosure (flood zones, hazards, etc.)
- Governmental compliance (permits, codes, etc.)
- Fixtures that remain (appliances, shrubs, etc.)
- Home warranty
- Pest control
- Septic (if applicable)
- Contingencies such as the sale of the buyers' home
- Backup offers
- Cancellation of contingencies (methods, times, etc.)
- Time frames for:
    Offer acceptance
    Inspections
    Loan approval
    Title report
    Disclosures
    Other
- Time frames for approval of inspections, disclosures, and reports
- Final inspection and approval of property
- Arbitration of disputes
- Attorney fees if arbitration or litigation occurs
- Contract changes
- Acceptance

Also, a separate addendum should address any personal property included in the transaction.

HOW MUCH SHOULD YOU OFFER?

If you read and understood the information in Chapter 6, you should feel confident that you can decipher the comparable sales information relating to the home for which you are interested in making an offer.

Let's take, for example, a home that is listed for $239,500. If the comparable sales show that the home should sell for no more than $225,000, a fair offer price would be around $220,000.

MAKING OFFERS

The most important thing to remember when making an offer is: *Everything is negotiable.*

The second most important thing to remember is that your agent, if he or she is a competent professional, will be able to guide you as to how your offer can be written most effectively.

If you choose to begin your offer process by asking the sellers to pay all closing costs, you can do so. These costs can include your loan organization fee, the escrow and title fees, all inspection fees and repairs required by the inspections, all of the incidental document preparation, and notary fees and attorney fees, if any—in other words, every possible cost to close the transaction.

However, unless it is an extremely weak sellers' market and those particular sellers are almost desperate, an offer of that type probably will not be accepted. Additionally, if you really want the home, you may create some animosity with the sellers because they will feel that you are trying to take advantage of them. Consequently, future negotiations may be more difficult.

Keep in mind that sellers are usually very emotional when it comes to selling their home. Even though you are submitting your offer based on factual, comparable sales data, the sellers may let their emotions get in the way of the selling facts.

As a buyer, you must be level-headed, tenacious, and, most important, patient!

> **SMART TIP:**
> When making offers, buyers must keep in mind the overall condition of the local real estate market. If it is a very strong sellers' market, an offer should be made closer to the market value that has been determined by using comparable sales data. If, on the other hand, it is a very weak sellers' market, an offer could be considerably below market value. Sellers in distressed markets usually are willing to consider any offer. Your agent should guide you in this critical offer process.

SMART TIP:

The best transaction is a win-win situation for all parties. If buyers or sellers continually take advantage of the other party, the transaction always seems to progress slowly and with much more difficulty. Also, litigation occurs much more often in such transactions. Try to give a little and take a little, but don't try to take too much.

SPECIAL OFFER STRATEGIES

One method that buyers can use to help convince sellers to accept an offer without countering is called "loading." This technique is used extensively by top-selling agents and brokers across the country, and it is easy, direct, and creates urgency on the part of the sellers.

"Loading" means simply that along with your offer, you include a separate statement that details information regarding the sellers' home in comparison with other similar properties that are either available or have sold possibly at an equivalent or lower price than the sellers' home.

In other words, you are saying to the sellers, "This is what's available out there and though we would like to buy your home, we have lots of other choices. Also, this is what has sold and for what price."

Give sellers so many reasons to say yes that it seems ridiculous for them to say no!

The following is an example of a "loading" statement letter that is to be included with an offer. The property on which the offer has been made was listed for $179,000; however, the buyer is offering $168,500.

Additional Information for the Sellers' Consideration

Dear Mr. and Mrs. Jones,

1. The following five homes are comparable sales that have sold in the past five months:

   2828 Valderas Street—$169,000

      hot tub, walk-in closets, new fence

1604 Arco Way—$179,800

pool, cabana, hot tub

1206 4th Avenue—$168,000

professional landscaping, new carpet, new paint and kitchen flooring

802 2nd Avenue—$168,200

hot tub, 3-car garage

46 Park Place—$168,500

RV parking, cul-de-sac

Each of the above listed-homes has amenities not offered in your property.

2. The following homes are for sale right now in your area, and these homes are comparable as well:

1294 Delong Way—$173,500

pool, built-in barbecue, oversize deck

894 8th Avenue—$169,500

large family room and new carpet

560 Rincon Way—$167,000

same floor plan and a much larger lot

158 Cotter Place—$169,000

same floor plan, covered patio, large lot

Again, each of these homes has amenities not offered in your home.

It is our commitment to purchase your property and make it our home. We are willing to pay a fair price and see that the purchase goes smoothly and quickly.

Please note that:

1. We are **not asking for any major changes or improvements** to be made to the home.

2. We **have been prequalified** for our loan.

3. We have the funds to close the sale **now** and there are **no contingencies** involving the sale of another property.

4. We **can allow you to stay in the home** (according to the terms of the offer) until June 15, which will delay your moving until your children are out of school.

This is our one and only offer and we do not want to receive a counteroffer.

Thank you for your consideration and we have high hopes that you will accept our offer as written and we can begin the closing process.

Sincerely,

John Doe and Mary Doe

Note that the buyers have stated that this will be their one and only offer. If the sellers do counter, it is a good indication that they really do not care if they lose those buyers.

Load your offer. It works!

UTILIZING A COUNTEROFFER

If sellers do prepare a counteroffer back to you as the buyer, you have to decide if you want to accept the counteroffer or prepare a counteroffer to the counteroffer.

Your agent should complete a new Estimated Closing Costs Worksheet so you can again know approximately how much it will cost you to close the transaction.

The Appendix contains a Counteroffer Form, which is copyrighted and should not be reproduced. For more information, contact your agent or your local Board of Realtors®.

Your counteroffer should be very specific with regard to any changes, alterations, or additions to the original offer or counteroffer that was presented to you. Once your counteroffer has been prepared, your agent will present it to the sellers with the sellers' agent.

The sellers will either accept the counteroffer or counter it again. If they counter, the process starts all over again.

HOW MANY COUNTEROFFERS?

You never know. If the negotiation process is working and each party is making an effort to agree on the terms of the sale, there could be a dozen or more counteroffers. Most likely there will be no more than two or three counters.

Again, be patient. The sellers may be adamant about certain terms or conditions, and you may have to look for alternatives to satisfy their desires and still accomplish your goals.

Remember, as long as offers and counteroffers are being sent back and forth, there is still an opportunity to put the transaction together. Don't become disappointed or frustrated during the offer or counteroffer process; it's simply all part of the game.

Offers are seldom written at the full listing price; therefore, both buyers and sellers must be willing to negotiate. The offer/counteroffer process can become frustrating in that both the buyers and the sellers want to make the best possible "deal" for themselves. Also, to add to the pressure of the situation, each offer and counteroffer will be written to expire in usually twenty-four to forty-eight hours.

Buyers and sellers need to be acutely aware of the importance in responding as quickly as possible to offers and counteroffers.

WHEN TO GIVE UP

When the counteroffers are not changing and sellers are not willing to bend with regard to the terms you desire, it may be time to walk away.

SMART TIP:
It is not uncommon for five or six counteroffers to be written before there is an acceptance. You should never be disappointed if your first offer is not accepted (especially if the terms and price of the offer are substantially different from the price and terms which the sellers have offered in their listing).

SMART TIP:
Offers and counteroffers usually are written for a short time (either one or two days). That means that the party who has received the offer/counteroffer must make a decision and respond quickly or the offer/counteroffer will be rescinded automatically. If either party has made an offer before the other party has accepted and communicated back to the offering party, the offering party can withdraw the offer. This is why on every deposit receipt or purchase contract, the following words are printed: Time Is of the Essence.

WITHDRAWING AN OFFER
OR COUNTEROFFER

After you have made a written offer to purchase, you may change your mind and decide that you want to withdraw the offer. Before you do so, be absolutely positive that you are not just suffering from a small case of that fateful disease known as "buyers' remorse." Anytime you commit to a major purchase, you will normally feel a little trepidation.

If, after you have really thought about it and you have good reason to withdraw the offer, you *may* be able to do so.

The law states that there must be an offer and an acceptance and the acceptance must be communicated back to the offering party. If you were to withdraw your offer before the offer acceptance is communicated back to you, you would legally not be responsible to complete the purchase.

On the other hand, if your agent delivered to you a copy of the purchase contract signed by the sellers to you and said, "Congratulations, you've bought a home," and then you mentioned the withdrawal . . . you may have a problem.

In any case, if you decide to withdraw an offer, do so as quickly as possible and notify all parties that you've changed your mind and that you no longer intend to purchase the property.

CHAPTER FOURTEEN

Home. Warranties

A home warranty works exactly like a warranty for other products. When you receive a warranty on a new stereo, the manufacturer or the store that sells the product guarantees that for a period of time, the product will not have defects and will work properly. If something should go wrong, the guarantor will fix the product at no cost or at a minimal predetermined service charge.

In the late 1960s, the home warranty business was pioneered by a man named David Smith and his company, American Home Shield. Since that time, the home warranty business has flourished and numerous companies now offer warranty policies to thousands of real estate buyers each year.

Properties that include a home warranty at no additional charge are well worth looking at.

Homes with warranties have become the norm. According to the National Home Warranty Association in St. Louis, Missouri, in 1995 alone, over 801,000 home warranties were purchased by consumers and real estate professionals. Most important, it was reported that these member warranty companies processed over 1,292,000 claims.

Considering that the average cost of a home warranty is less than $360, it is strongly recommended that buyers ask sellers to include a home warranty or guarantee with the sale of their home.

TYPES OF HOME WARRANTIES

Home warranties, like almost every product on the market, come in all shapes, sizes, and special coverages. Often warranties that cost less cover less; warranties that are more expensive have a much greater or more complete coverage.

Your real estate agent probably has several brochures (printed by home warranty companies) available for you. These brochures explain the exact coverages of different warranties available in your area. The brochures also should detail the cost of these warranties; if not, a quick call to the warranty company should answer any questions you may have.

WHAT IS COVERED?

Items that are specifically covered by home warranties protect buyers or home owners from having to pay the repair costs of built-in appliances, structural problems, roof leaks, plumbing, electrical systems, or any other problems that may occur in the home.

Some home warranties cover only specific items and exclude others. For example, one warranty would cover structural defects, electrical, plumbing, heating and cooling systems, and ventilation fans but would not cover appliances, fixtures, or built-in equipment.

Some warranties specifically also exclude swimming pools and spas or require an additional addendum or rider and fee if these items are to be covered. It is always in the best interest of buyers and sellers for these items to be covered.

Make sure that whatever warranty you have on your property covers a wide range.

Most home warranties are written for one year and sometimes may be extended at the mutual option of the warranty company and the home owner.

WHY SHOULD A WARRANTY
BE INCLUDED?

There are numerous reasons that a home warranty should be purchased and included with the sale of the home; however, the most important reason is that it will give the sellers and buyers "peace of mind" after the transaction has closed. The sellers will not have to be concerned with after-close buyer complaints, and the buyers can feel confident that their home will not turn into the proverbial "money pit."

HOW DO YOU CHOOSE A WARRANTY?

Your real estate professional will be able to advise you on the choices or warranty companies that are available in your area.

If you wish to purchase the home warranty yourself, you may look in the telephone directory under "Home Warranty Companies" or possibly in the real estate section of the newspaper.

However, in most cases, buyers ask sellers to pay for the warranty. In some cases, sellers and buyers might split the cost.

Every real estate professional, almost without exception, encourages all sellers to offer a warranty with their property. This is done primarily because it makes the home more salable. Also, the warranty gives the buyers the feeling that they are buying a good product. The warranty offers peace of mind for buyers, sellers, and agents at a very reasonable cost.

WHAT SHOULD THE WARRANTY INCLUDE?

Every home warranty should include the following:

- The name(s) of the person(s) who are warranted
- An explanation as to if or how this warranty can be transferred
- The term of the warranty
- Exactly what is covered by the warranty and specifically what items are included
- An explanation of exactly how a claim must be filed
- A statement of who will make necessary repairs. Is there a service company or does the warranty company have repair people on staff?
- How long it will take to have a service or repair person respond

- Any deductibles or service fees in addition to the original warranty policy cost
- Any specific limitations as to what will be covered as far as personal property items

Like any other guarantee, buyers should check out the warranty they will receive or purchase.

CHAPTER
FIFTEEN

Obtaining a Loan

Once your offer has been accepted, the real work begins. Now you must see that the loan process goes as smoothly and as quickly as possible. It will be important for you to try to do everything right the first time so nothing will have to be done twice or more and delay the closing of your transaction.

Remember, the main condition on which the purchase of your home is based is the line in the contract that reads: Buyer to obtain a loan in the amount of . . .

Your lender will ask for a great deal of information so the loan package can be completed properly. You must provide the lender with everything that is asked for (no matter how trivial it may seem). Sometimes borrowers mistakenly think that they really don't need to complete every item on the application, or that a particular verification is not important, or that a letter of explanation for a small mistake on the credit report can't make that much of a difference. This wishful thinking, however, will not help you obtain the loan quickly.

SMART TIP:
If you have been preapproved for your loan, the closing process will be much simpler and will certainly take much less time to complete. Preapproval can save as much as thirty days on a purchase.

THE APPLICATION

Your loan application is the most important item in your loan package. The application is to the loan

SMART TIP:
Don't forget, a lender (possibly someone who you have never worked with) is going to make a loan to you for a very large sum of money, based only on the loan package that you will provide. Make sure to cross every "T" and dot every "i" and leave nothing to chance when that package is submitted.

process what the engine is to your car . . . without it, the car goes nowhere! Therefore, it is very important that you fill out every item in the application, omitting nothing. If you have a question about any part of the paperwork, talk to your loan representative. *Do not leave any items blank.*

Sometimes you may have a meeting with your loan officer to review your application or package. In this case, write down all of your questions and see that you are clear on everything *before the application is submitted.*

To complete the application, you will need all of the information relating to your financial affairs, including account numbers; names, addresses and telephone numbers of financial institutions where you do business; present and previous address information; present and previous employment; and all present and previous credit information (credit cards, car purchases, etc.). In other words, you will need all past and present debt and liability information. Also, you will need to have all of the details about other real estate you may own (payments, rental income, etc.) and your current property purchase, including a description of the property, purchase price, and requested loan amount, and a signed copy of the purchase contract.

Most lenders also require a copy of your last two years' tax returns and a copy of your most current pay stubs showing your year-to-date income. If you are self-employed, you will need to provide not only two years' tax returns but also a year-to-date profit-and-loss statement.

SHOWING ALL OF YOUR INCOME

Without a doubt, the best way to show income is to have all of your income shown on your tax returns or pay stubs. However, certain income, such as child support, does not need to be claimed on taxes. In these situations, a copy of your

SMART TIP:
If you are applying for a loan with another person (husband/wife/cobuyer), it is important that everyone who is included as a borrower complete the application. This is especially true if the cobuyer is only a cosigner on the loan and will not occupy the home with the other borrowers.

divorce decree and court order coupled with your bank deposit records should suffice. Refer to Chapter 3 for more suggestions with regard to verifying income.

Most lenders who make conforming loans use a four-page loan application form. (See the Appendix for a sample loan application form.)

The worksheet in Figure 15.1, on the next page, will assist you in preparing the information you will need to complete your loan application. Use this worksheet, then transfer the information to the loan application form provided by your lender.

VERIFICATIONS

Certain verification forms will be mailed directly to the entity from which the verification is being requested. These items usually are sent to your current employer (sometimes your previous employer). If you have been employed for two years or less with your present employer, the financial institutions where you have deposits (banks, savings and loans, credit unions, etc.) and any other income-producing or financial holding entity will need to be verified to complete your loan package.

You will be asked to sign the verifications and to provide the mailing information. In the case of the employment verification, it is wise to provide the lender with the name of the person to whom the verification should be mailed. You should alert that person in your company that the verification will be coming to them. (See the Appendix for sample copies of typical employment verification and deposit verification forms that will be used with a loan application.)

CREDIT REPORTING

The lender will include a complete and current credit report with your loan application. (A sample credit report is shown in Chapter 3.)

Remember, to avoid any surprises on your credit report, you should have obtained a copy of that report *prior* to applying for the

FIGURE 15.1

BORROWERS' APPLICATION WORKSHEET

Borrower _____ Social Security # _____

Coborrower _____ Social Security # _____

Mailing Address _____

_____ Phone _____

Property Address _____

Property Contact Person _____ Phone _____

Real Estate Agent _____ Phone _____

Title or Escrow Company _____ Phone _____

Employment (List most recent employment first)

Name of Employer	Address	Date Employed	Current or Ending Salary

Bank Accounts (Savings, checking, etc.)

Institution	Address	Account #	Type of Account	Estimated Balance

Landlords (Past two years)

Name of Landlord	Address	Dates You Rented

Credit Cards (Department stores, banks, etc.)

Name of Creditor	Address	Account #	Monthly Payment	Estimated Balance Due

Loan Information (Car, Student, etc.)

Name of Lender	Address	Account #	Monthly Payment	Estimated Balance Due

Previous Credit References (Paid-off loans and other credit)

Name of Lender	Address	Account #	Type of Loan	Date Paid

loan. If you discover any problems or mistakes in the report, try to have them corrected before the lender obtains a copy.

Never try to cover up past credit problems, thinking that maybe the lender won't find them. Be completely truthful with the lender and he or she will work with you to help solve the problems. Remember, the lender doesn't make any money if he or she doesn't make the loan. The lender is on your side.

HANDLING MISTAKES
OR PROBLEMS
ON THE CREDIT REPORT

If you find a mistake on your credit report, contact the credit reporting agency immediately and ask what steps you must take to correct the mistake.

In most cases, you will be asked to submit a letter explaining the mistake. If a creditor (such as a bank card or department store) has indicated that you have an account that does not exist or that you have been late on payments, contact that creditor directly and try to solve the issue. Do not get mad! Be polite and do not be afraid to ask for a supervisor if you are not getting the results you want.

Lenders look favorably on borrowers who have established a good *recent* credit track record. Even if credit problems existed in the past, if borrowers have maintained a solid record for two to three years prior to the loan application, lenders most probably will base their decision on the satisfactory recent credit history.

SMART TIP:
Many companies sell their services claiming to repair past credit problems. Do not let a promoter mislead you into thinking that he or she has any control or power over the creditors or credit reporting agencies. If you have past credit problems, utilize the services of a nonprofit company such as Consumer Credit Counselors and begin to correct the problem areas properly.

TRUTH IN LENDING

Every lender is required by law to provide each borrower with a Truth in Lending Statement within three days of the application for a loan. This statement will show all of the terms of the proposed loan including the actual APR (remember, the APR may be different from the annual interest rate), costs to obtain the loan, the amount financed, and the total amount you will pay for the loan to the end of the term. Remember not to panic when you see the total amount to be paid. A $100,000 loan at 8 percent interest, with monthly payments of $733.76 for thirty years, actually costs the borrower $264,155.25, if it is paid to the end of the term.

> **SMART TIP:**
>
> If the actual APR varies by more than a small amount from the lender's original estimate, the lender is required to provide the borrowers with a corrected Truth in Lending Statement before the transaction's closing date.

THE APPRAISAL

In some cases, borrowers may be asked to pay for the appraisal. This can cost from $200 to $500, depending on the area and the lender. Remember, like most other costs related to a real estate purchase, who pays the cost of the appraisal is negotiable at the time the purchase contract is written.

If the borrower is asked to pay, the lender may request payment at the time the appraisal is ordered, or the payment may be included as a closing cost.

Depending on the market condition, the time it takes to obtain an appraisal could range from one to four weeks. Although many lenders have their own appraisers, in most situations an outside appraiser will provide the appraisal.

How to Handle a Low Appraisal

In some cases, an appraisal may come in at less than the sale price that has been agreed upon by the buyers and sellers. Buyers and sellers can approach such situations in several ways.

1. The buyers/borrowers can provide a larger down payment and buy the home for the price that was originally agreed upon.
2. The buyers, sellers, or lender can order a new appraisal.
3. The lender can ask the original appraiser to reconsider the value assessment.
4. The lender can decide to loan the original amount requested and override the appraiser's value assessment. (Usually this will happen only when the lender feels that the appraisal is not accurate and there is solid factual data to support that premise.)
5. The sellers can reduce their sale price to the appraised market value. (In most cases, agents and lenders recommend this action.)

> **SMART TIP:**
> Your offer should include a contingency clause stating that you can renegotiate the sale price if the appraisal is lower than the purchase price agreed upon by you and the sellers. This clause also should include your right to withdraw your offer without penalty if a low appraisal comes in.

LOCKING-IN RATE QUOTES

Some lenders allow buyers/borrowers to "lock-in" the quoted interest rate. This lock-in may occur at the time of the application or at the time of approval, depending on the particular lender. Lock-in periods usually range from fifteen to seventy-five days with some options for extending the period.

The lock-in assures borrowers that even if interest rates rise during the loan process period, the lower rate quoted will be honored by the lender. In some cases, a lender will charge for the lock-in guarantee.

Should the interest rate drop below the locked-in rate, most lenders will allow the borrower to receive the lower rate. A borrower should clarify this circumstance before they apply for a locked-in rate.

LOAN APPROVAL

When your loan has been approved, you will probably first receive a call of congratulations from your real estate professional and/or your loan officer.

Next you will receive a formal letter of approval that states that you have qualified for the loan. This letter will show:

- The loan amount for which you have qualified
- The term of the loan
- The annual interest rate that will be charged to the loan
- The loan origination fee that will be charged to obtain the loan
- Any points that will be charged additional to the loan origination fee
- The time that will be allowed for the buyers/borrowers to complete the home purchase and close the transaction (the date of the loan commitment expiration)
- Any other conditions that must be met before the loan will be funded

When you receive your loan approval or commitment letter, make sure everything is correct. Does the loan amount plus the down payment equal the sale price? Is the term for repayment correct? Is the annual interest rate correct? Are the costs to obtain the loan as you were quoted? Does the date on the expiration of loan commitment allow you enough time to close the transaction? Are there any conditions for funding that you did not expect?

CONTINGENCIES FOR LOAN FUNDING

If conditions or contingencies for loan funding have been stated in the loan commitment, you must address these requirements as soon as possible.

In many cases, repairs or improvements will be required on the

SMART TIP:

If contingencies for closing the loan are not met by the expiration date indicated on the loan commitment, the borrowers could lose not only their locked-in rate but their commitment as well. It is imperative that all conditions for closing be met within the time allowed by the lender.

property. It will be incumbent upon you to see that this required work is completed in a timely manner, so it does not delay the close of the transaction.

HANDLING LOAN REJECTION

Loan applications are denied for several common reasons, but there are also many ways for you to try to resurrect the application or save the transaction. Whatever the reason for the denial, don't give up until you have tried every possible recourse, including applying to another lender. Being rejected by one lender does not mean you can't get a loan from someone else. Like the inimitable baseball philosopher, Yogi Berra, said, "It's not over 'til it's over!"

Here are some of the most common reasons for loan rejection and some of the things you can do to correct them.

Poor or Insufficient
Credit Report

If your loan is denied due to information on your credit report, you are entitled to a free copy of the report from the credit reporting agency that issued the report. Sometimes a lender may simply ask you to provide an explanatory letter with regard to the derogatory information (called "derogs" in the business) that surfaced on your report. If the report contains incorrect information, correct it.

If you just have not established enough credit to build an acceptable history, try to put together as much information with regard to payments made on utility bills, rent, personal loans that were repaid to relatives or friends, and any other types of payments that could help establish an acceptable track record. Any series of payments that can be documented will help the lender.

If your credit history proves to be less than acceptable, remember that there are numerous ways to buy a property. You may be forced to use an alternative financing method, some of which were discussed in Chapter 11. Also, immediately begin to repair your deficient credit by working through a company such as Consumer Credit Counselors. It may take only a year or two (a few months in some cases) to improve your credit to an acceptable level. Your home purchase may be delayed for a while but it will happen even-tually if you are persistent. (See the Resources section for informa-tion on Consumer Credit Counselors.)

Insufficient Funds

Lenders may reject a loan application because they are unable to verify the funds that will be necessary to close the transaction. Sometimes buyers/borrowers count on funds to close from a tax return or the repayment of a debt, and the money is delayed for any number of reasons. In other cases, borrowers may have thought they were going to win the lottery and it just didn't happen. In either case, if the lender cannot verify that the funds are there, the loan will be rejected.

Here are some options to help close a transaction:

- Provide the lender with a way to verify the funds by giving him or her a copy of your tax return. (The lender should already have this but may not have looked at the refund portion.) The money may be there, but it must be proven.
- Ask the seller to pay part of the closing costs, which will help reduce the amount necessary to close the transaction.
- Ask the seller to agree to some type of seller financing, which could reduce the amount necessary to close the transaction.
- Ask the lender to reduce the cost to obtain the loan, or apply to another lender who charges less in fees.

Insufficient Income

As indicated in Chapter 3, lenders use formulas to determine if bor-rowers are qualified to obtain a loan. If the qualifying percentages are not met, the lender may be forced to decline the loan or accept the borrowers and be stuck with a nonconforming loan that will be difficult to sell in the secondary market.

First, be sure that the lender has properly calculated your income and that all of your income has been included. Have the qualifying ratios been calculated correctly?

If borrowers can demonstrate in some way that they have the ability to meet the payment obligation required on the loan, the lender may be able to provide the loan. For example, if the bor-rowers have been given a raise that has not yet taken effect but can be verified, this increase in income may be adequate to raise the qualifying percentages to an acceptable level.

Too Much Debt

Sometimes your existing obligations will cause your debt-to-income ratios to exceed acceptable levels. In this case, the best option is simply to figure out some way to pay off a portion of the debts. Remember, only debts that will require ten months or more for repayment are used in the calculation for debt-to-income ratios.

WHAT IF YOU SUSPECT DISCRIMINATION?

The Equal Credit Opportunity Act and the Fair Housing Act prohibit discrimination against a loan applicant on the basis of race, sex, age, religion, color, marital status, national origin, or receipt of public funds or assistance.

If you suspect that a lender has illegally denied your loan on a basis prohibited by law, you should file your grievance with the lender and with the regulatory agency that governs that lender. Also, file a copy of the complaint with U.S. Department of Housing and Urban Development (HUD), which is the government agency charged with the enforcement of the Fair Housing Act. (See the Resources section for information on HUD.)

Working with For Sale by Owners

Some potential home buyers have an inclination to work with For Sale by Owners (FSBOs). Most of these buyers believe they will get a better deal, prefer to work without the "middleman" agent or broker, or feel they can work more effectively if they negotiate directly with the seller. Whatever their reasons, buyers who choose to work directly with For Sale by Owners need to be extremely competent in the overall home purchase process or seek proper guidance to be sure that their transaction will be completed correctly.

WILL YOU GET A BETTER DEAL?

Usually most buyers decide to try to work with For Sale by Owners because they believe that they will get a better deal by working directly with the sellers and cut out the middleman, who is actually the agent or the broker.

Most buyers believe that if the sellers do not have to pay a commission, those sellers will be more apt to pass along the savings to the buyers. However, in most cases, sellers who are trying to sell their home without the services of a real estate agent are doing so in an attempt to make more money on the sale, not to be able to give the buyers a better deal.

Also, many times, For Sale by Owners sellers have their home priced considerably above market value, primarily because they have established the price of their home using the listing prices of homes in the area rather than actual comparable sale prices.

Another consideration, as I have mentioned previously, is that many sellers are emotionally attached to their property and consequently will not make decisions based purely and totally on the factual data relating to their home.

Most important, if buyers are going to get a good deal by working with For Sale by Owners, they must be effective negotiators and be able to remain calm, emotionally unattached, and extremely objective throughout the entire buying process.

WHY ARE THEY SELLING
THEIR HOME THEMSELVES?

There are several common reasons why sellers attempt to sell their home themselves. In most cases, they are simply trying to avoid paying a commission.

Another fairly common reason is that they have very little equity—possibly having owned the home only a short time—and they cannot afford to pay a commission when the home is sold.

A third reason is that some sellers are so completely unreasonable about pricing their property, agents simply won't take the listing. Often, in these cases, the home has previously been listed with one or more agents and the sellers were so unrealistic that they quickly developed a reputation within the real estate community. They became known as "taboo," and no agents will attempt to deal with them.

Sometimes sellers will try to sell their home themselves when it has problems. These sellers may have been informed that they need to make repairs or improvements to bring the home up to an acceptable standard or even to code before it can be sold, but they've chosen to ignore this advice and try to sell the home to an unwary buyer.

In rare cases, sellers are personally very difficult to deal with and agents just will not work with them. Usually the property of such sellers becomes a perennial listing that passes from one agent to the next until none will accept it and the sellers are forced to sell their home themselves. After two or three years of this nonsense, often you will see a "For Rent" sign posted in front of the home.

As a potential buyer of a For Sale by Owner home, make sure

that you always ask how long the home has been for sale, both as a For Sale by Owner and as a listing with agents. If it has been a long time (a year or more), ask the sellers why they believe the home has not sold. Most probably their excuse will be: the agents didn't do their job, the buyers just couldn't qualify, and/or there are no buyers for this type of home in the area.

In fact, in almost every case, the reason the home didn't sell is because it is overpriced, is not prepared properly, and/or the sellers are unrealistic.

CAN YOU USE AN AGENT?

If you are working with a competent and experienced real estate professional, he or she will know how to work with For Sale by Owners. If you see a For Sale by Owner home in which you are interested, advise your agent and allow him or her to make the initial contact.

In most states, an agent can take a "one person listing," which means that the agent will be paid a commission if the home sells to the one buyer who has been named by the agent. Most sellers, even those adamant about selling their home themselves, will not turn down the opportunity to sell to a buyer who is ready, willing, and waiting in the car outside, even if it does mean that there will be a commission or partial commission paid.

CAN YOU STILL SAVE MONEY
IF YOU USE AN AGENT?

If you decide to make an offer on an FSBO property, your agent should be the only agent involved in the transaction. In the normal course of business—working with an agent who is selling a home to you that is listed by other agents and brokers—your agent would normally share in the commission paid by the seller. In most areas, those commissions would range between 5 and 8 percent. When making an offer on an FSBO property using the services of an agent, always ask that agent to work for one-half of the commission he or she would normally charge to list and sell a property. If that agent normally charges 7 percent, ask that the transaction be written with a 3.5 percent commission and allow you to receive a 3.5 percent break on the sale price.

Keep in mind, you're buying a property that has cost the agent nothing to market. When agents take a listing and sell a home, they spend a considerable amount of time and of money marketing the property.

Never try to take advantage of an agent, but never allow the agent to take advantage of you, especially if you have found the home yourself and made it extremely easy for that agent to earn the commission.

As an example, if you were to purchase an FSBO property for $150,000, ask your agent to accept a 3 percent commission and ask the seller to reduce the sales price by 3 percent below market value. Your agent would earn $4,500 (or whatever percentage he or she is paid by the broker) on the sale price. The agent will make the same amount as if he or she had sold a $150,000 home listed by another agent. Most important, the sellers may reduce the price of the home since they are saving a substantial amount of money on the commission.

WHO WILL HANDLE THE PAPERWORK?

One of the major concerns you should have if you are working directly with FSBOs without the services of an agent is who will be responsible for preparing the deposit receipts or purchase contracts as well as the proper disclosure forms. Who will open the title orders, give the proper escrow/closing instructions, order the proper inspections, help the buyers and sellers interpret the inspections and reports, and in general handle the enormous amount of paperwork associated with a real estate transaction?

It is almost overwhelming for the average person to attempt to handle a home sale/purchase without an agent. However, it is possible to complete an FSBO sale/purchase if all parties to the transaction are willing to do their part to see that all requirements and responsibilities are completed in an effective and timely manner.

Sometimes real estate agents will offer their services to assist in an FSBO sale/purchase. Usually the agents will prepare the contracts, paperwork, and see that the closing process concludes smoothly. Normally in these cases, the agents will order the inspections and reports and generally handle all administration involved with the close of the transaction.

Agents who are willing to accept these responsibilities usually charge a flat fee ($500 to $1,500) or a small percentage of the sale price (normally between 1 and 1.5 percent).

Title officers, escrow/closing people, lenders, and inspectors are willing to explain their particular area of expertise with regard to the transaction. However, they cannot legally advise you as to how the inspections, reports, appraisals, or information adapts to your particular transaction.

> **SMART TIP:**
> In an FSBO transaction, to follow the procedures properly and legally, buyers and sellers should provide the instructions and directions for all aspects of the transaction to the inspectors, escrow/closing and title people, lenders, and any other parties to the transaction. The escrow/closing checklist in Chapter 19 will assist you in determining all of the procedures that must be completed.

SHOULD YOU USE AN ATTORNEY?

If you are not represented by a real estate agent or broker, it is a good idea to utilize the services of an attorney. The guidance of a qualified real estate lawyer can relieve some of the possibility of litigation that might occur long after the transaction has closed.

If you come to agreement with sellers on the terms by which you will purchase a property, you and the sellers should go to a real estate lawyer together and spell out in detail how the transaction will proceed. The attorney can then prepare all of the contracts, disclosures, escrow/closing instructions, warranties, and so on, and see that each item is completed properly.

Make sure that the attorney is well versed in real estate transactions and that he or she provides you with an estimate of the charges, up front, before any work has been completed. Do not ever accept only per-hour fee estimates, unless the attorney will put a maximum fee that will be charged for his or her services. At $150 to $350 per hour (the rates usually charged by real estate attorneys), it does not take long to surpass a full-blown commission, which a real estate broker would have charged to handle the entire transaction.

MAKING LOW-BALL OFFERS

Sometimes buyers, in trying to get a terrific deal with FSBOs, will make offers far below market value.

Occasionally, buyers will get lucky and find sellers who are desperate and will accept the offer. However, in most cases, FSBOs are no more apt to accept a ridiculously low offer than sellers who have their home listed by an agent or broker. And, in many cases, because those FSBOs are trying to save the commission and make more on the sale of their property, they may even be less receptive to low offers.

Whether a property is listed with a broker or is an FSBO, the sellers will be interested in low-ball offers only in extreme cases.

FINDING HOMES THAT ARE NOT LISTED BUT MIGHT BE FOR SALE

Just as a real estate agent obtains listings by finding sellers who are interested in selling their home, you, as a buyer, may be able to find those same sellers and possibly purchase a home directly from the owner.

The following letters can be used to make contact with other owners who may be interested in selling their homes. The best way to obtain the names and addresses of potential sellers is to work through a real estate agent and utilize the computer-generated information most agents and brokers have in their data bases.

Dear Mr. and Mrs. Jones,

We are looking to purchase a three- or four-bedroom, two-bath home in your neighborhood. We would like the home to have a large family room and a formal dining room. Also, we would prefer the property be located on a cul-de-sac or a very quiet street.

It would appear that your home may meet our desires and needs and we were wondering if you might be interested in selling your property in the near future.

Please understand, we are not real estate agents looking for listings. We are legitimate, qualified buyers seeking to find a nice home, in an acceptable area, for a fair price.

If you would be interested in speaking directly with us about the possibility of selling your home, please call us at (222) 333-4444, after 6:00 p.m.

Sincerely,

John and Mary Smith

Dear Mr. and Mrs. Jones,

We want to buy a home in your neighborhood!

Although there are several homes for sale, we have not yet found a property we wish to purchase.

If you are thinking of selling, we would very much like to discuss the possibility of purchasing your home.

We are not real estate agents looking for listings. We are legitimate, prequalified buyers looking to buy a home.

If you might be interested in selling your home in the near future, please call us after 6:00 p.m. at (222) 333-4444.

Sincerely,

John and Mary Smith

Dear Mr. and Mrs. Jones,

We have a difficult question and you may have the answer.

We are prequalified home buyers, looking for a three-bedroom home (or larger) in your neighborhood, yet we have been unable to find the home that we desire.

Our question is: Do you know anyone in your area who may have a home for sale that might meet our desires? If so, please call us. We would be willing to look at any home, listed or not, if the property met our needs.

Please call us at (222) 333-4444, if you have any information that might help in our search for a home in your beautiful area.

Sincerely,

John and Mary Smith

CHAPTER SEVENTEEN

New Home Purchases

Many buyers prefer to purchase newly constructed homes primarily because these homes seem to have fewer problems than previously owned homes or because, in many areas, new homes offer many more amenities.

Buyers need to be cautious when purchasing a new home and be sure that they will be satisfied with living in a newly established neighborhood. The most common complaint from home buyers nationwide is that new subdivisions seldom have the feeling of being completed until several years after the homes are built.

Also, buyers need to choose carefully the subdivision into which they buy, always keeping in mind whether the entire area appears to be growing and progressing into a neighborhood they will be happy in for several years.

CHOOSING THE SUBDIVISION

You should choose a new subdivision the same way you would choose a resale neighborhood, which was covered in Chapter 4. Do not just look inside the new tract, subdivision, or development itself; also look at the adjoining neighborhoods to be sure that the whole area is acceptable.

Consider the following items when choosing a subdivision:

> **SMART TIP:**
> Many times the schools your children will attend will be located outside of your development. Be sure that you feel comfortable with every area through which your children will pass en route to school.

- Are all of the adjoining neighborhoods acceptable?
- Are schools acceptable?
- Is the subdivision convenient to: shopping, freeways, your

place of work, family activities, churches, restaurants, recreation facilities, and repair services?

- What is the zoning in the areas surrounding the subdivision, and are there any major proposed changes in those zoning allowances? (In other words, what will be built around the subdivision: more single-family homes, a zillion apartments, or a sewage water treatment plant?)

- What specific covenants, conditions, and restrictions (CC & Rs) have been recorded and apply to that subdivision? The builder or developer should provide a copy of the CC & Rs at your request. If not, your agent can obtain a copy from the county or parish recorder's office. Some CC & Rs may be *very* restrictive, and buyers need to understand that these CC & Rs can, to a certain extent, alter the lifestyle of home owners in that area. Some examples might be restrictions as to the colors that the homes can be painted or a preclusion against cars parked overnight in the driveways; in one development in California, cats are not allowed in order to protect the nearly extinct marsh mouse that inhabits that area. One important CC & R should relate to the size of the homes allowed in an area. For example, you do not want a 1,000-square-foot home built next to a 5,000-square-foot mansion.

- If the city is growing near or around the subdivision, are you satisfied with the growth direction and the quality of the buildings that ultimately will surround your neighborhood?

- How close is the airport to the subdivision (noise, traffic, congestion)?

- How is the quality and availability of police and fire protection?

CUSTOM HOME PURCHASES

In some developments, the lots may be sold to a number of builders. If you are buying an existing new home, one that is already complete or close to completion, or a home built from the ground up with your specifications, you need to make sure that you are buying from a quality builder who will not only build a good home but will also back the work completely, even after the sale is completed.

GETTING LOAN APPROVAL FOR A HOME THAT IS NOT YET BUILT

In a custom home purchase, plans are submitted with the loan package and an appraisal is prepared from the comparable sales data available in that area. On a custom home sale, your loan can and should be approved before the home is actually started.

> **SMART TIP:**
> Some builders build for show and other builders build for quality. When you view custom homes, look for quality in construction and not flashy little touches that are designed to catch your eye. True quality in building goes much deeper than fancy wallpaper and upgraded carpet. If you have a friend or family member who knows construction, take that person along when you are viewing the homes. If you do not know anyone who can advise you on the quality of the construction, spend $200 to $300 and hire an expert for a few hours to guide you in your decision. It will be the best money you will ever spend.

CHOOSING A BUILDER

When you begin your search for a builder, make sure that you are looking at the homes from the proper perspective. Some builders do shoddy work yet their completed homes show beautifully, primarily due to the decorating in the model homes. However, when you look below the surface, the homes are just not built well.

As suggested previously, if you have a friend who knows construction, ask him or her to look at the homes with you or even hire a professional to guide you in your choice of builders.

Some homes in subdivisions are literally thrown together in a matter of weeks, and after two or three years the shoddy construction begins to surface. Make sure that you take time to talk to the people who are currently living in homes built by the builder you are considering. Ask these home owners:

- What problems have occurred with the home?
- How well has the contractor responded to and corrected these problems?

- Are they happy with the home overall?
- Would they buy another home from the same builder?

New homes (like new cars) will have little things go wrong. If a builder concentrates on quality in construction, is service-oriented, and follows up when problems do occur, most home owners will give glowing reports about the builder.

Look also at the previous subdivisions the builder has constructed. Did the homes sell well and are there many satisfied home owners? If so, you can feel fairly confident that the builder will continue to build homes that enhance his or her reputation.

You may check whether complaints have been filed against a particular builder with the State Contractors Board (the state department that handles contractor licensing), your local Better Business Bureau, and local real estate professionals who work with builders.

You may feel a little embarrassed about asking a total stranger rather personal questions pertaining to their home, but remember, you are probably making the biggest investment you have made in your life. It will pay for you to do your research well.

At your request, most builders are willing to give you the names and phone numbers of people who have purchased homes from them previously. Builders usually refuse for one of two reasons: either they want to protect the privacy of their clients or they do not want you to talk to dissatisfied clients.

In either case, you must have some references or past records or you would be a fool to purchase one of that builder's homes. Insist on a previous client list or at least the location of the previous subdivisions that the builder has constructed.

Do your homework!

CHOOSING YOUR LOT

The choice of a lot is based totally on your own personal desires. The most valuable lots in a subdivision are usually those with the best views. If there is a lake, stream, or canal in the subdivision, lots located on the waterways also may be the most desirable and valuable. However, many buyers are not concerned with the view or being on the water. Some buyers may want the largest lot, the most secluded lot, or a lot on the street with the least traffic.

When choosing your lot, some things to consider are:

- The traffic flow on the street.
- If you are specifically looking for a quiet area, a cul-de-sac may be your best choice.
- Will there be a lot of foot traffic across your yard if you choose a corner lot near a school or a store?
- What will adjoin your lot on the side and rear yards? (If the lot backs up to a busy street, a schoolyard, a recreation area, or a commercial business, will noise be a negative factor, not only while you live in the home but also financially when you sell the property?)
- Check everything that is to be built within a block of the lot you are considering. Things such as parks, recreational areas, or the subdivision pool can be positive or negative factors depending on your personal point of view.

Also, when you choose your lot and your home plan, if the adjoining properties are not yet constructed, find out what plans have been chosen for those lots.

SPECIAL FINANCING OPTIONS

Sometimes in a subdivision that is being constructed by one builder, prior to beginning the construction, the builder or the developer will arrange for special financing to be offered on the homes sold in that subdivision within a specified time.

You may remember "buy downs" from Chapter 8. Most times when builders offer special financing rates that are substantially below market interest rates, they have agreed to "buy down" the rates as the homes sell.

As an example, if homes were selling for $200,000 and loans were offered by a particular lender at 90 percent loan to value ($180,000 loan), at an annual interest rate of 1 percent below the current market interest rate, the builder might pay 2 to 4 points

($3,600 to $7,200) to "buy down" the interest rate offered to the buyers/borrowers.

Understand, most builders do not have a large profit margin on the homes they build. Therefore, if special financing is offered, there is a good chance that the builder has increased the prices of the homes to cover the cost of the financing. If you do not take advantage of the special financing options, you may be able to negotiate a better sale price on the home.

Make sure that you always ask if there are any special financing options available when you view the homes in a subdivision.

MAKING AN OFFER

When making an offer in a subdivision, the most important thing to remember is that builders will give up exactly what they must to make a deal. Consequently, you must ask for anything and everything that you expect to receive as part of that transaction.

Most homes in a subdivision that are being constructed by one builder will have established prices for each model, and there may not be much room for negotiation on these preset sale prices. However, in many cases, buyers may be able to negotiate a very good deal on the upgrades and improvements. Knowledgeable buyers can greatly enhance their deal in this area.

CAN YOU USE YOUR OWN AGENT WHEN BUYING IN A SUBDIVISION?

Most subdivision builders will cooperate with agents and brokers in the local Multiple Listing Service (MLS), which means that, in most cases, your agent will be able to work with you throughout the buying process. However (and this is a big however), many subdivision builders employ one or more sales representatives who work only for that builder. The primary job of these subdivision salespeople is to sell the homes and *get the best possible deal for the builder*. This means that they will give up as little as possible when it comes to price, terms, upgrades, special amenities, landscaping, or any other item that might be a cost factor for the builder. Some of these salespeople are actually paid a higher commission if they negotiate a deal that is less costly to the builder.

Because builders prefer that buyers work with their own salespeople, some builders pay outside agents and brokers a commission simply to deliver the buyers into the waiting arms of the subdivision salespeople. In some cases, that is like depositing Little Red Riding Hood into the arms of the Big Bad Wolf. This is not to say that all subdivision salespeople are waiting to take advantage of unsuspecting buyers. However, the question arises: Who is actually helping and representing the buyers to see that they get everything they should in the transaction?

Buyers must ask, ask, and ask again for everything that might be included at no extra cost and negotiate the very best possible price on every upgrade or improvement to the property.

Also, buyers in subdivisions need to be especially critical when they make their final walk-through. Every item that is not finished and in perfect order must be recorded with a time frame established as to when the items are to be completed.

Again, if possible, utilize the services of your own agent throughout the entire purchase process, even if the subdivision salespeople are willing to assist you.

NEGOTIATING AMENITIES, UPGRADES, AND PERSONAL PROPERTY

Many items will need to be negotiated during the purchase of a new home. Some of the areas that may require choices and decisions about upgrades include exterior items, such as exterior finish or siding, and/or roofing materials. Most basic exterior and roofing materials have at least a five-year guarantee. You must evaluate your own personal needs and judge how long you think you may own the home. Some exterior finishes offer guarantees for up to twenty years, and many types of tile roofs have guarantees for as long as fifty years. Choose your exterior and roofing upgrades carefully because these items can be costly to repair or replace.

Other upgrades include interior items, such as carpeting, floor coverings, cabinets, fixtures, tile, specialty lighting, and numerous other amenities, including appliances.

As you view a model home, take very detailed notes of the specific things you want in yours and be sure that all items are included in your purchase contract. Do not assume that certain lighting fixtures, cabinet tops, cabinets, sinks, tubs, special windows, and even a fireplace will be included in a standard home. Cover *every* option or upgraded feature in your purchase contract and leave nothing to chance.

> **SMART TIP:**
> When you view a model home, be sure to have the salesperson identify upgrades displayed. Most times model homes are professionally decorated and contain every available upgrade. A standard home in the subdivision may be quite different and much less appealing.

When negotiating upgrades, you may find yourself in a give-and-take situation. The offer/counteroffer process can be just as effective in the purchase of a new home as it is in a resale purchase. Ask for everything you want at no extra charge, but be ready to give a little here and there. Remember, if you are a strong, prequalified buyer who is ready to make a deal now, you will have some bargaining power. However, do not expect the subdivision salespeople to negotiate on your behalf. As mentioned, they work for the builder, and their job is get as much money out of you as possible.

Figure 17.1, the New Home Checklist, will help to guide you in asking salespeople about upgrades or improvements that may be offered in new homes.

Negotiate for the best upgrade you can get at no extra cost, then consider paying whatever is necessary to upgrade to the highest quality available.

GETTING THE BEST DEAL

The bottom line is, builders and developers are businesspeople. They are buying property and selling property for one reason: to make money. To that end, builders want to build homes and get

FIGURE 17.1

NEW HOME CHECKLIST

FEATURES	UPGRADE OFFERED	COST
Exterior Wall Finishes		
Roof		
Landscaping (Front)		
(Rear)		
Fencing		
Carpeting		
Floor Coverings (tile, wood, etc.)		
Wall Coverings (wallpaper, paneling, etc.)		
Special Lighting Features		
Cabinets		
Cabinet Tops		
Windows		
Doors		
Security System		
Fireplace/Wood Stove		
Ceiling Fans		

them sold as quickly as possible. Every day a builder delays selling a home, he or she is paying interest on the construction loan received to purchase the lot and to build the house.

Buyers who can purchase a property and close the deal quickly are very appealing to builders. The stronger the buyers appear on paper, the better negotiating position the buyers have. A builder does not want a home tied up for four to six weeks only to find that a buyer cannot qualify for the loan.

Here are a few suggestions to help you get the best deal possible when buying in a subdivision:

- Be prequalified, ready, willing, and able to buy on the spot. (A preapproved certificate in hand will help tremendously.)

- Buy in the early or late stages of a subdivision, which are the two best times to buy. In the beginning stages, the first homes are under construction and the builder really needs to get some properties sold. Also, subdivisions are less appealing when they are first under construction. After a few people buy and move into the area, the homes usually begin to sell better. Or, in the last stage, you can buy one of the last available homes because builders usually want to get these homes out of the way and move on to the next phase or subdivision. Also, in the last stages of a project, builders probably have made a substantial profit and may be willing to deal, especially on the upgrades and special features.

- Buy in a slow sellers' market. If you are buying in an area where the inventory of homes far exceeds the available buyers, often you can get an excellent deal on a subdivision home. Builders may have high interest construction loans, and their profit shrinks every month that the homes do not sell. If the homes sit long enough, builders may actually lose money on the sale of the homes.

- Buy in a future phase or an unbuilt home. Sometimes builders want to get a head start on a new phase or subdivision they are going to build. If you are willing to purchase a home in the new phase and give builders some security as to the sales in the new project, you may be able to get a better deal than you would if you waited to buy in there after construction had begun. Remember, you will have to wait a little longer for your home, but you may be able make a great deal.

- Buy a model home. Sometimes builders sell their model homes with all of the special amenities and upgrades for essentially the same price as a standard home. Usually buyers have to wait for possession until the subdivision is sold out. However, many times the deal on the home you will purchase is worth the wait.

WARRANTIES AND GUARANTEES

As explained in Chapter 14, warranties and guarantees are an extremely critical part of a home purchase. Especially with a new home, problems may occur, and it is important that buyers understand exactly what is warranted. Knowing and understanding the builder's reputation with regard to servicing the home after the sale is very important.

Some subdivisions are literally thrown together in a matter of weeks, and in two or three years the shoddy construction surfaces. Warranties and guarantees may play a major part in the ultimate satisfaction level of new home buyers.

HOW ARE NEW HOMES WARRANTED?

In every state in the United States, licensed contractors are bound by an implied warranty, which means that they must guarantee their construction to be sound and functional. In addition, most builders include, at no extra charge, a home owner's warranty, which offers additional specific guarantees for different periods of time.

The new home warranty may include coverages for things such as:

Year 1:   All electrical, plumbing, heating and cooling systems, structure, fixtures, and all workmanship and materials used in the construction
Year 2:   Most major structural defects
Years 3–15: Specified structural defects

Since there are many items not covered by most builders' warranties, you will probably want to consider asking for a complete homeowner's warranty, as explained in Chapter 14, to be included with the new home purchase. If the builder does not want to pay for the warranty, you may consider buying it yourself. For $300 or $400, it provides great peace of mind and may save you a great deal of money and frustration in the future.

WHAT SHOULD YOU EXPECT?

Anytime you purchase a new home, you should expect little things to go wrong, sometimes more than with a previously owned property. However, if the builder handles the problem situations quickly and efficiently, your aggravation and frustration should be minimized.

While you are waiting for your home to be finished, be patient. There will be delays and things always take longer than you think. However, if the builder is doing his or her job to see that everything is completed properly, the wait will be a small price to pay. Don't ever try to rush construction!

THE FINAL WALK-THROUGH

One of the most critical things in a new home purchase is the final walk-through. You may want to use the Home Inspection Form (located in the Appendix) to be sure that you do not miss anything on this final inspection before closing the transaction.

You will want to check everything from the baseboards, to the counter tops, to the electrical plates . . . everything in the home should be finished. Any necessary work or repairs that needs to be done must be recorded and made a part of the final closing instructions.

Make sure all appliances are working properly.

If you do find work that needs to be done, some builders will ask you to close the transaction and have the repairs completed after you occupy the home. If you agree to this arrangement, ask that a portion of the builder's funds be held in the escrow/closing until the repair is completed to your satisfaction.

Make sure your agent accompanies you during the walk-through. Also have your agent or the builder's agent sign or initial your notes with regard to repairs that need to be made.

Buying a Condominium or Cooperative Unit

Many home owners buy their properties primarily for the financial advantages in the form of a tax write-off and equity buildup. However, many of those same buyers do not really want the responsibility of the upkeep and care for a large home with a yard and extensive landscaping. In these cases, the most acceptable home purchase may be a condo or a co-op ownership.

WHAT IS A CONDOMINIUM (CONDO)?

A condo is an apartment-style home, a flat, a townhouse, a duplex, a four-plex, or even a freestanding, single-family home. Although most people envision a condo as a particular style of structure, a condominium is actually more a method of ownership.

Condominium ownership means simply that the owners buy airspace inside a building and receive a real estate deed for their particular unit. Included with the exclusive use of that airspace is a shared ownership of the exterior of the buildings and all grounds and common areas within the condominium project.

WHAT IS A COOPERATIVE OWNERSHIP (CO-OP)?

A co-op unit is similar to a condominium, in that the buyers purchase the right to use and occupy the interior of a particular housing unit. However, in a co-op purchase, the buyer is not buying any real estate. The buyer is actually buying shares in the corporation that owns and governs the cooperative units.

Condo buyers are given an actual title to the real estate. In a co-op purchase, buyers receive not only the stock ownership but also a lease that guarantees them the right to occupancy of a particular unit.

In most cases, all co-op buyers must be approved by the co-op board of directors, and, in some situations, that approval process extends to all shareholders. In other words, if one of the owners doesn't like you, you might not get in.

Unlike a condo, a co-op unit does not necessarily build individual equity per se. However, the value of the stock can increase, thereby creating an equity buildup situation for each stockholder/owner. Also, buyers in a co-op may pay additional monies to an individual seller for improvements that have been made to a unit.

Although a co-op owner does not actually own the real estate, the tax code does provide tax advantages for the cooperative ownership.

WHAT ARE THE ADVANTAGES?

Table 18.1 presents the advantages of condo and co-op ownership.

TABLE 18.1
ADVANTAGES OF CONDO/CO-OP OWNERSHIP

Advantages	Condo	Co-op
Less upkeep than a home	Yes	Yes
Equity increase	Possibly	Possibly stock value increase
Special shared amenities (pools, health clubs, spas, etc.)	Sometimes	Sometimes
Tax write-off	Yes	Yes
Lower maintenance cost	Yes	Yes
Lower purchase price	Sometimes	Sometimes
Availability	Yes	Not always
No yard or exterior upkeep	Yes	Yes

WHAT ARE THE DISADVANTAGES?

Table 18.2 details some of the disadvantages of condo or co-op ownership in comparison to home ownership.

TABLE 18.2
DISADVANTAGES OF CONDO/CO-OP OWNERSHIP

DISADVANTAGES	CONDO	CO-OP
Less Privacy	Yes	Yes
Usually smaller living spaces	Yes	Yes
Limited private yards	Yes	Yes
Sharing exterior amenities with others	Yes	Yes
Less control of your property	Yes	Yes
Condo association or co-op board has exterior power to govern	Yes	Yes
Less appreciation than single-family homes	Sometimes	Almost always
Actually own real estate	Yes	No
Buyer must be approved by the board	No	Yes
Financing is more difficult and sometimes more expensive	Sometimes	Yes
Must pay home owner's association dues	Yes	Yes
Higher down payment may be necessary	Sometimes	Yes
More controlled lifestyle	Sometimes	Usually
Home owner's association or co-ops sometimes have financial problems or go bankrupt	Yes	Yes

HOW ARE CONDOS OR CO-OPS FINANCED?

Financing for condos is very similar to financing available for any other home. Almost all conventional and government lenders loan on condos, usually at the same rate as single-family residences.

However, in some cases, lenders charge a slightly higher interest rate to finance condos. Also, the costs to obtain a loan are sometimes slightly higher than with a single-family home.

Co-ops, on the other hand, vary greatly from single-family homes in both the financing available and the cost to obtain that financing.

In some cases, co-ops are owned by cities, counties, or special government entities. In these cases, ownership usually is made available to low-income buyers and the financing is easily obtained, often with little or no money down.

However, at the other end of the spectrum are very expensive co-op units, selling for $500,000 up to $3,000,000 or more. For these, financing is expensive and often difficult to obtain. Many buyers for these types of units put at least 50 percent down when they make the purchase.

Sometimes when lenders receive a loan package involving the financing of a condo or co-op, they require an audited financial statement on the corporation that owns the co-op or the home owner's association that governs the condo. It is important to lenders that these managing bodies are well run and financially secure.

> **SMART TIP:**
> Sometimes a buyer of a condo or co-op unit may have difficulty meeting the required qualifying ratios and obtaining financing because of the homeowner's association fees. (See Chapter 3.) These fees are collected to maintain the common areas of the complex and can range from about $100 up to over $750 per month.

WHAT ABOUT
THE ASSOCIATIONS?

The condo homeowner's association and the governing board of the co-op corporation are established to protect the rights of the owners and to maintain the living standards within the condo or co-op. In both cases, the board of directors is usually elected by the homeowners or shareholders. However, co-ops sometimes are controlled by an outside entity, such as a county housing authority; in these cases, the governing board of directors usually is appointed by that outside agency.

As mentioned previously, some co-op complexes mandate that every potential buyer be screened and approved by every owner in the co-op. This can, in some cases, create a very unfair environment and may preclude a buyer from purchasing a co-op unit.

Condominium home owner's associations usually do not have the right to approve or disapprove of particular buyers who wish to buy in the complex.

In both cases, when the board of directors makes a decision, it is usually final. The board "rules," and unless an individual owner wishes to force a decision made by a board into actual litigation, he or she will have to abide by the board's decision.

CHOOSING A CONDO
OR CO-OP COMMUNITY

As with single-family residences, one of the most important aspects of choosing the right condo or co-op is the neighborhood in which the complex is located. However, in most cases, the condo or co-op is somewhat of a neighborhood or community within itself.

Second, most condos and some co-ops include common grounds that all residents of the complex can use. Potential buyers need to inspect these common areas prior to looking at the individual living units. Usually, if a condo or co-op is poorly maintained, it will be evident in the common areas and in the maintenance and repair of building exteriors. Be sure to check the pool and other recreation areas to be sure that all of the equipment is in good working order and repair.

Your third step in choosing a condo or co-op should be to determine what restrictions are in place that may affect the lifestyle of owners. Some examples might be restrictions on:

- Pets
- The use of common areas by children
- Window coverings

- Any changes, remodeling, or construction within your unit
- The number of occupants who can occupy the unit
- How many vehicles you can park on the grounds
- Motorcycles
- Use of decks or exterior ledges

Next, take some time to talk to home owners in the complex and determine if the current residents are happy living there. Does the home owner's association or board of directors do a good job managing the complex, and are they reasonable in their judgments and decisions? Do any occupants continually disturb the other owners with wild parties, loud music, or arguments?

Find out what goes on in the condo or co-op before you ever consider purchasing in the complex. As suggested previously, be sure to get the twenty-four-hour view, just as you would in a neighborhood of a single-family home.

Next, look at the construction of the units (both inside and out) in the same manner in which you would view a single-family home. (See Chapter 7.) How old are the buildings? How well are they maintained? What is the age and condition of the elevators? How are the roofs?

> **SMART TIP:**
> Throughout your decision and buying process for a condo or co-op unit, remember, your neighbor is not going to be one lot away from your exterior wall. Instead, your neighbor will *be* your exterior wall.

WHAT ELSE SHOULD YOU LOOK FOR?

One of the most critical factors in a condo or co-op is the sound insulation. In some units you can hear everything your neighbor says in a normal tone of voice; in other complexes you never know you have a neighbor. It is very important to spend enough time viewing the property to determine how well the units are insulated.

Use the Home Inspection Form from the Appendix when viewing the interior of the units. Often condos or co-ops have less closet and storage space than a single-family home. Be sure that you will have enough storage space.

WHAT ABOUT PARKING?

See that the parking facilities are adequate for your needs. If you have many guests often, how far will they have to walk to reach your unit? Also, if you must pay separately for parking, make sure that you understand how and when that cost can change.

Many co-ops do not offer any parking whatsoever, so buyers may have an additional cost of $100 to $300 per month per vehicle that must be parked off-site. In most condos, parking usually is in private garages, carports, or other assigned parking facilities. Check to be sure that these parking areas are secure and without leaks if it is covered.

WHAT ABOUT SECURITY
IN THE COMPLEX?

If the project provides security guards or a security service, how are the personnel paid? Is the cost included in your home owner's fees, or is there an additional charge? What hours are the security personnel on duty and what is their average response time to calls by residents? What are the actual duties of the security people? How are guests admitted? Are the security personnel armed? What is the training level and requirements for the security people? How many security personnel are employed? Is there a high turn-over rate?

THE CONDO OR CO-OP BY-LAWS

Read the condo or co-op laws carefully!

All rules, regulations, conditions, and restrictions associated with a condo or co-op are detailed in the by-laws that are recorded with CC & Rs when a condo or co-op receives approval for construction or conversion from the state, county, parish, or city that governs that type of project in the area.

Read and understand these by-laws before making an offer on a property, or else make an offer contingent upon your approval of the by-laws.

MAKING AN OFFER

Making an offer on a condo is very similar to making an offer on a single-family residence. Buyers should have been prequalified before beginning their search for a specific condo. If they are, the loan and the closing process should progress as quickly as would occur with the purchase of a single-family home.

Agents, brokers, and attorneys specialize in co-op sales, and buyers who are interested in a co-op unit should contact one of these professionals at the beginning of their home search.

Many times, co-op brokers will suggest that prospective buyers prepare a complete personal package for submission to the board of directors of a co-op. This package includes all information that would assist the board in making a positive decision about the co-op buyers.

SUGGESTIONS TO REMEMBER

- Always check to see how many units are for sale in a complex, what the average sale time for these units is, and how many units have actually sold. If many units are for sale and the sales times are excessive, and if very few units are selling, there may be a problem with the individual units or the entire complex.
- Be sure to determine if the condo home owner's association or the co-op corporation is financially sound and that there is enough money to run and maintain the complex properly.
- Find out if there are any proposed increases in the association or corporation home owner's fees.
- Check with the local police or sheriff's department and determine if an excessive number of complaints or incidents occur in or around the condo or co-op you are considering. Also, check with the local fire department and see if there have been an excessive number of calls from the complex.

Closing the Sale

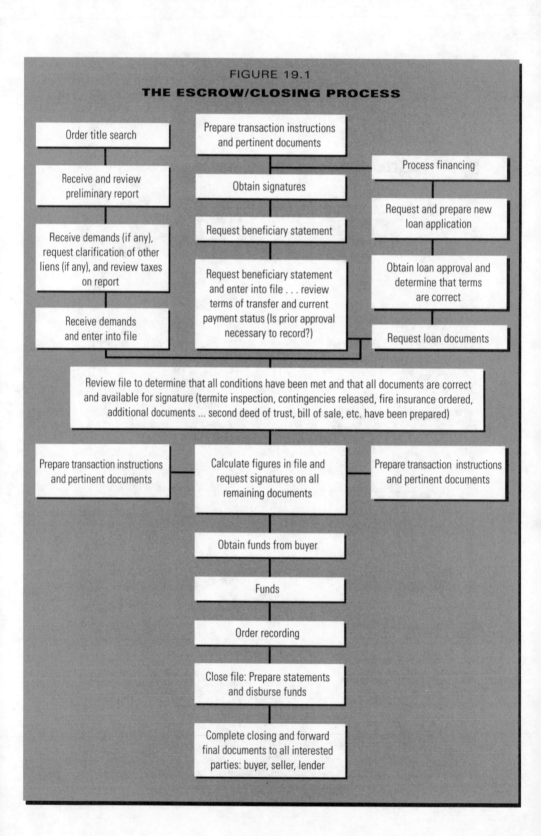

FIGURE 19.1

THE ESCROW/CLOSING PROCESS

Order title search

Receive and review preliminary report

Receive demands (if any), request clarification of other liens (if any), and review taxes on report

Receive demands and enter into file

Prepare transaction instructions and pertinent documents

Obtain signatures

Request beneficiary statement

Request beneficiary statement and enter into file . . . review terms of transfer and current payment status (Is prior approval necessary to record?)

Process financing

Request and prepare new loan application

Obtain loan approval and determine that terms are correct

Request loan documents

Review file to determine that all conditions have been met and that all documents are correct and available for signature (termite inspection, contingencies released, fire insurance ordered, additional documents ... second deed of trust, bill of sale, etc. have been prepared)

Prepare transaction instructions and pertinent documents

Calculate figures in file and request signatures on all remaining documents

Prepare transaction instructions and pertinent documents

Obtain funds from buyer

Funds

Order recording

Close file: Prepare statements and disburse funds

Complete closing and forward final documents to all interested parties: buyer, seller, lender

Finally, the time has come to start the closing process on your home purchase. If you are using the services of a real estate professional, he or she should be able to guide you through the final stages of your home purchase. However, you should understand what needs to be done by all parties to make the entire closing process go as smoothly as possible.

Figure 19.1 explains in detail what steps actually are involved in the escrow/closing process. You should be willing to help in any portion of this process where your assistance is needed.

WHO MUST DO WHAT?

At the beginning of the closing process, it is very important to see that the closing instructions are signed by the buyers and the sellers and submitted to the escrow/closing officer. These closing instructions should clarify for all parties exactly what will occur in the transaction, such as sale price, terms, conditions, and required inspections.

In some states, the closing agent/officer is an attorney. However, in most states, attorneys do not have to participate in the closing of a standard real estate transaction. In most cases, the escrow/closing is handled by either an escrow or a closing agent or a title company.

The closing/escrow agent acts as a neutral third party to the transaction to be sure that all documents have been prepared and submitted, all requirements for closing stated by the lender have been met, all inspections have been completed and reports submitted and approved, and all monies necessary to close the transaction have been received.

Once the parties to the transaction have taken all of the required actions, and the escrow/closing agent has received all documents, the closing/escrow is deemed to be *perfect*, or complete. Buyers and sellers sign the final closing documents and the escrow/closing agent sees that all documents that must be recorded are delivered to the county, parish, state, or province records offices and the recordation takes place.

The recording, in essence, makes the transaction public information and clarifies who has sold and who has purchased the subject property. Once the recordation process has occurred, the escrow/closing agent releases the monies owed to the sellers, pays all of the fees and charges that were to be paid out of the escrow/closing, and advises the agents to release possession of the property to the new buyers. As per the closing instructions, the transaction is complete after all fees, commissions, pro-rations, or charges are processed and paid by the escrow/closing agent.

The Escrow/Closing Checklist in Figure 19.2 will assist sellers, buyers, and agents in making sure that nothing is missed during this very important closing process.

You will note that a *target* date and a *completed* date are listed. All parties to the transaction should watch carefully to see that the target dates are met and that none of these critical steps is overlooked.

WATCHING ESCROW/CLOSING PROBLEM AREAS

If agents, buyers, or sellers find that one or more of the target dates have passed without completion of a checklist item, it should be addressed immediately with the party who is responsible for that particular item.

Problems that can come up during a closing process are numerous and should real estate agents, buyers, sellers, or escrow/closing agents recognize one of these obstacles, it should be brought to the attention of all parties immediately.

Figure 19.3 will give you an idea of the average time delays that can occur when certain difficulties arise.

FIGURE 19.2

THE ESCROW/CLOSING CHECKLIST

The following list is to confirm all the dates necessary to achieve a smooth closing. Please verify the dates with your clients and return a copy to me with your signature.

For Property at: _____	Goal Date	Actual Date
1. Contract acceptance with all decision makers present	_____	_____
2. Property inspection by buyer	_____	_____
3. Promissory note inspection and approval	_____	_____
4. Listing disclosure signed	_____	_____
5. Agency signed	_____	_____
6. Service contract approval	_____	_____
7. Income/expense approval	_____	_____
8. Permit approval	_____	_____
9. Inventory approval	_____	_____
10. Escrow instructions prepared	_____	_____
11. Escrow instructions signed	_____	_____
12. Deposit submitted	_____	_____
13. Deposit clears the bank	_____	_____
14. Professional property inspection	_____	_____
15. Inspection accepted	_____	_____
16. Estoppel certificates approval	_____	_____
17. Termite inspection	_____	_____
18. Earthquake and flood zones	_____	_____
19. Deposit increase to escrow	_____	_____
20. Preliminary title report approval	_____	_____
21. City approvals obtained	_____	_____
22. Loan submitted complete to lender	_____	_____
23. Appraisal made	_____	_____
24. Appraisal done	_____	_____
25. Termite work finished	_____	_____
26. Obtain insurance	_____	_____
27. Reappraisal done	_____	_____
28. Other work finished	_____	_____
29. PMI approval	_____	_____
30. FIRPTA signed	_____	_____
31. Other contingencies cleared	_____	_____
A. _____	_____	_____
B. _____	_____	_____
C. _____	_____	_____
32. Formal written loan approval	_____	_____
33. Loan documents signed	_____	_____
34. Cleared funds submitted for down payment	_____	_____
35. Buyer's occupancy	_____	_____

Buyer's Agent_____ Date _____

Seller's Agent_____ Date _____

FIGURE 19.3

ESCROW/CLOSING PROBLEM CHECKLIST

	Average Time Delay
1. Buyer and seller do not sign escrow/closing promptly.	5 days
2. Buyer's good-faith deposit check does not clear.	3 days
3. Buyer does not complete loan application in a timely manner.	10 days
4. Buyer or seller does not return calls of agent or lender.	10 days
5. Buyer or seller wants to change some terms of the transaction.	5 days
6. Buyer loses job.	30 days
7. Buyer lied on prequalification to lender.	10 days
8. Buyer cannot supply tax returns in timely manner.	10 days
9. Seller changes mind about selling.	5 days
10. Seller leaves town and does not leave a power of attorney with anyone.	5 days
11. Seller did not disclose all liens against him/herself.	20 days
12. Unknown problems with home are discovered.	10–30 days
13. Low appraisal.	15 days
14. Slow appraisal.	15 days
15. Difficult appraisal.	5 days
16. Incorrect appraisal.	15 days
17. Lender made a mistake on prequalification.	5 days
18. Lender decides not to loan on property or borrower.	10–30 days
19. Borrower does not qualify for loan.	10 days
20. Lender requires repairs on property.	15 days
21. Agents do not return calls.	5 days
22. Agents go on vacation.	5 days
23. Buyer or seller does not sign final closing papers in a timely fashion.	5 days
24. Escrow/closer/lender loses file.	10 days
25. Escrow/closer/title company/lender very busy.	5–20 days
26. Seller or buyer wants to change closing date.	5 days
27. Inspection companies too busy or slow.	5–10 days
28. Many things called on inspections.	5 days
29. Additional inspections required by appraiser or lender.	5–10 days
30. Title company finds problems with the title.	5–15 days

As you can see, it doesn't take much to slow up or completely destroy a transaction. Any of these or other problem areas can "blow the deal," so stay on top of the closing process and see that everything goes as planned.

Buyers and sellers will be asked to approve and sign several documents during the closing process, such as the Grant Deed, the HUD Statement, the Escrow/Closing Instructions, and the Net Proceeds Statement. (See the Appendix for these forms.)

As indicated previously, there may be numerous other closing documents to sign plus loan papers that may be delivered to the escrow/closing agent or the borrowers may be required to complete the lender's documents during a separate signing process.

CASUALTY INSURANCE

If you are obtaining a loan for the purchase of your property, you will be required to obtain hazard or casualty insurance.

In most cases, lenders will require hazard insurance to cover losses or damages to the home by fire, wind, theft, riot, and the like. Some lenders require a broader coverage policy that includes liability coverage in case someone is injured on your property.

Most buyers obtain a home owner's policy that includes several types of protection. Depending on which policy is chosen, coverage can be very extensive.

Homeowner's policies are divided into different categories, based on the coverage. Table 19.1 details the coverages extended by each policy.

When you are deciding what type of policy and coverage you desire, make sure you take some time to compare not just prices but

SMART TIP:
In certain areas, lenders may also require some special coverages, such as earthquake insurance if you live in Southern California or flood insurance if your home is located in a flood zone.

the quality of the policies. Look at the limits placed on certain

TABLE 19.1

HOME POLICY COVERAGES

TYPE OF POLICY	COVERAGES
Home owner 1 **HO–1**	Fire, theft, explosion, hail, wind, smoke, vandalism, glass, breakage, and liability
Home owner 2 **HO–2**	All of what is covered in HO–1 plus falling objects, structural collapses, exploding pipes, or heating or cooling devices and liability
Home owner 3 **HO–3**	The "everything is covered policy," almost a total coverage policy with a few exceptions
Home owner 4 **HO–4**	For renters, it covers personal possessions and liability
Home owner 5 **HO–5**	Covers everything in HO–3 plus has extended coverage with very few exceptions
Home owner 6 **HO–6**	Home owners' policy for condos or co-ops, can have coverages as broad as HO–3

items, such as cameras, guns, jewelry, computers, or other expensive personal property.

Most people are extremely underinsured when it comes to hazard and liability insurance. The cost of these types of insurance is minimal compared with a loss that could occur in a fire or even a burglary.

Prices for policies can vary considerably from company to company, so shop around, but remember, *don't just shop price*; shop for the best-quality policy at the lowest available cost.

The Insurance Information Sheet in Table 19.2 will help you obtain the proper information from the insurance companies.

SMART TIP:
Get an insurance "checkup" at least every two years and make sure you have enough coverage to protect your personal property as well as your liability. Increasing coverages and limits on policies is often inexpensive and well worth the extra cost.

TABLE 19.2

INSURANCE INFORMATION SHEET

	COMPANY 1	COMPANY 2	COMPANY 3
Company Name			
Name of Agent			
Address			
Phone			
Types of Policy			
What Is Covered			
What Is Excluded			
Limits on Personal Property			
Limits on Total Losses			
Limits on Liability			
Deductibles			
Cost of Policy			
Comments			

In most cases, you will be asked to pay the first year's insurance premium as a part of your closing costs. If your lender is going to require impounds, your monthly payment also will include an amount equal to approximately half of your insurance premium to assure that the policy is maintained. The actual bill for the insurance premium will be sent to and paid by the lender from the funds in the impound account.

SMART TIP:
Do not wait until the last minute to shop for casualty insurance. Do your homework and have the policy delivered to the escrow/closing agent at least a few days prior to the close of the transaction.

MORTGAGE INSURANCE PREMIUM (MIP)
OR
MUTUAL MORTGAGE INSURANCE (MMI)

This is the insurance that is required by the lender in cases where the borrowers are obtaining a loan of 81 percent or more, loan to value. The insurance guarantees for the lender that the loan obligation will be paid. If borrowers default on the payments, the private mortgage insurers will pay the obligation and proceed to recover their money from the borrowers or foreclose on and obtain the property.

Your lender will choose the mortgage insurer who will issue your policy; you need not concern yourself with shopping for this coverage.

The cost of the mortgage insurance ranges somewhere between .35 and .50 percent of the loan amount per year. In some cases, the MIP premium may be as high as 1 percent for the first year's coverage and then drop to a lower rate for subsequent years. Normally, when borrowers are making a down payment of at least 20 percent of the sale price, no mortgage insurance is required.

> **SMART TIP:**
>
> As you repay the loan balance and begin to build equity in a home, you may be able to delete the mortgage insurance premium (MIP) from your payment. Once home owners have at least 20 percent equity in their home (either from appreciation or loan reduction) and they can prove their equity position, lenders probably will rescind the mortgage insurance. Borrowers will need to make a formal request in writing to the lender and ask that the MIP be deleted. Lenders may require an appraisal to prove the equity position, and they also may require a perfect payment history.

TITLE INSURANCE

Title insurance guarantees the buyers of a property that they will receive title to the property, free and clear of any liens or judgments, except those of which they are aware (such as the loan that they are obtaining to purchase the property or items that were indicated on the title examination and report).

After a title company has done a complete and thorough inspection of the title on a property, it will issue a title insurance policy that guarantees that the title to the home is "clear."

Should another person show up (years subsequent to the home purchase) with a deed or claim to or on the property, the title company would be responsible to handle the claim.

The fee for title insurance often is paid by the sellers and is based on the sale price of the home.

> **SMART TIP:**
> In some areas of the United States, title insurance is not available. However, some type of title guarantee always is substituted as protection for buyers. These products may be called Guarantees for Title or Abstract Guarantees. Title insurance is by far the best coverage and should be utilized whenever available.

LENDER'S TITLE INSURANCE POLICY

This is a separate title insurance policy issued to and for the protection of the lender. This policy guarantees, for the lender, that the title to the property is "clear." Since the lender is putting the money out for a loan, he or she may want a separate title guarantee.

In most cases, buyers/borrowers usually pay for the lender's title policy, since the policy is a requirement to obtain the loan and is based on the loan amount. However, as indicated earlier, you may ask the sellers to pay this cost.

DOWN PAYMENT AND CLOSING COSTS

When the escrow/closing process begins, you should have a good idea as to how much money you will need to close the transaction once the escrow/closing has been perfected. However, in most transactions, the money to close will not need to be delivered to the escrow/closing agent until just before the closing date. At that time you will be given an exact figure that you will need to present to the escrow/closing agent, preferably in the form of a cashier's or certified check or a wire transfer.

Be sure to maintain the funds that will be necessary to close the transaction and be ready, upon request by the escrow/closing company, to present them.

GOOD FUNDS RULES AND LAWS

Escrow/closing companies are required to see that funds presented for closing a real estate transaction are in fact "good funds." In other words, the checks to close the transaction must have cleared the bank before the recording of the deed can take place. If a wire transfer occurs from your account directly into the escrow holder's account, the funds are considered "good" upon the confirmation of the wire transfer.

If a transaction is to close on time, deposit "good funds" into the escrow/closing agent's account at least two days prior to the closing date.

Cash is also considered "good funds;" however, most escrow/closing companies will not accept large sums of cash. If you present cash for the closing, the escrow/closing agent will probably request that you go to the nearest bank and obtain a cashier's check.

> **SMART TIP:**
> You can request that the escrow/closing company place the funds to close in an interest-bearing account while you are waiting for the transaction to close.

HOLDING SELLERS' FUNDS IF REQUIREMENTS ARE NOT MET

In some situations it is a good idea to have the escrow/closing company hold some of the sellers' funds after the close and recordation of the transaction. One such case is if sellers were required to make certain repairs and those repairs were not completed prior to closing. Funds in an amount large enough to cover the cost of repairs being made by an outside source should be set aside to ensure that the sellers will follow through on the required repairs.

You should never hesitate to ask that funds be held to cover required items that were conditions laid down for closing the transaction.

REPAIRS NOT MADE AS AGREED

Again, the best way to ensure that the required repairs will be made is to ask that a substantial amount of the sellers' funds be held in the escrow/closing account until the repairs have been completed and approved. If sellers will not agree to allow the funds to be held, you would be wise to delay the closing process until the sellers complete the repairs or agree to allow the funds to be held.

> **SMART TIP:**
> Never allow sellers to receive all of their proceeds from a sale if there are requirements, such as repairs to the property, that have not been met at the time of closing. You could be left "holding the bag" so to speak, if there is no way to force the sellers to meet their contractual requirements. Holding funds is the best action to ensure that all of the requirements are met.

SPECIAL LOAN REQUIREMENTS

In certain situations, when a lending package is approved, special requirements must be met before the transaction can close.

As an example, a lender might require as part of the loan approval that you pay off all or part of a debt(s). In that case, the escrow/closing agent would include the amount necessary to pay that debt or debts in the total amount that you would need to close the transaction. After the recording of the transaction, the escrow/closing agent would pay the debt from the funds you have paid. Sometimes this function is handled by the title company in a capacity known as a subescrow.

If the lender requires only proof that the requirements have been met, you can simply pay the debt directly to the creditor and receive a receipt for payment. This receipt can then be included in the completed package that is returned to the lender for final approval, just prior to closing.

NET PROCEEDS STATEMENT

The Net Proceeds Statement should be reviewed very carefully by buyers/borrowers, sellers, and agents, if any, who are participating in the transaction. This statement indicates exactly *who* is paying *what*. If any corrections need to be made, they must be made prior to the close of the transaction or the recordation. (See the Appendix for a Net Proceeds Statement.)

THE FINAL WALK-THROUGH

Just prior to closing, you will be given an opportunity to do a final walk-through inspection of the property. You should take all of the notes and inspection forms that you have prepared since the very first viewing of the home with you to the final walk-through.

All of the requirements for repairs, as well as closing and any other actions necessary by the sellers, should be completed prior to the final inspection. If all requirements are not met, some of the sellers' funds should be held in the escrow/closing account to ensure that these required items are completed.

THE RECORDING

After you have completed your final walk-through inspection and have reviewed and signed all of the closing papers, the recordation process will take place. This recording will be handled by the escrow/closing company, title company, or closing attorney who has handled your transaction. Certain documents, such as the grant deed and mortgage note, will be recorded at the county, parish, province, state, or federal government offices where specific documents are recorded. Most recordings in a residential real estate sale are done at county or parish level.

Once the actual recording process has occurred, the title will have passed from the seller to the buyer and you are officially a proud home owner.

Additionally, after the close of the transaction, you should receive a corrected copy of the HUD Settlement Statement that shows the exact figures for all items in the transaction. In some cases, a small check will accompany this statement that will balance the escrow/closing account in case you overpaid.

After the recording, the keys for your home should be delivered per the conditions of your purchase contract. If the sellers are allowed a certain period of time to vacate the property after the closing, you will receive possession once that time has elapsed.

If possession is not delivered to you as agreed in the contract and the seller requests time to move after the close, be sure to ask the seller to pay a per-day rental fee at least equivalent to your new loan payments. As an example, if your house payment is \$1,200 per month, \$1,200 $\div$ 30 = \$40 per day.

THE "WHAT-IFS"

Here's a quick reminder of some of the more common crises that could occur at this point and how you should handle them.

What if the appraisal by the lender who is making the loan for the buyers comes in at an evaluation lower than the sale price, and the loan amount is reduced?

A written appeal can be made to the lender for an increase in the appraisal and/or the loan amount. The lender who is making the loan can guide the buyers/borrowers as to how this process should be handled, or a new appraisal can be ordered if it appears that the original appraisal is incorrect.

What if after the appraisal or the review, the lender still will not increase the loan to the amount requested by the buyers/borrowers?

The buyers could complete the sale by paying an additional down payment and agree to close the sale at an above-appraisal price (this is not usually recommended), or the sellers can reduce the sale price of the property to match the appraisal value. (This is the fairest and likely scenario.)

If the sale price is altered due to a low appraisal, can the sellers renegotiate other items in the transaction, such as payment of closing costs, payment for repairs to be made, and even commissions and fees to be paid to the agents, brokers, or lenders?

Absolutely! When the sale price changes, all bets are off and the sellers can renegotiate all costs they had previously agreed to pay.

What if the buyers, although they were prequalified for a loan, ultimately do not qualify for the loan? (This can occur for a number of reasons, such as loss of job, divorce, reduction of income, etc.)?

The best action is to evaluate why the loan was rejected and solve the problem, if possible. Once the problem has been taken care of, the loan package can be resubmitted for approval, the buyer could apply to another lender who would be willing to make the loan, or the transaction could be renegotiated, possibly with a seller carry-back to allow the transaction to close with temporary financing until the problem can be corrected and the buyer can "cash out" the seller.

What if one or more of the parties or companies to the transaction is not completing its part of the sale efficiently and within the specified time, and it appears that these actions or inactions are going to delay the closing?

You should notify your agent and all other parties to the transaction if it appears that problems may jeopardize the timely closing. It may take numerous phone calls and/or a written contact, but be persistent with the person who is responsible for the delays until the closing is back on track. All you are asking is that all parties do as they agreed, when they agreed.

What if the sellers decide not to sell after the purchase contract has been signed and the closing process has already started?

If you are not willing to rescind the contract and release the sellers from their obligation to sell, you may have to take legal action against the sellers for damages that you may suffer or possibly even for specific performance. Also, the brokers involved in the transaction may have a possible action for the commission that they have earned.

What if the termite, roof, home, or other inspections result in more work than expected and the expense for these repairs is much greater than the sellers anticipated?

Obviously, the sellers can "bite the bullet" and make the repairs on the property. It is their problem, and it is probably fairest for them to take full responsibility. However, in some cases, the sellers may not financially be able to make all of the required repairs. In that case, if the buyers still want to purchase the home, they may offer to pay for or do some of the work or they may accept the home without some repairs being made. In this case, the lender also would have to agree to the loan on the home without the required work being completed.

What if the home suffers major damage or is destroyed by an earthquake, a flood, a hurricane, a fire, or some other act of nature?

Well, this is pretty much a deal "killer." You probably will not be willing to wait for the house to be rebuilt or repaired. Also, there is always the question if the sellers have enough insurance coverage to be able to rebuild the home to the buyers' satisfaction.

What if liens and encumbrances have been placed against the property? For example, what if the sellers were given a large tax lien that would need to be paid out of the proceeds of the sale of the property?

This, again, is the sellers' responsibility, and they should be willing to pay the liens and close the sale as per the contract. However, when the sellers are hit with a substantial unexpected expense, they may simply decide that they can't afford to sell. Again, you may have a course of action to recover damages you suffered and possibly for specific performance, but you probably will just find another home. The price of the litigation, both financially and emotionally, is seldom worth the reward.

THE ACTUAL MOVE

Figure 19.4, Checklist for Moving, will assist buyers to be sure that nothing is missed when the actual move occurs.

AFTER THE CLOSE

What about the taxes?

When you prepare your taxes at the end of the year, you will need your escrow/closing statement, which will indicate all of the nonrecurring closing costs you paid to obtain your loan and your property. Your tax preparer will know which of these expenses can be used as a write-off. Also, you will want to include the HUD Settlement Statement with tax information.

You also will receive a year-end statement from your lender, which will show exactly how much interest you paid for the year (a portion of which also can be used as a tax deduction).

Be sure to keep *every* receipt for any improvement you make to the property throughout the year. Some of these expenses will be added to the base value of the home when you sell the property. Your tax preparer or accountant will advise you as to which expenses can be used to help reduce your gain when the property is sold.

Should you have any losses to your property during the year that are not covered by insurance, you may be able to create some write-offs for them as well.

SMART TIP:

Should you decide to convert your home to a rental/income property, additional write-offs will be available, for things such as repairs and depreciation. Again, your tax person should be able to help you with this transition.

FIGURE 19.4
CHECKLIST FOR MOVING

ADDRESS CHANGE

❏ Give forwarding address to post office 2 to 3 weeks before moving.
❏ Charge accounts, credit cards.
❏ Subscriptions: Notice requires 6 to 8 weeks.
❏ Friends and relatives.

BANK

❏ Transfer funds, arrange check-cashing in new city.
❏ Arrange credit references.

INSURANCE

❏ Notify company of new location for coverages: life, health, fire, and auto.

UTILITY COMPANIES

❏ Gas, light, water, telephone, fuel, garbage.
❏ Get refunds on any deposits made.
❏ Return cable boxes.

DELIVERY SERVICE

❏ Laundry, newspaper, changeover of service.

MEDICAL, DENTAL, PRESCRIPTION HISTORIES

❏ Ask doctor and dentist for referrals, transfer needed for prescriptions, eyeglasses, X-rays. Obtain birth records, medical records, etc.

PETS

❏ Ask about regulations for licenses, vaccinations, tags, etc.

DON'T FORGET TO:

❏ Empty freezer, plan use of foods.
❏ Defrost freezer and clean refrigerator. Place charcoal inside to dispel odors.
❏ Have appliances serviced for moving.
❏ Clean rugs or clothing before moving. Have them wrapped.
❏ Check with your moving counselor, insurance coverage, packing and unpacking labor, arrival day, various shipping papers, method and time of expected payment.
❏ Plan for special care needs of infants or pets.
❏ Check with Agriculture Department of new area to see if there are restrictions on plants.

FIGURE 19.4 **CHECKLIST FOR MOVING** (continued)

ON MOVING DAY:

❏ Carry enough cash or traveler's checks to cover cost of moving services and expenses until you make banking connections in new city.

❏ Carry jewelry and documents yourself or use registered mail.

❏ Plan for transporting of pets; they are poor traveling companions if unhappy.

❏ Let close friends or relatives know the route and schedule you will be traveling, including overnight stops. Use them as message headquarters.

❏ Double-check closets, drawers, shelves to be sure they are empty.

❏ Leave old keys, garage door openers, broiler pans, landscape/house plans, and instruction manuals needed by new owner with real estate agent.

AT YOUR NEW ADDRESS:

❏ Obtain certified checks or cashier's checks necessary for closing real estate transaction (check transaction coordinator/title company for details.)

❏ Check on service of telephone, gas, electricity, water, and garbage.

❏ Check pilot light on stove, water heater, and furnace.

❏ Ask mailcarrier for mail he or she may be holding for your arrival.

❏ Have new address recorded on driver's license.

❏ Visit city offices and register for voting.

❏ Register car within 5 days after arrival in state, or you may have to pay a penalty when getting new license plates.

❏ Obtain inspection sticker and transfer motor club membership.

❏ Apply for state driver's license.

❏ Register family in your new place of worship.

❏ Register children in school.

❏ Arrange for medical services: doctor, dentist, veterinarian, etc.

Saving
Money When
You Buy

This chapter details numerous ways in which you can save hundreds or even thousands of dollars when you purchase a home as well as save a great deal of money on repairs that may need to be made after the purchase.

Here are some rules to follow when you are attempting to save money and get the best deal you can:

- Always negotiate fairly and honestly with all parties and always be truthful in your statements.
- Always negotiate any special discounts up front, before the deal is made.
- Never renege on any agreement that you have made.
- Don't try to get too much from any one person. A little discount from everyone will add up quickly.
- Try to always put your agreements in writing.
- Always offer to "give" before you ask to "get." Make every negotiation a "win-win" situation for all parties.
- Don't get greedy.

ASKING THE SELLERS TO PAY ALL COSTS

As indicated previously, in some purchase situations or market conditions, buyers may ask the sellers to pay all closing costs, possibly even including buyers' costs to obtain a loan. Most often this will be an acceptable request only when it is a very strong buyers' market and a very weak sellers' market. This type of offer often creates rather displeased sellers. However, in the proper market condition, the sellers may be happy to receive *any* offer.

Bear in mind that, at some time in the future, most probably you will become a seller and you will be dealing from a very different perspective. Try to put yourself in the sellers' place and evaluate your offer.

It is not uncommon, in a strong buyers' market, for sellers to pay a *major portion* of closing fees. However, if you are asked to pay some of the fees and other closing costs, you can use some methods that will be discussed in this chapter to reduce their cost.

ESCROW/CLOSING FEES

In some areas of the country, closings are handled by escrow/closing officers who are actually employees of title companies. In other areas, separate escrow/closing companies handle these duties. In still other areas, an attorney is required to handle the closing activities.

For example, in some states, such as New Jersey, closings have historically been handled by attorneys who charge between $250 and $1,000 or more for the closing process. More recently, title companies have begun to handle these closing activities; in most cases, their fees have been considerably less than those of closing attorneys.

If you are in a state that does not require the closing to be done by an attorney, you may want to choose a less expensive alternative. (See Appendix for information phone number.)

In states where escrow/closing officers handle the closing process, the fees are normally minimal, and there is not much room to negotiate for their services. However, some closing companies include additional fees such as typing and document preparation in addition to the escrow/closing fee. These additional costs often are referred to as "garbage fees"; sometimes they can be waived. Make sure you identify all fees you will be charged before you open your escrow/closing. Check your HUD Settlement Statement very carefully to be sure you were not charged any costs over what you were advised when you opened the transaction. If you find extra costs just thrown in, refuse to pay them. If it sounds like a *garbage fee*, looks like a *garbage fee*, smells like a *garbage fee* . . . it's probably a *garbage fee*.

However, some fees are necessary, such as a notary fee and a recording fee. A notary fee is charged to verify that you are indeed who you say you are. A recording fee is a fee paid to the recorder's office to record documents and usually will not be waived or discounted.

INSPECTION FEES

When you purchase your home, you may request several inspections, or they may be required by the lender.

For the most part, these inspection fees are minimal, and you should not ask for them to be reduced. Inspection companies in the state of Nevada charged $100 to $200 for roof inspection, $75 to $125 for termite inspection, and $200 to $300 for home inspection.

Saving money on these inspections and the subsequent work that might be required can get a little tricky, but here are a few inside secrets:

- Many of the companies that make these inspections do the repair work themselves or have an affiliate company complete the repairs. In other words, a roofing company may make a roof inspection, call for the work that needs to be done, actually do the work (new roof or repair), and finally issue the approved certificate for the work completed.
- If work that needs to be done is discovered during the inspection process, *the sellers should be willing to pay for the repairs.* However, in some cases, buyers may be asked to pay part of these expenses. If this occurs, and the buyers agree, the best way to save money would be to:
  1. Obtain a written estimate for the repairs that were called for during the inspection.
  2. Obtain a written estimate from two other companies for the repairs. Also, be sure that these other companies can issue an approval certificate when the work is completed. Sometimes companies that are not state licensed cannot issue approval certificates, and another inspection would be necessary.
  3. Take the lowest estimate back to the company that gave you the first estimate and ask that it be matched. In most

cases, the estimates will be very close, and the original company will very likely agree to match the low estimate.

4. After the estimator from the original company agrees to do the work for the lower estimate, ask that he or she waive the original inspection fee. (In many situations, he or she will agree.)

Table 20.1, at the end of this chapter, is an example of a buyer who saved almost $400 using these methods.

Some inspection companies are independent and make inspections but do not do any of the work which is required. In these cases, their inspection fees are nominal and are not usually negotiable.

COMMISSIONS AND SALES FEES

Commissions and sales fees are very sensitive areas to real estate agents and brokers since they earn 100 percent of their income from commissions. That means no salaries, no expense accounts, no bonuses . . . just pure commission. Now, if an agent sells thirty or forty homes a year, he or she can make a pretty good living. But if the agent sells only five or six homes a year, he or she is barely paying expenses.

In most situations, buyers should not have to ask agents or brokers to reduce their commission. However, in some cases, there may be no other way to salvage a transaction, and agents or brokers may even volunteer to reduce their sales fee.

As an example: Suppose you have made an offer on a $130,000 home, conditioned upon your receiving a 95 percent loan, $6,500 down payment, and closing costs not to exceed $1,500. You will have to pay no more than $8,000 at the close of escrow. The sellers agree but also are buying another property, and they must net not a penny less than $21,000 out of the sale or they cannot close on their new home. When the inspections are done, unexpected roof repair is called and the lowest quote to make the repairs is $1,250. If the sellers pay these costs, they will be $1,000 short of monies needed to buy their new home. They have no way to come up with the extra money and will not close on your purchase if they cannot buy their new home.

Here is a possible solution (taken from an actual sale situation): The lender agrees to reduce its origination cost from 1½ points to 1¼ points (savings of $325) because the buyers agree to pay ¹⁄₁₆ percent higher interest on their loan (monthly payment increase of approximately $10). The sellers' agent and the buyers' agent reduce their commission by approximately $325 each, and the transaction closes. Everyone wins!

> **SMART TIP:**
> In most situations, agents and brokers will suggest reducing their commission only as a last resort to save a transaction. You or the sellers may have to suggest that the agents and brokers participate in the necessary "give-and-take" negotiations. Bear in mind that on the $130,000 sale, it would not be uncommon to have a $7,800 commission. That commission split between two brokers would amount to $3,900 each. Brokers should be willing to give up a little to make the sale.

TITLE INSURANCE FEES

In some areas, it is customary for buyers to pay the cost of the title insurance. However, since this title inspection and insurance policy is issued to ensure that the title is free and clear of any liens or encumbrances (which might appear from past owners), it seems reasonable that the sellers pay all or at least a portion of this cost. Just because it is customary in an area doesn't mean it has to be that way. Direct your agent to write your purchase contract the way *you please*.

Most states require title insurance companies to post their rates with either the insurance commission or the corporation commission of the state. This means that once these rates are established and posted, they should not be discounted unless another rate filing is submitted to the state. However, the general public and many agents and brokers are unaware that within these filed rates are many allowable discounts that are actually filed and legally allowable. Sometimes the title company can legally charge you, the consumer, a full rate even when a discounted rate may apply.

As an example, most title companies have posted a filed-discounted rate for homes that have been insured (title insurance) within the previous two, three, or five years (depending on the individual companies filing). These rates are called "short-term rates," and usually the discounts are 10 to 25 percent off the standard rate. How much savings would this represent? On a title policy costing $900, the savings would range between $90 and $225.

HOW CAN YOU RECEIVE THESE DISCOUNTS?

Ask for discounts, have your agent ask for them, and have your lender ask for them. Get the picture? Ask, ask, and ask again!

CARPET AND FLOOR REPLACEMENTS OR REPAIRS

Again, if these repairs or replacements are called for in the appraisal or by an inspector, the sellers should be responsible for the cost. However, if repairs or replacements are not called for in the inspections or appraisal but you asked for the work (such as carpet replacement), the sellers might not be as likely to agree to pay for the entire cost.

You can save a great deal of money on carpeting and flooring simply by shopping at outlets. Prices will vary dramatically, so watch for sales, especially with major department stores.

Here is one suggestion on how to save even more on carpet replacement. Shop the local carpet stores or direct wholesale outlets (which are usually open to the public). Negotiate the very best price for the carpet and pad, excluding installation. Then ask for the very best price for the complete job, including installation.

Many floor covering companies utilize the services of independent contractor installers. Often these installers work for several carpet companies as well as private individuals when they can.

Also, many carpet companies make money on the installer's work. As an example, the carpet company may pay the installer an average of $20 to $30 per hour (usually based on a per square-yard installation fee). When the installation cost is tacked onto what the consumer pays, the carpet company earns a profit on the installer's work.

After you receive your quotes from the floor covering companies, call back and ask for the names and phone numbers of the carpet installers who do the work for them on a contract basis. Some companies will not give you the information, so it may take a few calls to get two or three names.

Call the installer direct (you may need to leave your name and number for a call back) and ask what he or she will charge to do the installation. Try to have the following information: number of square yards to be installed, type of carpet and pad, how many rooms, and the size and shape of the rooms.

Make sure that you ask if the installer works by the hour, per square yard, or by the job. You probably will get a better rate if you can pay a per-square-yard rate.

Compare the prices quoted from the floor covering companies and choose the highest quality carpet in your price range at the least cost. Compare the completely installed quote with the best quote for the carpet and pad only, installed by the least expensive installer.

The following example details one home buyer's research and ultimate decision for the choice of carpet and installation:

1st Floor Covering Company

Carpet and Pad alone:	$1,323
Carpet, Pad, and Installation:	$1,965

2nd Floor Covering Company

Carpet and Pad Alone:	$1,245
Carpet, Pad, and Installation:	$1,890

3rd Floor Covering Company

Carpet and Pad alone:	$1,680
Carpet, Pad, and Installation:	$2,060

Three installers quoted the following for the installation:

Installer 1:	$295
Installer 2:	$185
Installer 3:	$200

The home buyer went with the carpet from the first floor covering company and Installer 3.

Total cost:	$1,523
Savings:	$ 442 = 22.5%

The buyer saved $367 from the lowest bid that included installation, and $537 from the most expensive bid.

All of these estimates were done on essentially the same carpet and pad.

OTHER WORK OR REPAIRS

The very best way to save money on repairs, improvements, or work such as painting, electrical, plumbing, cement, landscaping, and so on, is to shop around for the best prices and quality. Get *several* estimates for *every* job that you need done. Keep in mind that the lowest estimate may not always be the best choice. You want a combination of quality and acceptable pricing.

"SWEAT EQUITY" ALLOWANCES

As indicated previously, sellers may reduce the sale price of their property if you are willing to take the responsibility for some or all of the work that was called during an inspection or appraisal and is required to close the transaction.

You must be sure that the lender has approved the sweat equity agreement and will allow you to complete the work and the allowance for the reduction in the sale price of the home. The reduced sale price should not adversely affect your requested loan amount. Be sure to get the lender's approval in writing.

AN EXAMPLE OF SAVINGS

Table 20.1 shows the savings one seller was able to achieve by utilizing the techniques explained in this chapter.

TABLE 20.1
EXAMPLE OF SAVINGS CHART

ITEM	SAVINGS
Title Insurance (seller paid)	$ 725
Title Insurance (lender policy—seller paid)	$ 185
Roof Inspection (reduced because roofer did the work)	$ 50
Roof Work (went with lower-price company)	$ 245
Carpet Installation (after close; seller would not replace)	$ 360
TOTAL SAVINGS	**$1,565**

These savings were in addition to the seller agreeing to pay the loan origination fee of $1,250 for the buyer.

Remember, to buy a home, for the best price, in any market, you must be patient and negotiate every item, from sale price to fees, costs, commissions, and repairs.

CHAPTER
TWENTY-ONE
The Joy of Home Ownership

Now you should understand that the process of successfully purchasing a good home, at a respectable price, and within a reasonable period of time can be quite an undertaking.

Throughout this book I have guided you through many of the normal (and sometimes not so normal) events that may occur when a person makes the commitment to buy a home. However, for every nuance I have discussed, there are fifty more that may occur in your actual transaction. The one rule for successful home buying is: *Be ready for the abnormal, the unexpected, and the sometimes unreasonable events that will happen and surprise everyone. Remember, no two transactions are ever the same.*

Home buyers who utilize the information in this book and go about their home purchase in a structured, systematic, and well-planned fashion will have a much more pleasant buying experience than the buyers who flounder about, just hoping everything will turn out okay.

The best plan that buyers can have is a *complete plan*: start to finish, from prequalification to the approval, and all the way through to the tax preparation after the close of the sale.

Utilize this publication as your own personal road map to a successful home purchase. The techniques, methods, and ideas that I shared with you have been tested and proven to work by thousands of real estate professionals and thousands of successful home buyers.

As I said earlier, there is a home out there for everyone as long as the buyer is willing to *be patient and reasonable and remain focused.*

For most people, home ownership is truly one of the greatest joys they will experience in their lifetime. If you wish to join the ranks of successful home buyers, don't wait, start preparing for your home purchase now!

A P P E N D I X
FORMS AND
WORKSHEETS

FIGURE A.1

HOME SEARCH CHECKLIST

	HOME 1	HOME 2	HOME 3
	Address	Address	Address
	ID Input	ID Input	ID Input
NEEDS			
WANTS			
COMMENTS			

FIGURE A.2
HOME INSPECTION FORM

Area or Item	OK	Work to be done	Comments
Floors (Check each room for the following)			
Carpets clean and in good repair			
No spots or discoloration			
Wood floors in good repair			
Baseboards clean and in good repair			
Floor electrical sockets clean and working			
Tile or linoleum no cracks or breaks			
No bubbles or sloping			
No discoloration			
Does furniture need to be moved for inspection?			
Walls (Check each room for the following)			
Do wall hangings need to be removed for inspection?			
Walls clean with no cracks			
Wallpaper seams (top and bottom) secure			
Holes patched and painted			
No discoloration			
Light fixtures in good repair			
Switch plates in good repair			
Socket plates in good repair			
Mirrors and glass unbroken and not stained			
Doors (Check each room for the following)			
Paint or finish in good repair			
No discoloration			
No chipping or loose panels			
Move smoothly and no dragging			
Handles, hinges, and locks work well			
No squeaks			
Windows and Window Coverings			
No broken glass			
No cracks in frames			
Open and close easily			
Hinges in good shape			
Latches, handles, and cranks in good shape			
Slide smoothly and tracks clean			
All locks working well			
Drapes and curtains clean and in good repair			
Blinds in good shape and working well			
Pull cords in good shape			
Drapes operating smoothly			

Area or Item	OK	Work to be done	Comments
Curtain rods straight and attached well	_____	_____	_____
No discoloration on walls or coverings	_____	_____	_____

Ceilings (Check each room for the following)

No stains or discoloration	_____	_____	_____
No damage	_____	_____	_____
Paint or finish in good repair	_____	_____	_____
Acoustic in good repair	_____	_____	_____
Light fixtures in good repair	_____	_____	_____
Track lighting working properly	_____	_____	_____

Kitchen

Refrigerator clean and in good repair (if it stays)	_____	_____	_____
Dishwasher clean and in good repair	_____	_____	_____
Stoves and ovens clean and in good repair	_____	_____	_____
Switches and buttons in good shape	_____	_____	_____
All drip pans in place and in good shape	_____	_____	_____
Sink in good shape (no chips or stains)	_____	_____	_____
Cupboards, shelves, etc. in good order	_____	_____	_____
Faucets not discolored or stained	_____	_____	_____
Faucets, sinks, and pipes no leaks or drips	_____	_____	_____
Window coverings in good shape	_____	_____	_____
Garbage disposal working properly	_____	_____	_____
All other appliances working properly	_____	_____	_____

Living Room

Does it have a good feel?	_____	_____	_____
Good traffic flow	_____	_____	_____
Enough room for furniture	_____	_____	_____
Good lighting	_____	_____	_____
Fireplace, hearth, and mantel is what you want	_____	_____	_____
Convenient to other rooms	_____	_____	_____
Drapes and curtains clean and in good shape	_____	_____	_____
Blinds in good repair	_____	_____	_____
Shelves secure	_____	_____	_____
Is noise a problem?	_____	_____	_____
Wet bar in good order	_____	_____	_____

Bathrooms

Bathtub clean (no stains or chips)	_____	_____	_____
Soap holders in place	_____	_____	_____
Tile walls (no chipping or peeling)	_____	_____	_____
Grout in good shape	_____	_____	_____
No mildew stains	_____	_____	_____
Shower curtains/doors clean and in good shape	_____	_____	_____
No water stains	_____	_____	_____
Faucets and handles in good order	_____	_____	_____
Cabinets and cupboards adequate	_____	_____	_____

FIGURE A.2 **HOME INSPECTION FORM** (continued)

AREA OR ITEM	OK	WORK TO BE DONE	COMMENTS
Any evidence of leaks or seepage?			
Toilet and toilet seat in good repair			
Towel holders affixed properly and secure			
All drains working well			
Any other devices working right			
Mirrors in good shape			

Bedrooms

Enough room for furniture			
Good lighting			
Sun faces room at the right time of the day			
Windowsills in good repair			
Curtains/drapes/blinds clean and in good shape			
Accessible to bathrooms			
Lots of privacy			
Closets large enough			
View is okay			
Good ventilation (heating and cooling)			

Closets

Enough closets			
Enough hanging space			
Well lit			
Hanging bars secure and straight			
Walls in good shape			
No odor			
All shelves in place and secure			

Laundry Area

No odor			
Well lit			
Exhaust connected properly			
No gas odor			
Cabinet and shelves in good order			
Proper connections for your appliances			
Sink in good repair (if there is one)			
No swelling in floors from leaks			

Staircases

Handrails, top and bottom posts secure			
Stairs tight and no squeaks			
Does sound carry through the house?			
Tile, carpet or other covering secure			
No rails protruding			
Side slats and vertical rail secure			
Decorative knobs and pieces secure			
Good lighting on entire staircase			
Plenty of head room			
Pull-down staircase working smoothly			

FIGURE A.2 **HOME INSPECTION FORM** (continued)

AREA OR ITEM	OK	WORK TO BE DONE	COMMENTS
Shelves, Bookcases, and Drawers			
Shelves level and secure	____	_____	_____
Finish or covering in good shape	____	_____	_____
Adequate lighting	____	_____	_____
Drawers move easily	____	_____	_____
Handles and knobs are tight	____	_____	_____
Fireplaces and Wood Stoves			
Chimney clean with no excessive burn marks	____	_____	_____
Grate in place and in good shape	____	_____	_____
Fireplace tools in good repair (if staying)	____	_____	_____
All fans and heating units in good repair	____	_____	_____
Any signs of leaks—no gas odor	____	_____	_____
Mantel and hearth in good shape	____	_____	_____
Screens or doors working well	____	_____	_____
Gas lighters and fans working properly	____	_____	_____
Electrical			
Adequate number of outlets in every room	____	_____	_____
All switches and plugs operative	____	_____	_____
Specialty lighting working properly	____	_____	_____
Any burned areas around switches or plugs?	____	_____	_____
No open wiring or plugs	____	_____	_____
Dimmers working properly	____	_____	_____
Wall plates in good repair	____	_____	_____
Pull cords in good shape	____	_____	_____
Heating and Cooling			
Units and thermostats working properly and recently serviced	____	_____	_____
If propane, is tank accessible year round?	____	_____	_____
Vent covers in place and working properly	____	_____	_____
Window units secure and sealed	____	_____	_____
Exposed ducting clean	____	_____	_____
Pilot lights stay lit	____	_____	_____
Basement			
Well lit	____	_____	_____
No odor	____	_____	_____
Dry	____	_____	_____
Is area usable?	____	_____	_____
Safe stairways	____	_____	_____
Easy entry and exit	____	_____	_____
Shelves and cabinets in good repair	____	_____	_____
Anything scary about the area?	____	_____	_____
Any live bugs or other critters?	____	_____	_____
Well ventilated	____	_____	_____
Sound Inspection			
Showers and tubs running—how much noise?	____	_____	_____

Area or Item	OK	Work to be done	Comments
Staircases—does sound carry?	___	_____	_____
Conversations in rooms—does it carry?	___	_____	_____
Does noise from appliances carry?	___	_____	_____
Noise from outside	___	_____	_____
Security System			
Operates properly	___	_____	_____
Instructions available	___	_____	_____
Attic			
No odor and well ventilated	___	_____	_____
Shelves and cabinets in good repair	___	_____	_____
No leaks	___	_____	_____
Anything scary about the area?	___	_____	_____
Easy entry and exit	___	_____	_____
Well lit	___	_____	_____
Porches, Patios, and Entryways			
Convenient access to other rooms	___	_____	_____
Is there a coat hanging area?	___	_____	_____
No uncomfortable steps	___	_____	_____
Well lit	___	_____	_____
No odor	___	_____	_____
Any rotting or damage?	___	_____	_____
Locks and doors in good repair	___	_____	_____
Stairs and guardrails in good shape	___	_____	_____
Deck or flooring in good repair	___	_____	_____
Floors and decks level	___	_____	_____
Glass and screens in good shape	___	_____	_____
Garage			
Well lit with doors open or closed	___	_____	_____
Neatly arranged with no excessive storage	___	_____	_____
Rafter area in good repair	___	_____	_____
Stains and spots removed from garage floor	___	_____	_____
All cabinets and shelves in good repair	___	_____	_____
Workbenches in good repair	___	_____	_____
Washer and dryer accessible with cars inside	___	_____	_____
Fans and ventilation in good order	___	_____	_____
Doors and windows secure	___	_____	_____
Doggy door in good repair	___	_____	_____
Good storage for tools, equipment, etc.	___	_____	_____
Electric outlets working	___	_____	_____
Garage door opener in good repair	___	_____	_____
Appliances out of the way (hot water heater, water softener, etc.)	___	_____	_____
Pools, Spas, and Saunas			
Decks in good repair	___	_____	_____
Proper chemical balance in the water	___	_____	_____
All pumps, heating, and drains in good repair	___	_____	_____

FIGURE A.2 **HOME INSPECTION FORM** (continued)

Area or Item	OK	Work to be done	Comments
Skimmers, hoses, cleaners operative	___	_____	_____
Ladders, slides, diving boards in good order	___	_____	_____
Pool furniture well maintained	___	_____	_____
Safety equipment and signs in place	___	_____	_____
Gates lock properly and doors close tightly	___	_____	_____
Lighting works properly	___	_____	_____
Heating units and timers work properly	___	_____	_____
Door closes and seals well	___	_____	_____
Good storage for equipment	___	_____	_____
No mildew or odor	___	_____	_____

Home Exterior

Area or Item	OK	Work to be done	Comments
Foundation in good shape and no cracks	___	_____	_____
Exterior finishes in good shape with no chipping, peeling, cracks, or holes	___	_____	_____
No discoloration from water splashes, drains, or the sun	___	_____	_____
Eaves not peeling, chipping, or molding	___	_____	_____
Window frames caulked well and in good shape	___	_____	_____
Crawl spaces covered and accessible	___	_____	_____
Vents and eave vents opened and screened	___	_____	_____
Any wooden structures against house? Termites?	___	_____	_____
Bushes and trees trimmed away from the house	___	_____	_____
Exterior doors (including garage door) clean, properly finished, and working well	___	_____	_____

Roof

Area or Item	OK	Work to be done	Comments
No low spots or sagging	___	_____	_____
No missing tiles or shakes	___	_____	_____
No leaks	___	_____	_____
No antennas or satellites causing damage	___	_____	_____
No stain or discoloration	___	_____	_____
No wires connected which cause damage	___	_____	_____
Gutters secure and clean	___	_____	_____
Caulking in good shape	___	_____	_____
No trees or bushes scraping the roof	___	_____	_____

Yard

Area or Item	OK	Work to be done	Comments
Do you like the yard?	___	_____	_____
Grass, bushes, and trees in good shape	___	_____	_____
Sprinkler system working properly	___	_____	_____
Driveways, sidewalks, and walkways free of stains	___	_____	_____
Fences in good repair	___	_____	_____
Parking areas in good shape	___	_____	_____
Animal areas in good shape	___	_____	_____

FIGURE A.2 **HOME INSPECTION FORM** (continued)

FIGURE A.3
COUNTEROFFER FORM

COUNTEROFFER

The offer made by _____

to purchase the real property commonly known as_____

_____

dated _____ is not accepted in its present

form, but the following counteroffer is hereby submitted: _____

_____

_____

_____

_____

_____

_____

_____

OTHER ITEMS: All terms to remain the same as original Offer and Acceptance.
RIGHT TO ACCEPT OTHER OFFERS: Seller reserves the right to accept any
other offer prior to purchaser's acceptance of this counteroffer and seller's agent
being so advised in writing.
EXPIRATION: This counteroffer shall expire unless a copy hereof with purchaser's written acceptance is delivered to seller or his/her agent within ___days
from date.

Date _____ Seller _____

Time_____ Seller _____

The above undersigned purchaser accepts the above counteroffer.

Date _____ Purchaser _____

Time_____ Purchaser _____

FIGURE A.4

REAL ESTATE PURCHASE CONTRACT (Sample - do not copy)

REAL ESTATE PURCHASE CONTRACT AND RECEIPT FOR DEPOSIT

THIS IS MORE THAN A RECEIPT FOR MONEY. IT IS INTENDED TO BE A LEGALLY BINDING CONTRACT. READ IT CAREFULLY.

DATE: _____ , 19 _____ AT _____ ,

RECEIVED FROM _____ ("Buyer")

THE SUM OF _____ Dollars $ _____

as a deposit to be applied toward the

PURCHASE PRICE OF _____ Dollars $ _____

FOR PURCHASED OF PROPERTY SITUATED IN _____ , COUNTY OF _____

DESCRIBED AS _____ ("Property").

1. FINANCING: THE OBTAINING OF THE LOAN(S) BELOW IS A CONTINGENCY OF THIS AGREEMENT. Buyer shall act diligent-
ly and in good faith to obtain all applicable financing.

   A. FINANCING CONTINGENCY shall remain in effect until (Check ONLY ONE of the following):

      1. ❑ (If checked). The designated loan(s) is/are funded and/or the assumption of existing financing is approved by Lender.

   OR 2. ❑ (If checked). _____ calendar days after acceptance of the offer. Buyer shall remove the financing contingency in writing
   within this time. If Buyer fails to do so, then Seller may cancel this agreement by giving written notice of cancellation to Buyer.

   B. OBTAINING OF DEPOSIT AND DOWN PAYMENT by the Buyer is NOT a contingency, unless otherwise agreed in writing.

   C. DEPOSIT to be deposited ❑ with Escrow Holder, ❑ into Broker's trust account, or ❑ _____

      BY ❑ Personal check, ❑ Cashier's check, ❑ Cash, or ❑ PAYABLE TO _____

      TO BE HELD UNCASHED UNTIL the next business day after acceptance of the offer, or ❑ _____ .

   D. INCREASED DEPOSIT, within _____ calendar days after acceptance of the offer, to be deposited ❑ with Escrow Holder,
   ❑ into Broker's trust account, or ❑ _____

   E. BALANCE OF DOWN PAYMENT to be deposited with Escrow Holder on demand of Escrow Holder.

   F. FIRST LOAN IN THE AMOUNT OF

      ❑ NEW First Deed of Trust in favor of ❑ LENDER, ❑ SELLER; or ❑ ASSUMPTION of existing First Deed of Trust; or
   ❑ _____ ; encumbering the Property, securing a note payable at approximately $ _____ per month (❑ or more), to include
   ❑ principal and interest, ❑ only, at maximum interest of _____ % ❑ fixed rate, ❑ initial adjustable rate with a maximum lifetime interest rate increase of _____ % over the initial rate, balance due in _____ years. Buyer shall pay loan
   fees/points not to exceed _____ .

   G. SECOND LOAN IN THE AMOUNT OF

      ❑ NEW Second Deed of Trust in favor of ❑ LENDER, ❑ SELLER; or _____ .
   ❑ ASSUMPTION of Existing Second Deed of Trust: or ❑ _____ ; encumbering the Property, securing a note
   payable at approximately $ _____ per month (❑ or more), to include ❑ principal and interest, ❑ interest only, at maximum
   interest _____ % ❑ fixed rate, ❑ initial adjustable rate, with a maximum lifetime interest rate increase of _____ % over the
   initial rate, balance due in _____ years. Buyer shall pay loan fees/points not to exceed _____ .

   H. TOTAL PURCHASE PRICE, not including costs of obtaining loans and other closing costs.

   I. LOAN APPLICATIONS: Buyer shall, within the time specified, submit to lender(s) (or to Seller for applicable Seller financing),
   a completed loan or assumption application(s), and provide to Seller written acknowledgment of Buyer's compliance. For Seller
   financing: (1) Buyer shall submit a completed loan application on FNMA Form 1003; (2) Buyer authorizes Seller and/or Broker(s) to
   obtain, at Buyer's expense, a copy of Buyer's credit report; and (3) Seller may cancel this purchase and sale agreement upon
   disapproval of either the application or the credit report, by providing to Buyer written notice within 7 (or ❑ _____) calendar days
   after receipt of those documents.

   J. EXISTING LOANS: For existing loans to be taken over by Buyer, Seller shall promptly request and upon receipt provide to
   Buyer copies of all applicable notes and deeds of trust, loan balances, and current interest rates. Buyer may give Seller written
   notice of disapproval within the time specified. Differences between estimated and actual loan balance(s) shall be adjusted at close
   of escrow by:

      ❑ Cash down payment, or ❑ _____ .

      Impound account(s), if any, shall be: ❑ Charged to Buyer and credited to Seller, or ❑ _____ .

   K. LOAN FEATURES: LOANS/DOCUMENTS CONTAIN A NUMBER OF IMPORTANT FEATURES AFFECTING THE
   RIGHTS OF THE BORROWER AND LENDER. READ ALL LOAN DOCUMENTS CAREFULLY.

   L. ADDITIONAL SELLER FINANCING TERMS: The following terms apply ONLY to financing extended by Seller under this
   agreement. The rate specified as the maximum interest rate in F or G above, as applicable, shall be the actual fixed interest rate for seller

financing. Any promissory note and/or deed of trust given by Buyer and Seller shall contain, but not be limited to, the following additional terms:

1. REQUEST FOR NOTICE OF DEFAULT on senior loans.
2. Buyer shall execute and pay for a REQUEST FOR NOTICE OF DELINQUENCY in escrow and at any future time if requested by Seller.
3. Acceleration clause making the loan due, when permitted by law, at Seller's option, upon the sale or transfer of the Property or any interest in it.
4. A late charge or 6.0 % of the installment due, or $5.00, whichever is greater, if the installment is not received within 10 days of the date it is due.
5. Title insurance coverage in the form of a joint protection policy shall be provided insuring Seller's deed of trust interest in the Property.
6. Tax Service shall be obtained and paid for by Buyer to notify Seller if property taxes have not been paid.
7. Buyer shall provide fire and extended coverage insurance during the period of the Seller financing, in an amount sufficient to replace all improvements on the Property, or the total encumbrances against the Property, whichever is less, with a loss payable endorsement in favor of Seller.
8. The addition, deletion, or substitution of any person or entity under this agreement, or to title prior to close of escrow, shall require Seller's written consent. Seller may grant or withhold consent in Seller's sole discretion. Any additional or substituted person or entity shall, if requested by Seller, submit to Seller the same documentation as required for the original named Buyer. Seller and/or Broker(s) may obtain a credit report on any such person or entity.
9. If the Property contains 1 to 4 dwelling units, Buyer and Seller shall execute a Seller Financing Disclosure Statement (Civil Code 2956-2967), if applicable, as provided by arranger of credit, as soon as practicable prior to execution of security documents.

M. ADDITIONAL FINANCING TERMS: _____

2. CONDITION OF PROPERTY: (Initial ONLY paragraph A or B; DO NOT initial both.)
Buyer's initials _____ Seller's initials _____ A. SELLER WARRANTY: (If A is initialled, DO NOT initial B.) Seller warrants that on the date possession is made available to Buyer: (1) Roof shall be free of KNOWN leaks; (2) built-in appliances (including free-standing oven and range, if included in sale), plumbing, heating, air conditioning, electrical, water, sewer/septic, and pool/spa systems, if any, shall be operative; (3) plumbing systems, shower pan(s), and shower enclosure(s) shall be free of leaks; (4) all broken or cracked glass shall be replaced; (5) Property, including pool/spa, landscaping, and grounds, shall be maintained in substantially the same condition as on the date of acceptance of the offer; (6) all debris and all personal property not included in the sale shall be removed; (7) _____

_____

NOTE TO BUYER: This warranty is limited to items specified in this paragraph A.
NOTE TO SELLER: Disclosures in the Real Estate Transfer Disclosure Statement and items discovered in Buyer's inspection do NOT eliminate Seller's obligations under this warranty unless specifically agreed in writing.

OR

Buyer's initials _____ Seller's initials _____ B. "AS-IS" CONDITION: (If B is initialled, DO NOT initial A.) Property is sold "AS-IS," in its present condition, without warranty. Seller shall not be responsible for making corrections or repairs of any nature except: (1) Structural pest control repairs, if applicable under paragraph 19, and (2) _____.
Buyer retains the right to disapprove the condition of the Property based upon items discovered in Buyer's Inspections under paragraph 9.
SELLER REMAINS OBLIGATED TO DISCLOSE ADVERSE MATERIAL FACTS WHICH ARE KNOWN TO SELLER AND TO MAKE OTHER DISCLOSURES REQUIRED BY LAW.

3. TRANSFER DISCLOSURE STATEMENT: Unless exempt, a Real Estate Transfer Disclosure Statement ("TDS") shall be completed by Seller and delivered to Buyer (Civil Code 1102-110.15). Buyer shall sign and return a copy of the TDS to Seller or Seller's agent: (a) ❑ Buyer has received a TDS prior to execution of the offer, OR (b) ❑ Buyer shall be provided a TDS within _____ calendar days after acceptance of the offer. If the TDS is delivered to Buyer after the offer is executed, Buyer shall have the right to terminate this agreement within three (3) days after delivery in person, or five (5) days after delivery by deposit in the mail by giving written notice of termination to Seller or Seller's agent.

4. PROPERTY DISCLOSURES: When applicable to the Property and required by law, Seller shall provide to Buyer, at Seller's expense, the following disclosures and information. Buyer shall then, within the time specified, investigate the disclosures and information and provide written notice to Seller of any item disapproved pursuant to A-C and E1(b) below.
A. GEOLOGIC-SEISMIC HAZARD ZONES DISCLOSURE: If the Property is located in a Special Studies Zone (SSZ), or in a locally designated geological, seismic, or other hazard zone(s) or area(s) where disclosure is required by law, Seller shall, within the time specified, disclose in writing to Buyer this fact(s) and any other information required by law. (GEOLOGIC, SEISMIC AND FLOOD HAZARD DISCLOSURE SHALL SATISFY THIS REQUIREMENT.) Construction or development of any structure may be restricted. Disclosure of SSZ and SHZs is required only where the maps, or information contained in the maps, are "reasonably available."

B. **SPECIAL FLOOD HAZARD AREAS:** If the Property is located in a Special Flood Hazard Area designated by the Federal Emergency Management Agency (FEMA), Seller shall, within the time specified, disclose this fact in writing to Buyer. (GEOLOGIC, SEISMIC AND FLOOD HAZARD DISCLOSURE SHALL SATISFY THIS REQUIREMENT.) Government regulations may impose building restrictions and requirements which may substantially impact and limit construction and remodeling of improvements. Flood insurance may be required by lender.

C. **STATE FIRE RESPONSIBILITY AREAS:** If the Property is located in a State Fire Responsibility Area, Seller shall, within the time speci fied, disclose this fact in writing to Buyer (Public Resources Code 4136). Disclosure may be made in the Real Estate Transfer Disclosure Statement. Government regulations may impose building restrictions and requirements which may substantially impact and limit construction and remodeling improvements. Disclosure of these areas is required only if the Seller has actual knowledge that the Property is located in such an area or if maps of such areas have been provided to the county assessor's office.

D. **MELLO-ROOS:** Seller shall make a good faith effort to obtain a disclosure notice from any local agencies which levy on the Property a special tax pursuant to the Mello-Roos Community Facilities Act, and shall deliver to Buyer any such notice made available by those agencies.

E. **EARTHQUAKE SAFETY:**

   1. **PRE-1960 PROPERTIES:** If the Property was built prior to 1960, and contains ONE-TO-FOUR DWELLING UNITS of conventional light frame construction, Seller shall, unless exempt, within the time specified, provide to Buyer: (a) a copy of "The Homeowner's Guide To Earthquake Safety" and (b) written disclosure of known seismic deficiencies (Government Code 8897-8897.5).

   2. **PRE-1975 PROPERTIES:** If the Property was built prior to 1975, and contains RESIDENTIAL, COMMERCIAL, OR OTHER STRUCTURES constructed of masonry or precast concrete, with wood frame floors or roofs, Seller shall, unless exempt, within the time specified, provide to the Buyer a copy of "The Commercial Property Owner's Guide to Earthquake Safety" (Government Code 8893-8893.5).

   3. **ALL PROPERTIES:** If the booklets described in paragraph E1 and E2 are not required, Buyer is advised that they are available and contain important information that may be useful for ALL TYPES OF PROPERTY.

F. **SMOKE DETECTOR(S):** State law requires that residences be equipped with operable smoke detector(s). Local ordinances may have additional requirements. Unless exempt, Seller shall, prior to close of escrow, provide to Buyer a written statement of compliance and any other documents required, in accordance with applicable state and local law. (SMOKE DETECTOR STATEMENT OF COMPLIANCE SHALL SATISFY THE STATE PORTION OF THIS REQUIREMENT.) Additional smoke detector(s), if required, shall be installed by Seller at Seller's expense prior to close of escrow.

G. **LEAD BASED PAINT:** Buyers obtaining new FHA-insured financing on residential properties constructed prior to 1978 are required to sign a lead paint disclosure form. (NOTICE TO PURCHASERS OF HOUSING CONSTRUCTED BEFORE 1978 (CAR FOR LPD-14) SHALL SATISFY THIS REQUIREMENT.)

H. **OTHER:** _____ .

5. **GOVERNMENTAL COMPLIANCE:** Seller shall promptly disclose to Buyer any improvements, additions, alterations, or repairs ("Improvements") made by Seller or known to Seller to have been made without required governmental permits, final inspections, and approvals. In addition, Seller represents that Seller has no knowledge of any notice of violations of City, County, State, or Federal building, zoning, fire, or health laws, codes, statutes, ordinances, regulations, or rules filed or issued against the Property. If Seller receives notice or is made aware of any of the above violations prior to close of escrow, Seller shall immediately notify Buyer in writing. Buyer shall, within the time specified, provide written notice to Seller of any items disapproved.

6. **RETROFIT:** Compliance with any minimum mandatory government retrofit standards, including but not limited to energy and utility effi-ciency requirements and proof of compliance, shall be paid for by ❑ Buyer, ❑ Seller.

7. **FIXTURES:** All existing fixtures and fittings that are attached to the Property or for which special openings have been made are INCLUD-ED IN THE PURCHASE PRICE (unless excluded below) and are to be transferred free of liens. These include, but are not limited to, elec-trical, lighting, plumbing and heating fixtures, fireplace inserts, solar systems, built-in appliances, screens, awnings, shutters, window coverings, attached floor coverings, television antennas/satellite dishes and related equipment, private integrated telephone systems, air cool-ers/conditioners, pool/spa equipment, water softeners (if owned by Seller), security systems/alarms (if owned by Seller), garage door open-ers/remote controls, attached fireplace equipment, mailbox, in-ground landscaping including trees/shrubs, and _____. ITEMS EXCLUDED:_____

8. **PERSONAL PROPERTY:** The following items of personal property, free of liens and without warranty of condition (unless provided in para-graph 10A) or fitness for use, are included: _____
_____
_____

9. **HOME WARRANTY PLANS:** Buyer and Seller are informed that home warranty plans are available. These plans may provide additional protection and benefit to Buyer and Seller. Broker(s) do not endorse, approve, or recommend any particular company or program. Buyer and Seller elect (Check ONLY ONE):

   ❑ To purchase a home warranty plan with the following optional coverage _____, at a cost not to exceed $ _____, to be paid by _____, and to be issued by _____ Company,

OR

   ❑ Buyer and Seller elect NOT to purchase a home warranty plan.

REAL ESTATE PURCHASE CONTRACT AND RECEIPT FOR DEPOSIT – page 4

10. SEPTIC SYSTEM: (If initialled by all parties.)

Buyer's initials _____ Seller's initials _____

❑ Buyer, ❑ Seller shall pay to have septic system pumped and certified. Evidence of compliance shall be provided to the other party before close of escrow.

❑ Buyer, ❑ Seller to pay for sewer connection if required by local ordinance.

11. PEST CONTROL: (If initialled by all parties.)

Buyer's initials _____ Seller's initials _____

A. Seller shall, within the time specified, provide to Buyer a current written Wood Destroying Pests and Organisms Inspection Report. Report shall be at the expense of ❑ Buyer, ❑ Seller, to be performed by _____, a registered Structural Pest Control Company, covering the main building and (If checked):

❑ detached garage(s) or carport(s); ❑ the following other structures on the Property: _____.

B. If requested by Buyer or Seller, the report shall separately identify each recommendation for corrective work as follows:

"Section 1": Infestation or infection which is evident.

"Section 2": Conditions that are present which are deemed likely to lead to infestation or infection.

C. If no infestation or infection by wood destroying pests or organisms is found, the report shall include a written Certification that on the inspection date no evidence of active infestation was found.

D. Work recommended to correct conditions shall be at the expense of ❑ Buyer, ❑ Seller.

E. Work recommended to correct conditions, if requested by Buyer, shall be at the expense of ❑ Buyer, ❑ Seller.

F. Work to be performed at Seller's expense may be performed by Seller or through others, provided that: (a) all required permits and final inspections are obtained, and (b) upon completion of repairs a written Certification is issued by a registered Structural Pest Control Company showing that the inspected property "is now free of evidence of active infestation or infection."

G. If inspection of inaccessible areas is recommended in the report, Buyer has the option to accept and approve the report, or request in writing within 5 (or ❑ _____) calendar days of receipt of the report that further inspection be made. BUYER'S FAILURE TO NOTIFY SELLER IN WRITING OF SUCH REQUEST SHALL CONCLUSIVELY BE CONSIDERED APPROVAL OF THE REPORT. If further inspection recommends corrective work, such work, and the inspection, entry, and closing of the inaccessible areas, shall be at the expense of the respective party designated in paragraphs (A), (D) and/or (E). If no infestation or infection is found, the inspection, entry, and closing of the inaccessible areas shall be at the expense of Buyer.

H. Inspections, corrective work, and certification under this paragraph shall not include roof coverings. Read paragraph 9A concerning inspection of roof coverings.

I. Work shall be performed in a skillful manner with materials of comparable quality, and shall include repair of leaking shower stalls and pans and replacement of tiles and other materials removed for repair. It is understood that exact restoration of appearance or cosmetic items following all such work is not included.

J. Funds for work agreed in writing to be performed after close of escrow shall be held in escrow and disbursed upon receipt of a written Certification that the inspected property "is now free of evidence of active infestation or infection."

K. Other: _____.

12. SALE OF BUYER'S PROPERTY: (If initialled by all parties.)

Buyer's initials _____ Seller's initials _____

This agreement is contingent upon the close of escrow of Buyer's property described as _____ situated in _____. Buyer's property is: ❑ Listed with _____ Company,

❑ In escrow No. _____ with _____ Company, scheduled to close escrow on _____, 19 _____.

A. (Check ONE:) ❑ Seller shall have the right to continue to offer the Property for sale, ❑ Seller shall NOT have the right to continue to offer the Property for sale (other than for back-up offers), ❑ Seller shall not have the right to continue to offer for sale (other than for back-up offers) until _____ calendar days after acceptance of the offer.

B. If Seller has the right to continue to offer the Property for sale (other than for back-up offers) and Seller accepts another offer, Seller shall give Buyer written notice to (1) remove this contingency in writing and (2) comply with the following additional requirements _____

_____.

If Buyer fails to complete those actions within _____ hours or _____ calendar days after receipt of such Notice from Seller, then this agreement and any escrow shall terminate and the deposit (less costs incurred) shall returned to Buyer.

C. If Seller does not give the Notice above the Buyer's property does not close escrow by the date specified in paragraph 3 for close of escrow of this Property, then either Seller or Buyer may cancel this agreement and any escrow by giving the other party written notice of cancellation, and the Buyer's deposit (less cost incurred) shall be returned to Buyer.

13. CANCELLATION OF PRIOR SALE/BACK-UP OFFER: (If initialled by all parties.)

Buyer's initials _____ Seller's initials _____

Buyer understands that Seller has entered into one or more contracts to sell the Property to a different buyer(s). The parties to any prior sale may mutually agree to modify or amend the terms of that sale(s). This agreement is contingent upon the written cancellation of the previous purchase and sale agreement(s) and any relate escrow(s).

(Check ONLY ONE of the following.)

❑ CANCELLATION OF PRIOR SALE: If written cancellation of the previous agreement(s) is not received on or before _____ , 19 _____ , then either Buyer or Seller may cancel this agreement and any escrow by giving the other party to this agreement written notice of cancellation. Buyer's deposit, less cost incurred, shall then be returned to Buyer.

❑ BACK-UP OFFER: This is a back-up offer in back-up position No. _____ , BUYER'S DEPOSIT CHECK SHALL BE HELD UNCASHED until a copy of the written cancellation(s) signed by all parties to the prior sale(s) is provided to Buyer. Until Buyer receives a copy of such cancellation(s), Buyer may cancel this agreement by providing written notice to Seller. Buyer's deposit shall then be returned to Buyer. AS RELATES TO BACK-UP OFFER, TIME PERIODS IN THIS AGREEMENT WHICH ARE STATED AS A NUMBER OF DAYS SHALL BEGIN ON THE DATES SELLER GIVES TO BUYER WRITTEN NOTICE THAT ANY PRIOR CONTRACT(S) HAS BEEN CANCELLED. IF CLOSE OF ESCROW OR ANY OTHER EVENT IS SHOWN AS A SPECIFIC DATE THAT DATE SHALL BE EXTENDED UNLESS BUYER AND SELLER SPECIFICALLY AGREE IN WRITING.

14. COURT CONFIRMATION: (If initialled by all parties)

Buyer's initials____ Seller's initials

This agreement is contingent upon court confirmation on or before _____, 19___. The court may allow open, comjpetitive bidding, resulting in the Property being sold to the highest bidder. Buyer had been advised to be in court when the offer is considered for confirmation. Court confirmation may be required in a probate, conservatorship, guardianship, receivership, bankuptcy, or other proceeding. Buyer understands that the Property may continue to be marked by Broker(s) and others may represent other competitive bidders prior to and at the court confirmation. If court confirmation is not obtained by date shown above, Buyer may cancel this agreement by giving written notice of cancellation to Seller.

15. NOTICES: Notices given pursuant to this agreement shall, unless otherwise required by law, be deemed delivered to Buyer when personally received by Buyer _____, who is authorized to receive it for Buyer, or to Seller when personally received by Seller or _____, who is authorized to receive it for Seller. Delivery may be in person, by mail, or facsimile.

16. TAXWITHHOLDING:

A. Under the Foreign Investment in Real Propery Tax Act (FIRPTA), IRC 1445, every Buyer must, unless an exemption applies, deduct and withhold 10% of the gross sales price from Seller's proceeds and send it to the Internal Revenue Service, if the Seller is a "foreign Person" under that statute.

B. Penalties may be imposed on a responsible party for non-compliance with the requirements of these statutes and related regulations. Seller and Buyer agree to execute and deliver any instrument, affidavit, statement, or instruction reasonably necessary to carry out these requirements, and to withholding of tax under those statutes if required.

17. RISK OF LOSS: Except as otherwise provided in this agreement, all risk of loss to the Property which occurs after the offer is accepted shall be borne by Seller until either the title has been transferred, or possession has been given to Buyer, whichever occurs first. Any damage totalling 1.0 (one)% or less of the purchase price shall be repaired by Seller in accordance with paragraph 10, if applicable. If the land or improvements to the Property are destroyed or materially damaged prior to transfer of title in an amount exceeding 1.0 (one)% of the purchase price, then Buyer shall have the option to either terminate this agreement and recover the full deposit or purchase the Property in its then present condition. Any expenses paid by Buyer or Seller for credit reports, appraisals, title examination, or Inspections of any kind shall remain that party's responsibility. If Buyer elects to purchase the Property and the loss is covered by insurance, Seller shall assign to Buyer all insurance proceeds covering the loss. If transfer of title and possession do not occur at the same time, BUYER AND SELLER ARE ADVISED TO SEEK ADVICE OF THEIR INSURANCE ADVISORS as to the insurance consequences thereof.

18. CONTINGENCIES/COVENANTS: METHODS OF SATISFACTION/REMOVAL, TIME FRAMES, DISAPPROVAL/APPROVAL:

A. METHOD OF SATISFYING/REMOVING CONTINGENCIES: Contingencies are to be satisfied or removed by one of the following methods:

(1) PASSIVE METHOD: IF BUYER FAILS TO GIVE WRITTEN NOTICE OF DISAPPROVAL OF ITEMS OR OF CANCELLATION OF THIS AGREEMENT WITHIN THE STRICT TIME-PERIODS SPECIFIED IN THIS AGREEMENT (except financing contingency, if paragraph 1A(2) is checked), THEN BUYER SHALL CONCLUSIVELY BE DEEMED TO HAVE COMPLETED ALL INSPECTIONS AND REVIEW OF APPLICABLE DOCUMENTS AND DISCLOSURES AND TO HAVE MADE AN ELECTION TO PROCEED WITH THE TRANSACTION WITHOUT CORRECTION OF ANY ITEMS WHICH THE SELLER HAS NOT OTHERWISE AGREED TO CORRECT; OR

(2) ACTIVE METHOD: IF BUYER AND SELLER INITIAL THIS PARAGRAPH, THEN PARAGRAPH A(1) SHALL NOT APPLY. Buyer's initials _____ Seller's initials _____ BUYER'S DISAPPROVAL OF ITEMS OR REMOVAL OF CONTINGENCIES SHALL BE IN WRITING (except financing contingency, if paragraph 1(A)(1) is checked). IF BUYER FAILS TO REMOVE OR WAIVE ALL CONTINGENCIES IN WRITING WITHIN THE STRICT TIME PERIODS SPECIFIED IN THIS AGREEMENT, THEN SELLER MAY CANCEL THIS AGREEMENT BY GIVING WRITTEN NOTICE OF CANCELLATION TO BUYER.

B. TIME FRAMES: Buyer and Seller agree to be bound by the following time periods:

BUYER has the following number of calendar days to take the action specified, BEGINNING ON THE DATE OF ACCEPTANCE OF THE OFFER:

1. _____ Loan Application(s) submit to lender(s) for new loan(s) and assumption(s), submit to Seller for seller financing), submit written acknowledgment to Seller

FIGURE A.4 **REAL ESTATE PURCHASE CONTRACT** *(continued)*

REAL ESTATE PURCHASE CONTRACT AND RECEIPT FOR DEPOSIT – page 6

2. ____ Buyer Inspections of Property (complete inspections, except GEOLOGIC, and give notice of disapproval)

3. ____ Buyer Inspections of Property (complete GEOLOGIC inspections and give notice of disapproval)

4. _____

BUYER has the following number of calendar days to DISAPPROVE the items listed below, BEGINNING ON THE DATE OF BUYER'S RECEIPT OF EACH ITEM:

5. ____ Existing Loans Documents,
    Preliminary (Title) Report,
    Condominium/Planned Development Documents,
    Geological/Seismic/Flood/State Fire Zones/Areas,
    Governmental Notices Disclosure

6. _____

SELLER has the following number of calendar days to PROVIDE to Buyer, as applicable, the information listed below, BEGINNING ON THE DATE OF ACCEPTANCE OF THE OFFER:

7. ____ Geologic/Seismic/Flood/State Fire Zones/Areas Disclosures, if applicable, Homeowner's Guide to Earthquake Safety and/or Commercial Property Owner's Guide to Earthquake Safety

8. ____ Pest Control Report

9. _____

The items listed below, as applicable, shall promptly be requested and upon receipt provided to Buyer:

10. Existing Loan Documents,
    Preliminary (Title) Report,
    Condominium/Planned Development Documents,
    Mello-Roos Disclosure

11. _____

C. **DISAPPROVAL/APPROVAL OF ITEMS:** (1) If, within the time specified, Buyer provides written reasonable disapproval to Seller of any item for which Buyer has a disapproval right, Seller shall respond in writing within ____ calendar days after receipt of Buyer's notice. If Seller is unwilling or unable to correct the items disapproved by Buyer, then Buyer may cancel this agreement by giving written notice of cancellation to Seller within ____ calendar days (after receipt of Seller's response, or after expiration of the time for Seller's response, whichever occurs first), in which case Buyer's deposit shall be returned to Buyer. If paragraph A2 is initialled, then Buyer shall provide Seller with a written notice of either cancellation or election to proceed. If Buyer elects to proceed with the transaction without Seller's correction of items, Buyer shall assume all liability, responsibility, and expense for repairs or corrections, including the expense of compliance with governmental agency requirements. This does not, however, relieve the Seller of any contractual obligations to repair of correct items otherwise agreed upon. (2) If a MELLO-ROOS DISCLOSURE notices delivered to Buyer after the offer is executed, Buyer shall have three (3) days after delivery in person or five (5) days after delivery by deposit in the mail to give written notice of termination to Seller.

D. **FOR ALL TIME PERIODS:**

1. Buyer and Seller understand that time periods can be changed only by mutual written agreement.

2. If this is a back-up offer (paragraph 21), time periods which are shown as a number of days beginning on the date of acceptance of the offer shall instead begin on the date Seller gives to Buyer written notice that any prior contract(s) has been cancelled.

19. **FINAL VERIFICATION OF CONDITION:** Buyer shall have the right to make a final inspection of the Property approximately 5 (or ❑ ____) calendar days prior to close escrow, NOT AS A CONTINGENCY OF THE SALE, but solely to confirm that: (a) Seller has completed alterations, repairs, replacements, or modifications ("Repairs") as agreed in writing by Buyer and Seller, and has complied with warranty obligations, if any, in paragraph 10, and (b) the Property is otherwise in substantially the same condition as on the date of acceptance of the offer. Repair under this agreement shall be completed prior to close of escrow unless otherwise agreed in writing, and shall comply with applicable building code and permit requirements. Materials used shall be of comparable quality to existing materials.

20. **MEDIATION OF DISPUTES:** BUYER AND SELLER AGREE TO MEDIATE ANY DISPUTE OR CLAIM BETWEEN THEM ARISING OUT OF THIS CONTRACT OR ANY RESULTING TRANSACTION BEFORE RESORTING TO ARBITRATION OR COURT ACTION. Mediation is a process in which parties attempt to resolve a dispute by submitting it an impartial, neutral mediator who is authorized to facilitate the resolution of the dispute but who is not empowered to impose a settlement on the parties. Mediation fee, if any, shall be divided equally among the parties involved. Before the mediation begins, the parties agree to sign a document limiting the admissibility in arbitration or any civil action of anything said, any admission made, and any documents prepared, in the course of the mediation. In addition, if paragraph 22 is initialled by Broker(s), Buyer and Seller agree to mediate disputes or claims involving an initialling Broker, as defined by that paragraph, consistent with this provision. The election by Broker(s) to initial or not initial paragraph 22 shall not affect the applicability of this mediation provision between Buyer and Seller and shall not result in the Broker(s) being deemed parties to the purchase and sale agreement. IF ANY PARTY COMMENCES AN ARBITRATION OR COURT ACTION BASED ON A DISPUTE OR CLAIM TO WHICH THIS PARAGRAPH APPLIES WITHOUT FIRST ATTEMPTING TO RESOLVE THE MATTER THROUGH MEDIATION, THEN IN THE DISCRETION OF THE ARBITRATOR(S) OR JUDGE, THAT PARTY SHALL NOT BE ENTITLED TO RECOVER ATTORNEY'S

FIGURE A.4 **REAL ESTATE PURCHASE CONTRACT** *(continued)*

FEES EVEN IF THEY WOULD OTHERWISE BE AVAILABLE TO THAT PARTY IN ANY SUCH ARBITRATION OR COURT ACTION.

However, the filing of a judicial action to enable the recording of a notice of pending action, for order of attachment, receivership, injunction, or other provisional remedies, shall not in itself constitute a loss of the right to recover attorney's fees under this provision. The following matters are excluded from the requirement of mediation hereunder: (a) a judicial or non-judicial foreclosure or other action or proceeding to enforce a deed of trust, mortgage, or installment land sale contract, (b) an unlawful detainer action, (c) the filing or enforcement of a mechanic's lien, and (d) any matter which is within the jurisdiction of a probate court.

21. **ARBITRATION OF DISPUTES:** Any dispute or claim in law or equity between Buyer and Seller arising out of this contract or any resulting transaction which is not settled through mediation shall be decided by neutral, binding arbitration and not by court action, except as provided by California law for judicial review or arbitration proceedings. In addition, if paragraph 22 is initialled by Broker(s), Buyer and Seller agree to arbitrate disputes or claims involving an initialling Broker, as defined by that paragraph, consistent with this provision. The election by Broker(s) to initial or not initial paragraph 30 shall not affect the applicability of the arbitration provision between Buyer and Seller, and shall not result in the Broker(s) being deemed parties to the purchase and sale agreement.

The arbitration shall be conducted in accordance with the rules of either the American Arbitration Association (AAA) or Judicial Arbitration and Mediation Services, Inc. (JAMS). The selection between AAA and JAMS rules shall be made by the claimant first filing for the arbitration. The parties to an arbitration may agree in writing to use different rules and/or arbitrator(s). Judgment upon the award rendered by the arbitrator(s) may be entered in any court having jurisdiction thereof.

"NOTICE: BY INITIALLING IN THE SPACE BELOW YOU ARE AGREEING TO HAVE ANY DISPUTE ARISING OUT OF THE MATTERS INCLUDED IN THE ARBITRATION OF DISPUTES PROVISION DECIDED BY NEUTRAL ARBITRATION AS PROVIDED BY CALIFORNIA LAW AND YOU ARE GIVING UP ANY RIGHTS YOU MIGHT POSSESS TO HAVE THE DISPUTES LITIGATED IN A COURT OR JURY TRIAL. BY INITIALLING IN THE SPACE BELOW YOU ARE GIVING UP YOUR JUDICIAL RIGHTS TO DISCOVERY AND APPEAL, UNLESS THOSE RIGHTS ARE SPECIFICALLY INCLUDED IN THE ARBITRATION OF DISPUTES PROVISION. IF YOU REFUSE TO SUBMIT TO ARBITRATION AFTER AGREEING TO THIS PROVISION, YOU MAY BE COMPELLED TO ARBITRATE. YOUR AGREEMENT TO THIS ARBITRATION PROVISION IS VOLUNTARY."

"WE HAVE READ AND UNDERSTAND THE FOREGOING AND AGREE TO SUBMIT DISPUTES ARISING OUT OF THE MATTERS INCLUDED IN THE 'ARBITRATION OF DISPUTES' PROVISION TO NEUTRAL ARBITRATION."

22. **BROKERS:** (initialled.) Any Broker who initials below agrees to (a) mediate any dispute or claim with Buyer, Seller, or other initialling Broker, arising out of this contract or any resulting transaction, consistent with paragraph 20, and (b) arbitrate any dispute or claim with Buyer, Seller or other initialling Broker arising out of this contract or any resulting transaction, consistent with paragraph 21. However, if the dispute is solely between the Brokers, it shall instead be submitted for mediation and arbitration in accordance with the Board/Association of REALTORS® or MLS rules. If those entities decline to handle the matter, it shall be submitted pursuant to paragraphs 20 and 21. The initialling of this paragraph shall not result in any Broker being deemed a party to the purchase and sale agreement. As used in this paragraph, "Broker" means a brokerage firm and any licensed persons affiliated with that brokerage firm.

Selling Broker By: _____   Listing Broker By: _____

23. **LIQUIDATED DAMAGES:** (If initialled by all parties.)

Buyer's Initials _____   Seller's Initials _____   Buyer and Seller agree that if Buyer fails to complete this purchase by reason of any default of Buyer:

A. Seller shall be released from obligation to sell the Property to Buyer.

B. Seller shall retain, as liquidated damages for breach of contract, the deposit actually paid. However, the amount retained shall be no more than 3% of the purchase price if Property is a dwelling with no more than four units, one of which Buyer intends to occupy as Buyer's residence. Any excess shall be promptly returned to Buyer.

C. Seller retains the right to proceed against Buyer for specific performance or any other claim or remedy Seller may have in law or equity, other than breach of contract damages.

D. In the event of a dispute, Funds deposited in trust accounts or escrow are not released automatically and require mutual, signed release instructions from both Buyer and Seller, judicial decision, or arbitration award.

24. **ATTORNEY'S FEES:** In any action, proceeding, or arbitration between Buyer and Seller arising out of this agreement, the prevailing party shall be entitled to reasonable attorney's fees and costs.

25. **MULTIPLE LISTING SERVICE:** If Broker is a Participant of a multiple listing service (MLS), Broker is authorized to report the sale, price, terms, and financing for publication, dissemination, information, and use of the MLS, its parent entity, authorized members, participants, and subscribers.

26. **OTHER TERMS AND CONDITIONS:** _____

_____

27. **TIME OF ESSENCE; ENTIRE CONTRACT; CHANGES:** Time is of the essence. All prior agreements between the parties are incorporated in this agreement, which constitutes the entire contract. Its terms are intended by the parties as a final, complete and exclusive expression of their agreement with respect to its subject matter and may not be contradicted by evidence of any prior agreement or contemporaneous oral agreement. The captions in this agreement are for convenience of reference only and are not intended as part of this agreement. This agreement may not be extended, amended, modified, altered, or changed in any respect whatsoever except by a further agreement in writing signed by Buyer and Seller.

REAL ESTATE PURCHASE CONTRACT AND RECEIPT FOR DEPOSIT – page 8

28. **AGENCY CONFIRMATION:** The following agency relationship(s) are here by confirmed for this transaction:

Listing Agent: _____ is the agent of (check one): ❑ the Seller exclusively; or ❑ both the Buyer and Seller.

Selling Agent: _____ (if not same as Listing Agent) is the agent of (check one): ❑ the Buyer exclusively; ❑ the Seller exclusively; or ❑ both the Buyer and Seller.

(If the property contains 1-4 residential dwelling units, buyer and seller must also be given one or more disclosure regarding real estate agency relationships forms.)

29. **OFFER:** This is an offer to purchase the Property. All paragraphs with spaces for initials by Buyer and Seller are incorporated in this agreement only if initialled by both parties. If only one party initials, a Counter Offer is required until agreement is reached. Unless acceptance is signed by Seller and a signed copy delivered in person, by mail, or facsimile, and personally received by Buyer or by _____, who is authorized to receive it, by _____ , 19 _____ at _____ AM/PM, the offer shall be deemed revoked and the deposit shall be returned. Buyer and Seller acknowledge that Broker(s) is/are not a party(ies) to the purchase and sale agreement. Buyer has read and acknowledged receipt of a copy of the offer and agrees to the above confirmation of agency relationships. This agreement and any supplement, addendum, or modification, including any photocopy or facsimile, may be executed in two or more counterparts, all of which shall constitute one and the same writing.

Receipt for deposit is acknowledged: Broker: _____ Buyer: _____

ACCEPTANCE

The undersigned Seller accepts the above and agrees to sell the Property on the above terms and conditions and agrees to the above confirmation of agency relationships (❑ subject to attached counter offer). Seller agrees to pay compensation for services as follows: _____ to _____ , Broker, and _____ to _____ , Broker, payable: (a) on recordation of the deed or other evidence of title, or (b) if completion of sale is prevented by default of Seller, upon Seller's default, or (c) if completion of sale is prevented by default of Buyer, only if and when Seller collects damages from Buyer, by suit or otherwise, and then in an amount equal to one-half of the damages recovered, but not to exceed the above compensation, after first deducting title and escrow expenses and the expenses of collection, if any. Seller hereby irrevocably assigns to Broker(s) such compensation from Seller's proceeds in escrow. In any action, proceeding, or arbitration relating to the payment of such compensation, the prevailing party shall be entitled to reasonable attorney's fees and costs, except as provided in paragraph 20. The undersigned Seller has read, acknowledges receipt of a copy of this agreement, and authorizes Broker(s) to deliver a signed copy to Buyer.

Date_____ Telephone_____ Fax _____ Seller_____

Real Estate Broker(s) confirm(s) agency relationship(s) as above. (Real Estate Brokers are not parties to the purchase and sale agreement between Buyer and Seller.):

Real Estate Broker (Selling) _____ By _____ Date _____

Address _____ Telephone _____ Fax_____

Real Estate Broker (Selling) _____ By _____ Date _____

Address _____ Telephone _____ Fax_____

FIGURE A.4 **REAL ESTATE PURCHASE CONTRACT** *(continued)*

ESCROW/CLOSING INSTRUCTIONS

Excrow #: _____

TO: ABC TITLE COMPANY
     123 10th Street
     Anywhere, CA 90000

Date of Deposit Receipt: _____

RE: Property Known As _____ Deposit Amount: $_____

Gentlemen:

You are advised that we have negotiated the purchase of real property referred to above.

We hereby hand you a check payable to ABC Title Company for the above deposit amount.

You are to deposit the check and hold the funds represented thereby and any additional funds deposited with you in your escrow trust account. You are instructed not to release any funds until mutually acceptable instructions are received by you from the undersigned Sellers and Buyers.

Any principal instructing you to cancel this escrow shall file notice of cancellation in your office, in writing, and so state the reason for cancellation. Upon receipt of such request, you shall prepare cancellation instructions for signatures of the principals and shall forward same to the principals. If no written objection is filed with you upon receipt of the mutually agreeable cancellation instructions signed by all principals and after payment of your cancellation charges, you are authorized to comply with such instruction and cancel your escrow. If, after 30 days from date of notice of cancellation, you have not received mutually agreeable cancellation instructions, the principals hereto expressly agree that you, as escrow holder, have the absolute right at your election to file an action in interpleader requiring the principals to answer and litigate their several claims and rights among themselves, and you are authorized to deposit with the clerk of the court all documents and funds held in this escrow. In the event such action is filed, the principals jointly and severally agree to pay your cancellation charges and costs, expenses, and reasonable attorney's fees which you are required to expend or incur in such interpleader action, the amount thereof to be fixed and judgment therefor to be rendered by the court. Upon the filing of such action, you shall thereupon be fully released and discharged from all obligations to further perform any duties or obligations otherwise imposed by the terms of this escrow.

We hereby apply for a California Land Title Association standard form policy of title insurance to be issued on closing the sale and request that a preliminary report be issued for the purpose of disclosing the terms and conditions upon which you are willing to provide such title insurance policy.

BUYER : _____ SELLER : _____

x _____ x _____

FIGURE A.6

NET PROCEEDS STATEMENT

Escrow No.: _____ Filing Date: _____

Escrow Settlement	Debit	Credit
Total Consideration		
Deposit		
Deposit		
Deposit		
Paid Outside of Escrow to		
Principal Balance of First Trust Deed of Trust of Record		
Principal Balance of Second Trust Deed of Trust of Record		
Amount of New Loan		
Purchase Money Deed of Trust		
Taxes $ per from to		
Personal Property Tax		
Insurance on $ Premium $ per		
from to		
Interest on $ @ from to		
Interest on $ @ from to		
Impounded Funds Held by Lending Institution		
Rents		
# $ per from to		
# $ per from to		
Rental Deposits:		
#		
Deducted by Lender:		
Commission to		
Commission to		
Termite Company Paid		
Payment of Demand to		
Interest on $ @ from to		
Prepayment		
Forwarding Fee		
County Tax Collector		
Title Policy/ATA Policy		
Revenue Stamps		
Recording		
Reconveyance Fee		
Tax Service		
Sub Escrow Fee		
Completing Documents		
Notary Fee		
Insurance Endorsement Fee		
Reconveyance Fee		
Loan Escrow Fee/Beneficiary/Demand Processing Fee		
Balance - Check Herewith		
TOTAL		

FIGURE A.7

UNIFORM RESIDENTIAL LOAN APPLICATION

Uniform Residential Loan Application

This application is designed to be completed by the applicant(s) with the lender's assistance. Applicants should complete this form as "Borrower" or "Co-Borrower," as applicable. Co-Borrower information must also be provided (and the appropriate box checked) when ☐ the income or assets of a person other than the "Borrower" (including the Borrower's spouse) will be used as a basis for loan qualification or ☐ the income or assets of the Borrower's spouse will not be used as a basis for loan qualification, but his or her liabilities must be considered because the Borrower resides in a community property state, the security property is located in a community property state, or the Borrower is relying on other property located in a community property state as a basis for repayment of the loan.

I. TYPE OF MORTGAGE AND TERMS OF LOAN

Mortgage Applied for:	☐ VA ☐ Conventional ☐ Other: ☐ FHA ☐ FmHA		Agency Case Number	Lender Case No.
Amount $	Interest Rate %	No. of Months	Amortization Type: ☐ Fixed Rate ☐ GPM ☐ Other (explain) ☐ ARM (type):	

II. PROPERTY INFORMATION AND PURPOSE OF LOAN

Subject Property Address (street, city, state, & zip code) **②** — County — No. of Units **③**

Legal Description of Subject Property (attach description if necessary) **④** — Year Built

Purpose of Loan	☐ Purchase ☐ Construction ☐ Refinance ☐ Construction-Permanent	☐ Other (explain):	Property will be: ☐ Primary Residence ☐ Secondary Residence ☐ Investment

Complete this line if construction or construction-permanent loan.

Year Lot Acquired	Original Cost $	Amount Existing Liens $	(a) Present Value of Lot $	(b) Cost of Improvements $	Total (a + b) $

Complete this line if this is a refinance loan.

Year Acquired	Original Cost $	Amount Existing Liens $	Purpose of Refinance	Describe Improvements ☐ made ☐ to be made Cost: $

Title will be held in what Name(s) **⑤** — Manner in which Title will be held **⑥** — Estate will be held in: ☐ Fee Simple ☐ Leasehold (show expiration date) **⑧**

Source of Downpayment, Closing Costs and/or Payoff Funds (explain) **⑦**

III. BORROWER INFORMATION

⑨ Borrower — Co-Borrower

Borrower's Name (include Jr. or Sr. if applicable)	Co-Borrower's Name (include Jr. or Sr. if applicable)

Social Security Number	Home Phone (incl. area code)	Age	Yrs. School	Social Security Number	Home Phone (incl. area code)	Age	Yrs. School

☐ Married ☐ Unmarried (include single, divorced, widowed) ☐ Separated	Dependents (not listed by Co-Borrower) no. / ages	☐ Married ☐ Unmarried (include single, divorced, widowed) ☐ Separated	Dependents (not listed by Borrower) no. / ages

Present Address (street, city, state, zip code) ☐ Own ☐ Rent ___ No. Yrs.	Present Address (street, city, state, zip code) ☐ Own ☐ Rent ___ No. Yrs.

If Mailing Address is different from above, please list on page 4. | If Mailing Address is different from above, please list on page 4.

If residing at present address for less than two years, complete the following:

Former Address (street, city, state, zip code) ☐ Own ☐ Rent ___ No. Yrs.	Former Address (street, city, state, zip code) ☐ Own ☐ Rent ___ No. Yrs.

Former Address (street, city, state, zip code) ☐ Own ☐ Rent ___ No. Yrs.	Former Address (street, city, state, zip code) ☐ Own ☐ Rent ___ No. Yrs.

IV. EMPLOYMENT INFORMATION

Borrower — Co-Borrower

Name & Address of Employer **⑩** ☐ Self-Employed	Yrs. on this job	Name & Address of Employer ☐ Self-Employed	Yrs. on this job
	Yrs. employed in this line of work/profession		Yrs. employed in this line of work/profession
Position/Title/Type of Business	Business Phone (incl. area code)	Position/Title/Type of Business	Business Phone (incl. area code)

If employed in current position for less than two years or if currently employed in more than one position, complete the following:

Name & Address of Employer ☐ Self-Employed	Dates (from-to)	Name & Address of Employer ☐ Self-Employed	Dates (from-to)
	Monthly income $		Monthly income $
Position/Title/Type of Business	Business Phone (incl. area code)	Position/Title/Type of Business	Business Phone (incl. area code)

Name & Address of Employer ☐ Self-Employed	Dates (from-to)	Name & Address of Employer ☐ Self-Employed	Dates (from-to)
	Monthly income $		Monthly income $
Position/Title/Type of Business	Business Phone (incl. area code)	Position/Title/Type of Business	Business Phone (incl. area code)

MARRIED APPLICANTS ARE HEREBY NOTIFIED THAT THEY ARE ENTITLED TO APPLY FOR A SEPARATE ACCOUNT.

Borrower's Initials X ___
Co-Borrower's Initials X ___

V. MONTHLY INCOME AND COMBINED HOUSING EXPENSE INFORMATION

Gross Monthly Income	Borrower	Co-Borrower	Total	Combined Monthly Housing Expense	Present	Proposed
Base Empl. Income*	$	$	$	Rent	$	
Overtime				First Mortgage (P & I)		$
Bonuses				Other Financing (P & I)		
Commissions				Hazard Insurance		
Dividends/Interest				Real Estate Taxes		
Net Rental Income				Mortgage Insurance		
Other (before completing, see the notice in "describe other income," below)				Homeowner Assn. Dues		
				Other:		
Total	$	$	$	Total	$	$

*Self Employed Borrower(s) may be required to provide additional documentation such as tax returns and financial statements.

Describe Other Income **Notice:** Alimony, child support, or separate maintenance income need not be revealed if the Borrower (B) or Co-Borrower (C) does not choose to have it considered for repaying this loan.

B/C		Monthly Amount
		$

VI. ASSETS AND LIABILITIES

This statement and any applicable supporting schedules may be completed jointly by both married and unmarried Co-Borrowers if their assets and liabilities are sufficiently joined so that the Statement can be meaningfully and fairly presented on a combined basis; otherwise separate Statements and Schedules are required. If the Co-Borrower section was completed about a spouse, this Statement and supporting schedules must be completed about that spouse also.

Completed ☐ Jointly ☐ Not Jointly

ASSETS Description	Cash or Market Value	Liabilities and Pledged Assets. List the creditor's name, address and account number for all outstanding debts, including automobile loans, revolving charge accounts, real estate loans, alimony, child support, stock pledges, etc. Use continuation sheet if necessary. Indicate by (*) those liabilities which will be satisfied upon sale of real estate owned or upon refinancing of the subject property.		
Cash deposit toward purchase held by:	$	LIABILITIES	Monthly Payt. & Mos. Left to Pay	Unpaid Balance
		Name and address of Company	$ Payt./Mos.	$
List checking and savings accounts below				
Name and address of Bank, S&L, or Credit Union				
		Acct. no.		
Acct. no.	$	Name and address of Company	$ Payt./Mos.	$
Name and address of Bank, S&L, or Credit Union				
		Acct. no.		
Acct. no.	$	Name and address of Company	$ Payt./Mos.	$
Name and address of Bank, S&L, or Credit Union				
		Acct. no.		
Acct. no.	$	Name and address of Company	$ Payt./Mos.	$
Name and address of Bank, S&L, or Credit Union				
		Acct. no.		
Acct. no.	$	Name and address of Company	$ Payt./Mos.	$
Stocks & Bonds (Company name/number & description)	$			
		Acct. no.		
		Name and address of Company	$ Payt./Mos.	$
Life insurance net cash value				
Face amount: $				
Subtotal Liquid Assets	$			
Real estate owned (enter market value from schedule of real estate owned)	$	Acct. no.		
Vested interest in retirement fund	$	Name and address of Company	$ Payt./Mos.	$
Net worth of business(es) owned (attach financial statement)	$			
Automobiles owned (make and year)	$			
		Acct. no.		
Other Assets (itemize)	$	Alimony/Child Support/Separate Maintenance Payments Owed to:	$	
		Job Related Expense (child care, union dues, etc.)	$	
		Total Monthly Payments	$	
Total Assets a.	$	Net Worth (a minus b) ▶		Total Liabilities b. $

Borrower's Initials X _____
Co-Borrower's Initials X _____

N34020

③② **Schedule of Real Estate Owned** (if additional properties are owned, use continuation sheet.)

Property Address (enter S if sold, PS if pending sale or R if rental being held for income) ▼	Type of Property	Present Market Value	Amount of Mortgages & Liens	Gross Rental Income	Mortgage Payments	Insurance, Maintenance, Taxes & Misc.	Net Rental Income
		$	$	$	$	$	$
	Totals	$	$	$	$	$	$

List any additional names under which credit has previously been received and indicate appropriate creditor name(s) and account number(s):

Alternate Name	Creditor Name	Account Number

---

②⑤ **VII. DETAILS OF TRANSACTION**

a. Purchase price	$
b. Alterations, improvements, repairs	
c. Land (if acquired separately)	
d. Refinance (inc. debts to be paid off)	
e. Estimated prepaid items	
f. Estimated closing costs	
g. PMI, MIP, Funding Fee	
h. Discount (if Borrower will pay)	
i. Total costs (add items a through h)	
j. Subordinate financing	
k. Borrower's closing costs paid by Seller	
l. Other Credits (explain)	
m. Loan amount (exclude PMI, MIP, Funding Fees financed)	
n. PMI, MIP, Funding Fee financed	
o. Loan amount (add m & n)	
p. Cash from/to Borrower (subtract j, k, l, and o from i)	

②⑥ **VIII. DECLARATIONS**

If you answer "yes" to any questions a through i, please use continuation sheet for explanation.

	Borrower		Co-Borrower	
	Yes	No	Yes	No
a. Are there any outstanding judgments against you?	☐	☐	☐	☐
b. Have you been declared bankrupt within the past 10 years?	☐	☐	☐	☐
c. Have you had property foreclosed upon or given title or deed in lieu thereof in the last 7 years?	☐	☐	☐	☐
d. Are you a party to a law suit?	☐	☐	☐	☐
e. Have you directly or indirectly been obligated on any loan which resulted in foreclosure, transfer of title in lieu of foreclosure, or judgment? (This would include such loans as home mortgage loans, SBA loans, home improvement loans, educational loans, manufactured (mobile) home loans, any mortgage, financial obligation, bond, or loan guarantee. If "Yes," provide details, including date, name and address of Lender, FHA or VA case number, if any, and reasons for action.)	☐	☐	☐	☐
f. Are you presently delinquent or in default on any Federal debt or any other loan, mortgage, financial obligation, bond, or loan guarantee? If "Yes," give details as described in the preceding question.	☐	☐	☐	☐
g. Are you obligated to pay alimony, child support, or separate maintenance?	☐	☐	☐	☐
h. Is any part of the down payment borrowed?	☐	☐	☐	☐
i. Are you a co-maker or endorser on a note?	☐	☐	☐	☐
j. Are you a U.S. citizen?	☐	☐	☐	☐
k. Are you a permanent resident alien? # _____	☐	☐	☐	☐
l. Do you intend to occupy the property as your primary residence? If "Yes," complete question m below.	☐	☐	☐	☐
m. Have you had an ownership interest in a property in the last three years? **②⑦**	☐	☐	☐	☐
(1) What type of property did you own—principal residence (PR), second home (SH), or investment property (IP)?				
(2) How did you hold title to the home—solely by yourself (S), jointly with your spouse (SP), or jointly with another person (O)?				

---

②⑧ **IX. ACKNOWLEDGEMENT AND AGREEMENT**

The undersigned specifically acknowledge(s) and agree(s) that: (1) the loan requested by this application will be secured by a first mortgage or deed of trust on the property described herein; (2) the property will not be used for any illegal or prohibited purpose or use; (3) all statements made in this application are made for the purpose of obtaining the loan indicated herein; (4) occupancy of the property will be as indicated above; (5) verification or reverification of any information contained in the application may be made at any time by the Lender, its agents, successors and assigns, either directly or through a credit reporting agency, from any source named in this application, and the original copy of this application will be retained by the Lender, even if the loan is not approved; (6) the Lender, its agents, successors and assigns will rely on the information contained in the application and I/we have a continuing obligation to amend and/or supplement the information provided in this application if any of the material facts which I/we have represented herein should change prior to closing; (7) in the event my/our payments on the loan indicated in this application become delinquent, the Lender, its agents, successors and assigns, may, in addition to all their other rights and remedies, report my/our name(s) and account information to a credit reporting agency; (8) ownership of the loan may be transferred to successor or assign of the Lender without notice to me and/or the administration of the loan account may be transferred to an agent, successor or assign of the Lender with prior notice to me; (9) the Lender, its agents, successors and assigns make no representations or warranties, express or implied, to the Borrower(s) regarding the property, the condition of the property, or the value of the property.

Certification: I/We certify that the information provided in this application is true and correct as of the date set forth opposite my/our signature(s) on this application and acknowledge my/our understanding that any intentional or negligent misrepresentation(s) of the information contained in this application may result in civil liability and/or criminal penalties including, but not limited to, fine or imprisonment or both under the provisions of Title 18, United States Code, Section 1001, et seq. and liability for monetary damages to the Lender, its agents, successors and assigns, insurers and any other person who may suffer any loss due to reliance upon any misrepresentation which I/we have made on this application.

Borrower's Signature	Date	Co-Borrower's Signature	Date
X		X	

---

②⑨ **X. INFORMATION FOR GOVERNMENT MONITORING PURPOSES**

The following information is requested by the Federal Government for certain types of loans relating to a dwelling, in order to monitor the Lender's compliance with equal credit opportunity, fair housing and home mortgage disclosure laws. You are not required to furnish this information, but are encouraged to do so. The law provides that a Lender may neither discriminate on the basis of this information, nor on whether you choose to furnish it. However, if you choose not to furnish it, and you apply in person, under Federal regulations this Lender is required to note race and sex on the basis of visual observation or surname. If you do not wish to furnish the above information, please check the box below.

BORROWER ☐ I do not wish to furnish this information.

Race/National Origin: ☐ American Indian or Alaskan Native ☐ Asian or Pacific Islander ☐ Black, not of Hispanic origin ☐ Hispanic ☐ White, not of Hispanic origin ☐ Other (specify)

Sex: ☐ Female ☐ Male

CO-BORROWER ☐ I do not wish to furnish this information.

Race/National Origin: ☐ American Indian or Alaskan Native ☐ Asian or Pacific Islander ☐ Black, not of Hispanic origin ☐ Hispanic ☐ White, not of Hispanic origin ☐ Other (specify)

Sex: ☐ Female ☐ Male

This application was taken by:
☐ face-to-face interview
☐ mail
☐ telephone

Interviewer's Name (print or type)	Name and Address of Interviewer's Employer
	☐ Bank of America _____
Interviewer's Signature Date	☐ Loan Agent for Bank of America, _____
Interviewer's Phone Number (incl. area code)	☐ Other (specify) _____

Borrower's Initials X _____
Co-Borrower's Initials X _____

N34030

FIGURE A.7 **UNIFORM RESIDENTIAL LOAN APPLICATION** (continued)

307

Continuation Sheet/Uniform Residential Loan Application

Use this continuation sheet if you need more space to complete the Residential Loan Application. Mark **B** for Borrower or **C** for Co-Borrower.	Borrower:	Agency Case Number:
	Co-Borrower:	Lender Case Number:

If Mailing Address is different from property address, please list below (street, city, state & zip code)

I/We fully understand that it is a Federal crime punishable by fine or imprisonment, or both, to knowingly make any false statements concerning any of the above facts as applicable under the provisions of Title 18, United States Code, Section 1001, et seq.

Borrower's Signature	Date	Co-Borrower's Signature	Date
X		X	

Borrower's Initials X _____
Co-Borrower's Initials X _____

N34040

FIGURE A.7 **UNIFORM RESIDENTIAL LOAN APPLICATION** *(continued)*

FIGURE A.8

REQUEST FOR VERIFICATION OF DEPOSIT

INSTRUCTIONS TO LENDER:
1. Fill out Part I - Request
2. Have Applicant(s) sign each copy (no carbon signatures)
3. Forward both copies to Depository

VMP MORTGAGE FORMS • (800)521-7291

Ply 1 Printed on Recycled Paper

INSTRUCTIONS TO DEPOSITORY
1. Complete Part II - Verification
2. Return both completed copies to Lender

VMP -47 (8908).02

OMB No. 2502-0059

DEPARTMENT OF VETERANS AFFAIRS AND U.S. DEPARTMENT OF HOUSING AND URBAN DEVELOPMENT
HUD COMMUNITY PLANNING AND DEVELOPMENT
HUD HOUSING - FEDERAL HOUSING COMMISSIONER

REQUEST FOR VERIFICATION OF DEPOSIT

PRIVACY ACT NOTICE STATEMENT - This information is to be used by the agency collecting it in determining whether you qualify as a prospective mortgagor for mortgage insurance or guaranty or as a borrower for a rehabilitation loan under the agency's program. It will not be disclosed outside the agency without your consent except to financial institutions for verification of your deposits and as required and permitted by law. You do not have to give us this information, but, if you do not, your application for approval as a prospective mortgagor for mortgage insurance or guaranty or as a borrower for a rehabilitation loan may be delayed or rejected. This information request is authorized by Title 38, U.S.C., Chapter 37 *(if VA)*; by 12 U.S.C., Section 1701 et seq., *(if HUD/FHA)*; and by 42 U.S.C., Section 1452b *(if HUD/CPD)*.

INSTRUCTIONS

LENDER OR LOCAL PROCESSING AGENCY: Complete Items 1 through 8. Have applicant(s) complete Item 9. Forward directly to the Depository named in Item 1. DEPOSITORY: Please complete Items 10 through 15 and return DIRECTLY to Lender or Local Processing agency named in Item 2.

PART I REQUEST

1. TO *(Name and Address of Depository)*	2. FROM *(Name and Address of Lender or Local Processing Agency)*

I certify that this verification has been sent directly to the bank or depository and has not passed through the hands of the applicant or any other party.

3. Signature of Lender or Official of Local Processing Agency	4. Title	5. Date	6. Lender's Number *(Optional)*

◄ FOLD

7. INFORMATION TO BE VERIFIED

Type of Account and/or loan	Account/Loan in Name of	Account/Loan Number	Balance
			$
			$
			$
			$

TO DEPOSITORY: I have applied for mortgage insurance or guaranty or for a rehabilitation loan and stated that the balance on deposit and /or outstanding loans with you are as shown above. You are authorized to verify this information and to supply the lender or the local processing agency identified above with the information requested in Items 10 through 12. Your response is solely a matter of courtesy for which no responsibility is attached to your institution or any of your officers.

8. NAME AND ADDRESS OF APPLICANT(S)	9. SIGNATURE OF APPLICANT(S)
	X
	X

TO BE COMPLETED BY DEPOSITORY

PART II - VERIFICATION OF DEPOSITORY

10. DEPOSIT ACCOUNTS OF APPLICANT(S)

Type of Account	Account Number	Current Balance	Average Balance for Previous Two Months	Date Opened
		$	$	
		$	$	
		$	$	
		$	$	

◄ FOLD

11. LOANS OUTSTANDING TO APPLICANT(S)

Loan Number	Date of Loan	Original Amount	Current Balance	Installments (Monthly/Quarterly)	Secured by	Number of Late Payments within Last 12 months
		$	$	$ per		
		$	$	$ per		
		$	$	$ per		

12. ADDITIONAL INFORMATION WHICH MAY BE OF ASSISTANCE IN DETERMINATION OF CREDIT WORTHINESS: *Please include information on loans paid-in-full as in Item 11 above)*

13. Signature of Depository Official	14. Title	15. Date
X		

The confidentiality of the information you have furnished will be preserved except where disclosure of this information is required by applicable law. The completed form is to be transmitted directly to the lender or local processing agency and is not to be transmitted through the applicant or any other party.

VMP -47 (8908).02

VA-26-8497-a (7-80) HUD-92004-F (11-85) HB 4155.1

FIGURE A.9

REQUEST FOR VERIFICATION OF EMPLOYMENT

INSTRUCTIONS TO LENDER:
1. FILL OUT PART 1 - REQUEST
2. HAVE APPLICANT(S) SIGN EACH COPY (No Carbon Signatures)
3. FORWARD 2 COPIES CARBON INTACT TO EMPLOYER

VMP MORTGAGE FORMS - (800)521-7291

VMP-29 (9505)

Request for Verification of Employment

U. S. Department of Housing and Urban Development
Veterans Administration
USDA, Farmers Home Administration

HUD OMB Approval No. 2502-0059
VA OMB Approval No. 2900-0460
FmHA OMB Approval No. 0575-0009

Privacy Act Notice: This information is to be used by the agency collecting it in determining whether you qualify as a prospective mortgagor under its program. It will not be disclosed outside the agency except to your employer(s) for verification of employment and as required and permitted by law. You do not have to give us this information, but if you do not, your application for approval as a prospective mortgagor or borrower may be delayed or rejected. The information requested in this form is authorized by Title 38, USC, Chapter 37 (if VA); by 12 USC, Section 1701 et. seq. (if HUD/FHA); and Title 42 USC, 1471 et. seq., or 7 USC., 1921 et. seq. (if USDA, FmHA).

Public reporting burden for this collection of information is estimated to average 10 to 30 minutes per response, including the time for reviewing instructions, searching existing data sources, gathering and maintaining the data needed, and completing and reviewing the collection of information. Send comments regarding this burden estimate or any other aspect of this collection of information, including suggestions for reducing this burden, to the Reports Management Officer, Office of Information Policies and Systems, U.S. Department of Housing and Urban Development, Washington, D.C. 20410-3600 and to the Office of Management and Budget, Paperwork Reduction Project (2502-0059), Washington, D.C. 20503.

Lender or Local Processing Agency (LPA): Complete items 1 through 7. Have the applicant complete items 8 and 9. Forward the completed form directly to the employer named in item 1.
Employer: Complete either parts II and IV or parts III and IV. Return the form directly to the lender or local processing agency named in item 2 of part I.

Part I - Requested of:

Requested by:

1. Name & Address of Employer

2. Name & Address of Lender or Local Processing Agent (LPA)

3. Name & Address of Applicant

4. I certify that this verification has been sent directly to the employer and has not passed through the hands of the applicant or any other interested party.

Signature of Lender, Official of LPA, or FmHA Loan Packager

FOLD

I have applied for a mortgage loan or rehabilitation loan and stated that I am/was employed by you. My signature in the block below authorizes verification of my employment information.

X

5. Title

8. Applicant's Signature	9. Employee Identification Number	6. Date	7. HUD/FHA/CPD, VA or FmHA No.
X			

Part II - Verification of Present Employment

10. Present Position	11. Date of Employment	12. Probability of Continued Employment	13a. Salaried ☐ Yes ☐ No Commission ☐ Yes ☐ No	13b. Is overtime/bonus likely to continue? Overtime: ☐ Yes ☐ No Bonus: ☐ Yes ☐ No

14. Current Base Pay ☐ Annual ☐ Monthly ☐ Weekly ☐ Hourly
$ ____ ☐ Other (specify):

16a. Monthly Taxable Pay (for Military Personnel Only)

15a. Base Earnings Year-to-Date	Past Year	Base Pay	Career C Pay	Pro Pay
$	$	$	$	$
b. Overtime Year-to-Date	Past Year	Flight Pay	Other (specify)	
$	$	$	$	

16b. Monthly Nontaxable Pay (for Military Personnel Only)

c. Commissions Year-to-Date	Past Year	Quarters	VHA	Clothing
$	$	$	$	$
d. Bonuses Year-to-Date	Past Year	Rations	Other (specify)	
$	$	$	$	

17. **Remarks:** If paid hourly, please indicate average hours worked each week during current and past year.

FOLD

Part III - Verification of Previous Employment

18. Salary/Wage at Termination: ☐ Yearly ☐ Monthly ☐ Weekly	Base Pay $	Overtime $	Commissions $	Bonus $

19. Dates of Employment
from: ____ to: ____

20. Reasons for Leaving

21. Position Held

Part IV - Certification

Federal statutes provide severe penalties for any fraud, intentional misrepresentation, or criminal connivance or conspiracy purposed to influence the issuance of any guaranty or insurance by the VA or USDA, FmHA Administrators, or the FHA Commissioner.

22. Signature	23. Title of Employer	24. Date
X		

Previous editions may be used until supply is exhausted.
If copied, this form must be reproduced on BLUE paper.
VMP-29 (9505)

FmHA form 410-5   VA form 26-8497

VMP MORTGAGE FORMS - (800)521-7291

form HUD-92004-G (12/90)
ref. HUD Handbooks 4155.1, 4310.5

EMPLOYER-RETURN BOTH COMPLETED COPIES TO LENDER
LENDER-DETACH THIS COPY AND FILE FOR FOLLOW-UP

FIGURE A.10
GRANT DEED

RECORDING REQUESTED BY

And when recorded, mail this deed and, unless otherwise shown below, mail tax statement to:

SPACE ABOVE THIS LINE
RECORDER'S USE

Name
Address

Documentary Transfer Tax $ _____
_____ Computed on full value of property conveyed,
_____ or computed on full value less liens and
        encumbrances remaining at time of sale.

_____
Signature of Declarant or Agent determining tax. Firm Name

GRANT DEED

FOR A VALUABLE CONSIDERATION, receipt of which is hereby acknowledged,

hereby GRANT(s) to

the following described real property in the _____
County of _____ , State of _____

Assessor's Parcel No:

Dated _____   X _____

_____

_____
State of _____
County of _____

_____

On _____ before me,
_____ personally appeared

_____

_____
personally known to me (or proved to me
on the basis of satisfactory evidence) to be
the person(s) whose name(s) is/are sub-
scribed to the within instrument and
acknowledged to me that he/she/they executed the same in his/her/their authorized
capacity(ies), and that by his/her/their signa-
ture(s) on the instrument the person(s), or
the entity upon behalf of which the per-
son(s) acted, executed the instrument.

WITNESS my hand and official seal.

_____   (Space above for official notarial seal)

MAIL TAX STATEMENTS TO PARTY SHOWN ON FOLLOWING LINE;

IF NO PARTY SHOWN, MAIL AS DIRECTED ABOVE.

FIGURE A.11

HUD STATEMENT

OMB No. 2502-0265

U.S. DEPARTMENT OF HOUSING AND URBAN DEVELOPMENT

A. Settlement Statement

B. Type of Loan

1. ❏ VA 2. ❏ FmHA 3. ❏ Conv. Unins. 4. ❏ FHA 5. ❏ Conv. Ins.	6. File Number	7. Loan Number	8. Mtg. Insurance Case Number

C. NOTE: This form is furnished to give you a statement of actual settlement costs. Amounts paid to and by the settlement agent are shown. Items marked "(p.o.c)" were paid outside the closing; they are shown here for informational purposes and are not included in the totals.

D. Name and Address of Borrower	E. Name and Address of Seller	F. Name and Address of Lender

G. Property Location	H. Settlement Agent	
	Place of Settlement	I. Settlement Date

J. Summary of Borrower's Transaction		K. Summary of Seller's Transaction	
100. Gross Amount Due From Borrower		400. Gross Amount Due To Seller	
101. Contract sales price		401. Contract sales price	
102. Personal property		402. Personal property	
103. Settlement charges to borrower (1400)		403.	
104.		404.	
105.		405.	
Adjustments for items paid by seller in advance		Adjustments for items paid by seller in advance	
106.		406.	
107. County taxes		407. County taxes	
108. Assessments		408. Assessments	
109.		409.	
110.		410.	
111.		411.	
112.		412.	
120. Gross Amount Due From Borrower		420. Gross Amount Due To Seller	
200. Amounts Paid By Or In Behalf of Borrower		500. Reductions in Amount Due To Seller	
201. Deposit or earnest money		501.	
202. Principal money of new loan(s)		502. Settlement charges to seller (1400)	
203. Existing loan(s) taken subject to		503. Existing loan(s) taken subject to	
204.		504. Payoff of first mortgage loan	
205.		505. Payoff of second mortgage loan	
206.		506. Mortgage loan to Borrower	
207.		507.	
208.		508.	
209.		509.	

U.S. DEPARTMENT OF HOUSING AND URBAN DEVELOPMENT - page 2

Adjustments for items unpaid by seller		Adjustments for items unpaid by seller	
210.		510.	
211. County taxes		511. County taxes	
212. Assessments		512. Assessments	
213.		513.	
214.		514.	
215.		515.	
216.		516.	
217.		517.	
218.		518.	
219.		519.	
220. Total Paid By/For Borrower		520. Total Reduction Amount Due Seller	
300. Cash At Settlement From/To Borrower		600. Cash At Settlement To/From Seller	
301. Gross amount due from borrower (120)		601. Gross amount due to seller (420)	
302. Less amounts paid by/for borrower (220)		602. Less reductions in amount due seller (520)	
303. Cash ❏ From ❏ To Borrower		603. Cash ❏ To ❏ From Seller	

L. Settlement

700. Total Sales/Broker's Commission based on price $ @ % =		Paid from Borrower's Funds at Settlement	Paid from Seller's Funds at Settlement
Division of Commission (700) as follows			
701. $ to			
702. $ to			
703. Commission paid at Settlement			
704.			
800. Items Payable In Connection With Loan			
801. Loan Origination Fee %			
802. Loan Discount %			
803. Appraisal Fee to			
804. Credit Report to			
805. Lender's Inspection Fee			
806. Mortgage Insurance Application Fee to			
807. Assumption Fee			
808.			
809.			
810.			
811.			
900. Items Required By Lender To Be Paid In Advance			
901. Interest from to @$ /day			
902. Hazard Insurance Premium for years to			
903. Flood Ins. Premium years to			
905.			
906.			
907.			
908.			

FIGURE A.11: **HUD Statement** *(continued)* 313

U.S. DEPARTMENT OF HOUSING AND URBAN DEVELOPMENT - page 3

1000. Reserves Deposited With Lender			
1001. Hazard Insurance	months @$	per month	
1004. County property taxes	months @$	per month	
1005. Annual assessments	months @$	per month	
1006.			
1007.			
1008.			

1100. Title Charges		
1101. Settlement or closing fee to		
1102. Abstract or title search to		
1103. Title examination to		
1104. Title insurance binder to		
1105. Document preparation to		
1106. Notary fees to		
1107. Attorney's fees to		
(includes above items numbers):)		
1108. Title insurance to		
(includes above items numbers:1102, 1103, 1108, and endorsements, if any)		
1109. Lender's coverage $		
1110. Owner's coverage $		
1111.		
1112.		
1113.		
1114.		

1200. Government Recording and Transfer Charges		
1201. Recording fees: Deed $; Mortgage $; Release $		
1202. City/county tax/ stamps: Deed $; Mortgage $		
1204.		
1205.		
1206.		

1300. Additional Settlement Charges		
1301. Survey/Inspection to		
1302. Survey/Inspection to		
1303.		
1304.		
1305.		
1306.		
1307.		
1308.		
1309.		
1310.		
1311.		

1400. Total Settlement Charges (enter on 103, Section J and 502, Section K)

To the best of my knowledge, the HUD-1 Settlement Statement which I have prepared is a true and accurate account of the funds which were received and have been or will be disbursed by the undersigned as part of the settlement of this transaction.

Escrow Officer   Date

RESOURCES

The following companies and government agencies can provide additional information.

APPRAISAL INFORMATION

American Society of Appraisers
555 Herndon Parkway, Suite 125
Herndon, VA 20170
(704) 478-2228
Private organization to which appraisers belong.

Appraisal Foundation
1029 Vermont Avenue NW, Suite 900
Washington, DC 20005-3517
(202) 347-7722
Private nonprofit foundation funded by 14 separate appraisal organizations. Sets uniform standards for appraisers. Offers training as well as subscription service for "what's happening" in the appraisal field.

Appraisal Institute
875 N. Michigan Avenue, Suite 2400
Chicago, IL 60611-1980
(312) 335-4100
Issues MAI and SRA designations. Provides a list of members upon request.

CO-OP LENDING

National Cooperative Bank (NCB)
1630 Connecticut Avenue, NW
Washington, DC 20009
(202) 336-7700
Provides information on co-op lending services.

CREDIT COUNSELING

Consumer Credit Counseling
(800) 388-2227
Provides phone numbers for credit counselors in your area.

CREDIT REPORTING

Equifax
P.O. Box 740256
Atlanta, GA 30374
(800) 685-1111
Provides free credit report to consumers whose credit is denied.

TRW
P.O. Box 2350
Chatsworth, CA 91313-2350
(800) 682-7654
Provides free credit card report once a year.

HOME INSPECTIONS

American Society of Home Inspectors (ASHI)
85 W. Algonquin Road
Arlington Heights, IL 60005-4423
Provides information on home inspections.

HOME WARRANTY

National Home Warranty Association (NHWA)
20 Ellerman Road
Lake St. Louis, MO 63367
(800) 325-8144
Private organization to which warranty companies belong.

NHWA/Fischman Public Relations
1141 Lake Cook Road, Suite C-1
Deerfield, IL 60015
(847) 945-1300
> *Provides a free brochure on home warranties upon receipt of a self-addressed, stamped envelope.*

GOVERNMENT OR GOVERNMENT-ASSOCIATED AGENCIES

Fair Housing Information Clearing House
P.O. Box 6091
Rockville, MD 20850
(800) 343-3442
> *Provides free brochures on numerous aspects of home buying, fair housing and lending.*

Federal Consumer Information Center
Pueblo, CO 81009
(719) 948-3334
> *Provides free catalog of information and brochures published by the government (thousands of free listings).*

Federal Housing Administration (FHA)
Washington, DC 20410
(202) 401-0388
> *Provides information on the many FHA loans available for both home purchases and home improvements.*

Federal National Mortgage Association (Fannie Mae)
Consumer Information and Education
3900 Wisconsin Avenue, NW
Washington, DC 20016
(202) 752-7000
> *Provides free information on loans and home buying.*

Government National Mortgage Association (Ginnie Mae)
c/o HUD Consumer Information
451-7th Street SW
Washington, DC 20410
(202) 708-0926
  Provides free information on loans and home buying.

U.S. Department of Housing and Urban Development (HUD)
451 7th Street SW, Room B100
Washington, DC 20410
(800) 767-7468
Fax (202) 708-2313
  Provides free information on housing and handles complaints of discrimination. Also provides a list of local HUD offices.

U.S. Department of Veteran's Affairs (VA)
810 Vermont Avenue, NW
Washington, DC 20420
(202) 273-5400
  Provides information on VA loans or other services available for qualified veterans.

NON-ATTORNEY
CLOSING INFORMATION

Realty Guardian Title
Josh Elkes, President
(908) 780-0900
  Provides information on non-attorney closings in New Jersey and can provide names of companies in other states.

GLOSSARY

Absentee Owner: A person who owns property and resides elsewhere, usually in another community.

Abstract of Title: A summary of all conveyances, transfers, and other facts (of record) relied on as evidence of title or which would impair title of real property.

Acceleration: To hasten or speed up an event that normally would have occurred at a later date.

Acceleration Clause: A clause or provision in an agreement (note, deed of trust, mortgage) which would hasten or speed up the date of maturity (shall become all due and payable) upon the occurrence of a certain event.

Acceptance: The voluntary act of receiving something tangible or the voluntary agreement to specific terms and conditions.

Access Right: The right of a landowner to have "ingress to" and "egress from" privileges and right of way from his/her property to a public street.

Accretion: The gradual and imperceptible addition of land on a shore or riverbank by the natural action of water.

Accrue: The growing, adding to, accumulating, or causing to come into fact or existence.

Accrued Interest: All interest accumulated and unpaid to date.

Acknowledgment: A formal declaration made before an authorized official (usually notary public) by the person who has executed (signed) a document, that such execution is his or her own act and deed. In most instances, document must be acknowledged (notarized) before it can be accepted for recording.

Acquisition: The act of obtaining property; becoming an owner.

Acre: A measure of land equal to 160 rods, 4,840 square yards, 43,560 square feet, or 208.71 linear feet square.

Action: A judicial proceeding wherein one party prosecutes another for protection or enforcement of a right, the prevention or redress of a wrong, or the punishment of a public offense.

Action to Quiet Title (Quiet Title Action): A court action to remove a "cloud" from the title or to determine the actual status of the title.

Adjustable Rate Mortgage: Any real estate loan in which the interest rate varies over time according to a prescribed formula or set of conditions, usually changes in economic conditions (also known as a variable-rate mortgage).

Adjusted Basis: The cost or value of property for taxation purposes after allowable expenses are deducted.

Administrator: A male who has been appointed (by the court) to handle the affairs of an estate for a person who died intestate (without a will).

Administratrix: A female who has been appointed (by the court) to handle the affairs of an estate for a person who died intestate (without a will).

Affiant: A person who makes and subscribes to a statement under oath; makes an affidavit.

Affidavit: A written statement taken under oath before an officer of the court or a notary public.

Affidavit of Mailing: Certifies that a copy of the Substitution of Trustee has been mailed (prior to its recordation) to all parties who also would receive a copy of any recorded Notice of Default.

Affidavit of Personal Service: In lieu of the record trustee's acknowledgment or an affidavit of publication of notice, this certifies that a copy of the Substitution of Trustee was personally served on the trustee who is being replaced.

Affirmation: A written declaration under penalty of perjury.

Agency: A relationship where one person acts (with authority) on behalf of another.

Agent: Someone who has the authority to represent another (the principal).

Agreement of Sale: An agreement entered into between two or more parties for the sale and purchase of property.

AKA: Abbreviation for "also known as."

Alienate: To voluntarily transfer one's interest in real property.

Alienation: The voluntary transfer of one's real property.

Alienation Clause: A provision in a note or a security document that automatically calls for maturity of the note (all due and payable) in the event of sale or title transfer by the borrower.

Allegation: An assertion or statement of fact in a pleading that the contributing party is prepared to prove.

All-Inclusive Deed of Trust: A security document for a new encumbrance that encompasses an existing debt ("wraparound" or secures payment of a senior or prior deed of trust). Upon recordation, the all-inclusive deed of trust is junior to said existing lien: also known as a "wrap-around deed of trust" or "wraparound mortgage."

A.L.T.A.: Acronym for the American Land Title Association.

Amenities: A property's desirable or attractive features; visible and/or hidden.

Amortization: The gradual payoff of a debt through regular and scheduled payments of principal and interest over a stated period of time until paid in full.

Amount of Judgment: The dollar amount awarded as settlement by the court.

Ancillary: Something that is "in addition to" or auxiliary to the main body or subject.

And When Recorded Mail To: After recording, the document will be mailed by the county to the addressee shown.

Annexation: The addition of property to an area already established by boundaries; the joining of one property to another.

Annuity: A payment of money made annually for a specified term.

Annum: Latin, meaning a year; a period of time (per annum used to mean per year).

Ante: Latin, meaning "before."

Appearance: The presence of a party in court, either through summons or on a voluntary basis.

Appellant: One who files an appeal in a court of law.

Appraisal: An opinion or statement (written or oral) of the value of property.

Appraiser: A person who is qualified to determine the relative value of property.

Appreciation: An increase in the value of property.

Appurtenance: Anything incidental to, belonging to, or attached to land and therefore considered a part of the property (whether it is real property or a burden such as a covenant or an easement).

Appurtenant: Incidental to, belonging to, or attached to.

Arbitrary Map: An unofficial parcel map made by a title company for its own convenience in identifying parcels of land; sometimes known as arb map.

Arbitrator: An impartial person chosen by the parties in a dispute to resolve and make a final determination of the issues.

Assessed Value: Value of property for taxation purposes as determined by the tax assessor.

Assessments: Specific and special taxes (in addition to normal taxes) imposed on real property to pay for public improvements within a specific geographical area.

Assessor: The county official who determines the value of property for taxation purposes.

Assessor's Parcel Number (APN): Number assigned by the county assessor; in some counties, it must appear on the document as a prerequisite to recording.

Assets: Any property (real or personal) with value.

Assign: To transfer all of one's interest in property.

Assignee: The person to whom property interest has been assigned or transferred.

Assignor: The person who is transferring or assigning an interest in property.

Assumpsit: A promise or undertaking (expressed or implied, oral or written) to do an act or make a payment.

Assumption Agreement: An agreement to assume or take responsibility for a debt or obligation that was contracted originally by another person.

Assumption Fee: The fee charged by a lender when a buyer assumes or takes responsibility for an existing loan.

Assumption of Loan (Mortgage or Deed of Trust): An agreement wherein the buyer assumes or takes responsibility (becomes liable) for payment of an existing note secured by a mortgage or deed of trust.

ATA Title Policy: An American Title Association insurance policy that has greater coverage than a standard policy because it includes unrecorded liens and encumbrances.

Attachment: A judicial process wherein a creditor obtains a lien upon property prior to adjudication of the debt.

Attest: To bear witness to the execution of a document, to affirm as true.

Attestation Clause: A clause within a deed stating that the subscribing persons are witnesses-in-fact.

Attorn: The acceptance and acknowledgment of a new landlord.

Attorney-in-Fact: Identifies the party(s) (attorney-in-fact) designated to act on behalf of the principal as specified in a Power of Attorney. Identifies the party(s) whose specific authority is being revoked in the Revocation of Power of Attorney.

Authorization: The official statement of approval for the attorney-in-fact to act for the principal.

Avulsion: The sudden tearing away of land by the violent action of river or other watercourse; the abrupt change in the course of a waterbed that forms a boundary between two parcels of land, resulting in a change of land for each parcel (a gain for one and a loss for the other).

Balance Sheet: A statement of financial condition showing assets, liabilities, and net worth as of a specific time.

Balloon Payment: Any payment that is greater than twice the amount of the normal and periodic payment. Generally used to refer to the final payment of a note with an advanced due date.

Bankruptcy: A legal process in the U.S. District Court wherein assets of the debtor are liquidated to pay off the claims of his or her creditors.

Base Lines: Imaginary lines running east to west that intersect meridians (imaginary lines between the North and South poles) to form a starting point for the survey or measurement of land.

Basis: Usually the property owner's original cost, plus capital improvements, less depreciation, computed for income tax purposes according to one of many possible formulas. Also known as book value.

Benchmark: A durable and reliable location marker used by land surveyors.

Beneficiary: Generally, one who is in receipt of benefit, profit, or advantage. Used to identify the party to whom the trustor is obligated (beneficiary)—usually the lender or the person intended to benefit from a trust.

Beneficiary Information — Notice of Default: The name, address, and phone number of the beneficiary who should be contacted to determine the amount necessary to reinstate or pay off the deed of trust in foreclosure.

Beneficiary Receives Damage Award: In the event the property or a portion of the property is condemned for public use, any award of damages connected with such action is assigned (by the trustor) to the beneficiary, who may apply said award to any indebtedness secured or, at beneficiary's option, may release the entire award, or a portion thereof, to the trustor.

Beneficiary's Demand: Usually the full payment (remaining balance including any accrued interest charges) required by a beneficiary (under a deed of trust) before authorizing a reconveyance.

Beneficiary's Statement: Statement by the beneficiary as to the principal balance due on a promissory note secured by a deed of trust. It also may contain other pertinent loan information. Also known as bene statement or offset statement.

Beneficiary Under the Deed or Trust: Identifies the present beneficiary on the Substitution of Trustee document.

Bequeath: The act of making a gift of personal property through a will.

Bilateral Contract: An agreement wherein promises are exchanged between the two parties.

Bill of Sale: A written instrument that transfers title of personal property from one person to another.

Binder: Memorandum of agreement to issue insurance that provides temporary coverage until the complete and formal policy can be issued; something that obligates or constrains the bound individual.

Blanket Deed of Trust or Mortgage: A security document that binds more than one parcel of land as the security for the loan obligation.

Blanket Policy: An insurance policy covering an entire subdivision for which individual policies are issued on separate parcels.

Blighted Area: A neighborhood in which the property values are declining due to economic or natural forces such as inharmonious property usages, rapidly depreciating buildings, and/or an influx of "undesirable inhabitants."

Body of Document: Generally, the main or operative text of provisions within a legal instrument.

Bona: Latin, meaning "good," "virtuous."

Bona Fide: Made in good faith.

Bona Fide Purchaser: A person who purchases in good faith for a valuable consideration and has no notice of outstanding rights or claims of any third-party members.

Bond: A written agreement with sureties that guarantees faithful performance of acts or duties, including the payment of a certain sum of money.

Bonded Debt: A debt contracted under the obligation of a bond.

Breach: The breaking of a law, contract, or duty by omission or commission.

Brief: A written argument of legal points used by an attorney to convey to the court the essential facts of his or her client's case.

Broker: A person who brings parties together and assists in negotiating contracts between them for a commission or fee.

Building Code: A set of regulations setting forth minimum building construction standards in a city, county, or state.

Building Contract: An agreement for the construction or improvement of a structure.

Building Lines: Imaginary lines established by ordinance or by statute beyond which the building of structures is not permitted; also known as setback lines.

Building Restrictions: Zoning ordinances and regulatory laws that require that construction be protective of people's health and safety.

By-Law: A standing rule governing the regulation of a corporation's or society's internal affairs.

Call: To require payment of loaned money on demand.

Capacity: A person's capability or qualifications to enter into agreements —by being competent, of sound mind or legal age.

Capita: Latin, meaning "heads" or "persons," as in "per capita" (per person).

Capital Gain: Profit gained from the increase in value of a capital asset.

Capitalization: The process of amassing the funds necessary to purchase a property. Also, a means of appraising that determines the value of property by estimating net annual income and dividing by a capitalization rate; the "cap rate" usually is determined from current market prices.

Capital Loss: Loss resulting from the sale of an asset for a dollar amount below its purchase price or adjusted basis.

Caption: Heading or introduction to the main body of document that identifies the parties of interest.

Carryback: Usually known as seller carryback; seller acts as a lender of purchase money and holds or carries back a loan for the purchaser.

Case Number: The case number as assigned by the court. Some documents also contain an explanation of the purpose of the document, which, for all practical purposes, becomes the title for the document.

Cause (of Action): A claim in law with sufficient facts to demand judicial attention; an action or suit.

Cautionary Notes — Rights in Foreclosure: Notations within a document regarding foreclosure due to default, rights to reinstate, rights to stop foreclosure, and the amount necessary to reinstate the obligations secured by the deed of trust under foreclosure.

Cautionary Note — Seek Legal Counsel: Note to all parties that legal rights and duties are established through the execution of this contract, and, therefore, all parties are advised to seek independent legal counsel.

Cautionary Note — Subordination Agreement: Note to the subordinating party as to the effect of the Subordination Agreement on his or her security interest (becomes subject to and of lower priority than the new Deed of Trust).

Caveat: Latin, meaning "let him beware."

Caveat Emptor: Latin, meaning "let the buyer beware;" the basic rule of commerce and law; the purchaser buys at his or her own risk.

Certificate of Sale: Document issued as evidence of purchaser's acquisition of legal title at a judicial sale, subject to redemption rights, if any exist.

Certificate of Title: Document issued as evidence of landownership according to examination of record title.

Certification: A certification by a deputy of the clerk of the Superior Court that the decree is a full, true, and correct copy of the original on file in the clerk's office. The date of filing and entering of the document in the judgment books is also shown (a requirement for recordation).

Chain of Title: The chronological list of recorded documents affecting title to a specific parcel of real property.

Change of Venue: The movement of a trial from one judicial jurisdiction to another.

Character of the Property: Includes a description of the nature or character of the property being homesteaded. Examples of character would include: nature of residence (single family or multiresidential), type of construction (stucco, brick, frame), and so on.

Chattel: Any tangible, movable, personal property article.

Chattel Mortgage: An obsolete name for a mortgage or security interest in personal property.

Chattel Real: An interest in real property that is less than a freehold or fee interest (estate at sufferance, and so on.)

Chose: A thing either presently possessed or claimed as a possession.

Chose in Action: A claim or debt of which recovery may be made in a lawsuit.

Civil Law: Roman law now used in most Western European states; also distinguishes noncriminal (civil) and criminal law.

Claim: The assertion of a right to money or property.

Class Action: A lawsuit wherein the plaintiff is bringing suit on behalf of all persons in similar situations.

Clear Title: A title that is free from any encumbrance, obstruction, or limitation that would "cloud the title."

Closing: Closing of escrow; the final act of a transaction wherein papers are signed, monies are exchanged, and the title is transferred.

Closing Costs: The expenses incurred in a real estate transaction including costs or title examination, title insurance, attorney's fees, lender's service charges, documentary transfer tax, and so on.

Cloud of Title: An outstanding claim of title that has yet to be proven invalid.

Coadministrator: One of two or more administrators.

Code: A systematic compilation or collection of laws on a specified subject, organized for clarity and understanding.

Codicil: An instrument that amends a will without revoking it. A codicil may add to, enlarge, alter, restrict, qualify, and so on.

Coexecutor: One of two or more executors.

Collateral: The property secured as a security interest for a debt.

Collateral Assignment: The transfer of interest in personal property for security reasons.

Collusion: An attempt by two or more people to defraud another of his or her rights.

Color of Title: Lending the appearance of title; an instrument that appears to pass title when, in effect, there is no legal basis for said title transfer.

Commercial Acre: In land development terms, that net portion of an acre remaining after deducting areas devoted to streets, sidewalks, and the like.

Commissioner's Deed: A deed executed by a court-appointed official in consummation of a court-ordered sale.

Commitment: Something given in trust; a pledge, promise, a firm agreement. A title insurer's contractual obligation to insure title to real property.

Common Law: The English system of jurisprudence, which is based on judicial precedent rather than legislative enactments; therefore, it is generally derived from principles rather than rules.

Community Property: Property acquired after marriage by either party (husband or wife), other than by gift or by inheritance.

Competent: The capacity to reason, understand, and do a certain thing; therefore, the capacity to enter into a contract with legal basis.

Completion Bond: A bond posted by a contractor as a guarantee that he or she will complete a project satisfactorily and it will be free of any liens.

Composition: Negotiated agreement between a debtor and creditors wherein the creditors each agree to mutually accept a certain percentage less than is due or an altered payment schedule and/or structure.

Comprehensive Coverage: An insurance policy that covers a range of contingencies.

Conclusive Presumption: A conclusion drawn by a court of law from a set of facts that cannot be overcome by contrary proof.

Concurrent: To run together, in conjunction with, as in concurrent closing of a new deed of trust and a subordination agreement; must record together.

Condemnation: Under the laws of eminent domain, a municipality takes over private property for public use. Also: Result of official determination that a building is unfit for human habitation.

Condemnation Guarantee: A document executed as evidence of title issued to a governmental agency naming defendants in an eminent domain proceeding.

Condition: A qualification or restriction attached to the conveyance of property wherein it is predetermined that upon the occurrence of a specified event, an estate shall commence, enlarge, or be defeated.

Conditional Sales Contract: Also known as a contract of sale or a land-sales contract; title remains in the name of the vendor (seller) until the vendee (buyer) fulfills all the conditions of the contract.

Condition Precedent: A condition wherein an act or event must exist or occur before a right accrues or an estate vests.

Condition Subsequent: A condition that defeats a previously vested estate or accrued right.

Condominium: Fee ownership of an individual unit (within the confines of the perimeter walls) and tenants-in-common ownership in all the underlying fees and in the common building and grounds designated for use for all the unit owners.

Confirmation of Sale: Court approval of a sale through a personal representative, guardian, or conservator.

Congressional Grant: A grant of public land or the United States via an act of Congress.

Conservatee: A person without capacity to care for self and/or property and for whom the probate court has appointed a conservator.

Conservator: A person appointed by the probate court to handle the affairs (take care of person and/or property) of a conservatee.

Consideration: Something of value that is given in return for a specific performance or a promise of performance by another in the formation of a contract.

Constructive: That which is not actual but is accepted in law as if it actually were real; inferred or implied.

Constructive Notice: Public notice given by public records.

Constructive Trust: A trust imposed by law to prevent unjust enrichment or to redress a wrong.

Contiguous: That which is bordering, touching, adjacent to.

Contingency: An item in a contract dependent on a specific condition for its fulfillment.

Contingent: That which is dependent on a future event that may never occur.

Contingent Beneficiary: A person who may or may not share in an estate or trust based on the occurrence of a specific yet uncertain event.

Contingent Estate: An interest in land that may or may not begin at some time in the future based on the occurrence of a specific yet uncertain event.

Contingent Interest: An interest in an estate that may or may not occur at some time in the future based on the occurrence of a specific yet uncertain event.

Contract: A promise, or a set of promises; an agreement to do or not to do certain things, as between two or more parties.

Contract of Sale: Also known as a conditional sales contract and a land contract of sales; title remains in the name of the vendor (seller) until the vendee (buyer) fulfills certain conditions of the contract.

Convey: To transfer title to property from one person to another.

Conveyance: A written document that transfers title to property from one person to another.

Co-Owner — Pertinent Information: Sets forth the full name and address of anyone holding title to the property as co-owner with the person giving notice. This applies only if title is held as joint tenants or tenants-in-common. If there are no co-owners, the word "none" should be inserted.

Corporate Seal: The purpose of a seal is to attest in a formal manner the execution of a document; thus a corporate seal attests said execution by the corporation.

Corporation: An artificial being created by law and endowed with certain rights, privileges, and duties of natural person and yet is entirely separate and distinct from the individuals who compose it. A corporation has the unique quality of continuous existence or succession.

Corporeal Hereditaments: Anything that can be inherited, including real or personal property or a combination of both.

Cost: The actual purchase price paid for a property.

Cotenancy: Ownership interests by two or more persons.

Cotrustee: One of two or more trustees.

Counteroffer: A new offer as to price, terms, and/or conditions made in reply to and supersedes a prior offer.

County Recorder's Stamps: The large stamp reflects the recording reference of the document and refers to the names of the county and the county recorder. The smaller stamps are placed on the document by the clerk in the county recorder's office.

Courses and Distances: Description of land measurement, angles, and parameters by metes and bounds.

Court Identification: Identifies the court and the judicial district number where the court case was conducted.

Court Seal: The official seal of the court handling the case is placed over the date of issuance of the abstract.

Covenant: To enter into a formal agreement to do or not to do a certain thing; a promise.

Coverage: Items insured under a policy. "Additional coverage" refers to extra premiums charged where extraordinary risk or labor is involved in issuance of a policy.

Creditor: One to whom a debt is owed; a person who grants credit.

Credit Report: A report on the credit history of a person or business.

Custody: The personal control, care, guarding, inspection, preservation, and security of a property or person under the delegated authority and responsibility of the custodian.

Cut Out: A parcel or a portion of a property taken or "cut out" from a larger parcel on an arbitrary map.

Damages: The amount of money ordered by a court to be paid to a person who sustained an injury, either to property, person, or relative rights, through the actions or failures to act of another.

Date Down: The date through which an examination of title is to be conducted.

Date of Approval: Date the decree is prepared and also usually the date of approval by the judge of the Superior Court.

Date of Completion: The actual date of completion to the improvement work done on the property. In order to be valid, the Notice of Completion must be recorded within ten days of the date of actual completion.

Date of Delivery: Date on which a document was officially received.

Date of Entry: The date on which the judgment was entered in the judgment books of the court.

Date of Execution: Usually the date on which the document is executed (signed); however, quite often it is the date on which it is prepared (drawn).

Date of Issuance of Abstract: Specifies the date on which the abstract of the judgment was executed by the court.

Debit: A charge or debt.

Debtor: Someone who owes a debt or is liable for a claim.

Debt Service: The amount of money periodically required as payments to amortize.

Decedent: A deceased person.

Declarants: Identifies the individuals who are recording the Declaration of Homestead as well as the name of the head of the family and a mention of other family members. A statement is included that identifies the city and county where the property is located and that the person or persons are now residing on the premises on which the homestead is being declared.

Declarants Abandoning: Identifies the original declarants who recorded the Declaration of Homestead, certifies their relationship (husband and wife, etc.), and states that they do hereby abandon the homestead of the subject property.

Declaration: At common law, the formal document that sets forth the plaintiff's cause of action.

Declaration of Homestead: A legal, written and recorded document that provides the homesteader certain protections against a forced sale of a primary residence.

Declaration of Trust: A written document wherein a person acknowledges that he or she holds title to the subject property (as trustee) for the benefit of someone else (beneficiary).

Decree: A judicial decision.

Decree of Distribution: A judicial decision of probate court that distributes the assets of the deceased to the proper persons (distributees).

Dedication: Donation of private property (by the landowner) to a municipality for public usage.

Deed: A written document that transfers the interest in property from one person to another.

Deed in Lieu of Foreclosure: The conveying of title to a mortgage or beneficiary in order to prevent foreclosure.

Deed of Trust: A security document used to transfer "bare legal" title from the trustor (borrower) to the trustee (a neutral party, usually a corporation) to be held in trust for the benefit of the beneficiary (lender) until the trustor completes performance of an obligation (monetary or otherwise).

Deed of Trust — Pertinent Information: Cross-reference information regarding the deed of trust in question. It includes: recording reference, date of execution, names of original trustor and beneficiary, and the county in which said deed of trust was recorded. This same basic identification information is listed whenever any of the following notices are filed: request for notice; notice of default; notice of recession; assignment of deed of trust.

Deed Restrictions: Limitations on the use of real estate written into the deed.

De Facto: Latin, meaning "in fact," "in reality," "actually."

Default: Anything wrongful; failure to discharge a duty; failure in the performance of an obligation.

Default/Breach Statement: Statement containing information regarding the specifics of the obligation that has been placed into default.

Default Judgment: A judgment entered against a defendant who failed to respond to the plaintiff's action or failed to appear in court.

Defeasance: An instrument that negates or reverses the effectiveness of another document.

Defeasance Clause: A provision in a deed of trust of mortgage that allows the trustor/mortgagor to redeem the title to the subject property upon satisfaction of the obligation that it secures.

Defeasible: Subject to being defeated, annulled, or revoked if certain conditions are not met.

Defeat: To make null and void.

Defective Title: A title that is unmarketable; a title that cannot be transferred in its present condition.

Defendant: The party against whom the court action was initiated; the party being sued.

Deferred Payments: Payments that are extended over a period of time or put off until some date in the future.

Deficiency Judgment: A personal judgment against a debtor for the difference between the amount owed and the amount received in a foreclosure.

Definition of Obligation: Defines the trustor's obligation. Since the obligation to be performed is usually the payment of a promissory note, the amount is set forth here.

Defunct: No longer in effect or use; dead.

De Jure: Latin, meaning "by right," "lawful and legitimate."

Demand: A term used in escrow to identify the consideration payoff required to execute a reconveyance, relinquishment of an interest, or a right to property.

Demand of Claimant: Specifies the total amount owing to the claimant along with any interest rate that might be assigned to the debt if it is being paid through an installment arrangement.

Demurrer: A formal allegation that the pleadings of the opponent are not legally sufficient to allow the case to proceed any further.

Deponent: A witness, one who gives information under oath.

Deposition: Out-of-court question-and-answer testimony (usually held before court proceedings) taken under oath.

Depository Statement: Escrow instructions directing the usage and flow of documents, instruments, or property.

Deposit Receipt: A written document used to secure a firm offer to purchase property and provide a receipt for the buyer's earnest money; also known as a purchase agreement or purchase offer.

Depreciation: A decline in the value of a property.

Deraign: To dispute or contest a claim; to trace; to prove.

Dereliction: The recession of waters of the sea, a navigable river, or stream wherein the land that was previously covered by water is now dry.

Descent: The orderly manner of title succession of an intestate decedent.

Determinable Fee: An interest in property that may last forever; however, if certain contingencies are not satisfied, title automatically terminates. Also known as fee simple determinable.

Devise: A gift of real property by a will.

Devisee: A person who receives a gift of real property by a will.

Dictum: A judicial opinion that is not necessary for the decision of the case.

Diluvian: The gradual washing away and loss of soil along the banks of a river.

Discharge Statement: A statement indicating that the obligation secured by mortgage has been fully paid; therefore the mortgage is satisfied and discharged (released).

Divestiture: A remedy wherein the court orders the offending party to rid itself of rights or title to property or assets prior to the time when it would normally do so.

Divisa: A recognized boundary.

Documentary Transfer Tax: Tax levied by the county (sometimes also by the city) on the transfer of title of real property.

Domicile: The fixed and permanent home of a person.

Domiciliary Administrator: A probate court–appointed administrator of a decedent's domicile.

Dominant Tenement: The land benefited by an appurtenant easement; an estate whose owners are entitled to the beneficial use or another property.

Dona: A gift.

Donee: A person who receives a gift.

Donor: A person who gives a gift.

Down Payment: The portion of the purchase price of a home that the buyer pays in cash and does not finance.

Draft: A written order directing a person other than the maker (of the draft) to pay a specified amount of money to a named person.

Dragnet Clause: A provision in a security document making it applicable to all past and present obligations between a debtor and creditor.

Due Date: Fixed time for a payment.

Due-on-Sale Clause: A provision in a security document calling for the automatic maturity (note is all due and payable) in the event of sale or transfer of title.

Durable Power of Attorney: A power of attorney that will exist for an indefinite period of time; one where the duration is not limited.

Earnest Money: Something of value given as part of the purchase price to show "good faith" and to secure an agreement.

Easement: A limited right or interest in the land of another entitling the holder to some use, privilege, or benefit.

Easement Appurtenant: A "pure easement" created for the benefit of and attaching to a parcel of land known as the dominant tenement.

Easement in Gross: An easement created for the benefit of a person rather than for a parcel of land; therefore, often it is not assignable or inheritable.

Economic Life: The time remaining during which a property is expected to yield a return on an investment or to be used profitably.

Economic Obsolescence: A loss in value of property due to such causes as high unemployment, unfavorable zoning, deteriorating neighborhood, and so on.

Economic Rent: The estimated income that a property should generate in the current rental market, based on the rent for comparable properties.

Effective Age: The age assigned to a building by an appraiser, based on the physical condition of the property rather than its chronological age.

Egress: The means of exiting from a property.

Ejectment: Legal action brought about by one claiming a right to possess real property against the one who currently possesses it.

Eminent Domain: The legal right and procedures for a municipality to take title and possession of private property for public use.

Emptor: Latin, meaning "buyer."

Encroachment: The unlawful extension of an improvement onto the land owned by another.

Encumber: To place a legal claim on a property.

Encumbrance: A right, interest in, or legal liability upon land limiting the fee simple title without hindering or affecting its sale or transfer.

Endorsement: The placing of a signature on the back of a check, bill, or promissory note in order to transfer to another party the value represented on the face of the instrument.

Enfeoff: The conveyance of fee title to land; sometimes used on deeds as the "granting" verbiage.

Entirety: The ownership of property (real or personal) by a husband and wife (unity of one) wherein neither party is allowed to alienate any part of the property without the consent of the other.

Equal Credit Opportunity Act (ECOA): A federal law that prohibits lenders from denying mortgages on the basis of the borrower's race, color, religion, national origin, age, sex, marital status, or receipt of income from public assistance programs.

Equitable Lien: A lien recognized in a court of equity.

Equitable Owner: One who has pledged property as security for a debt while retaining the right to use and enjoy the property.

Equitable Title: Ownership of property that is recognized by a court of equity; the right to acquire legal title.

Equity: Natural right or justice based on ethics and morals: also commonly used to denote the difference between the value of property and the amount owed on the property.

Equity of Redemption: The right of the judgment debtor to redeem property (within specific guidelines) after a judicial sale.

Equity Sharing: A type of purchase wherein two or more parties (absentee investor-owner and owner-occupant) share in the equity and appreciation of the property.

Erosion: The gradual eating away of soil by natural causes.

Escalator Clause: A provision in a contract or lease that provides for an upward or downward adjustment of price, costs, rents, expenses, prorations, and so on, based on factors beyond the control of the parties.

Escheat: The reversion of title to the state, usually upon death of a person without heirs; however, can also be by virtue of a breach of condition.

Escrow: A transaction wherein an impartial third party (escrow agent) acts as agent to both parties (seller/buyer—lender/borrower, etc.) acting only under instructions in delivering papers, drawing and/or recording documents, and disbursing funds.

Estate: The degree, quantity, nature, and extent of a person's interest and/or ownership in real property.

Estate at Will: The right of possession by a tenant for an indefinite time that is terminable upon notice by either landlord or tenant.

Estate for Life: An estate that is measured in time by the uncertain duration of a specific person's lifetime.

Estate for Years: An estate that is created and is measured for a certain, definite, and fixed period of time.

Estate of Inheritance: A freehold estate of indefinite duration, of absolute inheritance to particular heirs (free of any condition, limitations or restrictions); fee simple.

Estate Tax: A tax on the transfer of title to a decedent's property rather than a tax on the property itself.

Estoppel: A bar (preclusion) that prevents a person from denying the truth of a fact (or an action of a right) that already has become settled in judicial proceedings.

Et Al.: Latin; abbreviation for "and others."

Et Con.: Latin; abbreviation for "and husband."

Et Seq.: Latin; abbreviation for "and the following."

Et Ux.: Latin; abbreviation for "and wife."

Examination of Title: The process of determining the vesting, encumbrances, and liens upon a title.

Examiner: A person who analyzes a chain of title to land and offers an opinion on said chain of title.

Exception: Allowance for a deduction, subtraction, or exclusion from the main body or group.

Exchange Agreement: A contract for the exchanging of title and equity positions in properties, as compared to selling and buying.

Exclusive Agency Agreement: A written agreement between an owner and an agent that gives the agent the right to sell a property within a specified period of time, while allowing the owner the right to sell the property him- or herself without paying the agent a commission.

Exclusive Right to Sell: A written agreement between an owner and a broker that gives the broker the exclusive right to sell the property. If the property is sold to anyone during the specified listing period, the broker is entitled to receive the specified commission.

Exculpatory Clause: A contract provision that absolves a party from liability.

Execute: To perform that which is required in order to have and demonstrate completion or validity.

Executed: Complete, fully performed, nothing unfulfilled.

Execution Proceedings: Judicial enforcement of a money judgment wherein the debtor's property is seized and sold.

Executor: A male who is appointed by a testator (one who dies leaving a will) to handle the affairs of the testator's estate.

Executory: An agreement or contract that is contingent upon the occurrence of a specific event(s) or performance of some act(s) before it is fully accomplished or completed.

Executrix: A female who is appointed by a testator (one who dies leaving a will) to handle the affairs of the testator's estate.

Exemption: Something that is set aside or immune from a burden or obligation.

Ex Officio: Latin, meaning "from the office of" or "by virtue of the office."

Expediente: A Spanish or Mexican land grant file.

Ex Post Facto: Latin, meaning "after the fact" (event); when an event or decision is affected by something that occurs after the first event is finished.

Expropriate: To take land or other property from a property owner for public use.

Extension Agreement: A mutual agreement that grants additional time for the completion of performance.

Facsimile: An exact copy of the original.

Facto: Latin, meaning "in fact," "by an accomplishment/deed."

Fair Credit Reporting Act: A consumer protection law that sets a procedure for correcting mistakes on one's credit record.

False Personation: The unauthorized assumption of another's identity for fraudulent purposes.

Federal Housing Administration: FHA. A federal agency that sets guidelines and insures loans on residential housing.

Fee: An estate of inheritance; one in which ownership can be sold or devised to heirs.

Fee Simple: Absolute ownership without limitations, conditions, or restrictions burdening particular heirs.

Fee Simple Absolute: The clearest, most recognized estate in land without any limitations.

Fee Simple Defeasible: A fee simple estate subject to being defeated, annulled, or revoked if certain conditions are met or not met.

Femme Sole: An unmarried woman.

Femme Covert: A married woman.

Fictitious: Artificial or contrived; that which is false, feigned, or pretended.

Fictitious Deed of Trust: A deed or trust that is recorded to have "on record" all the general terms and conditions that never change during the life of this specific document. It generally represents the second page of a deed of trust and eliminates the unnecessary repetitious recording of this page as it can be referred to by recording reference identification.

Fictitious Name: A name created for business or other usage and not the true name of the owner or individual.

Fiduciary: One who holds a position of trust and confidence to act primarily for the benefit of another in matters of responsibility.

Final Decree: The final and complete judicial decision.

Financing Statement: A personal property security instrument that replaced the chattel mortgage (as a security instrument) upon the adoption of the Uniform Commercial Code.

Fixed Expense: The ongoing and normally stable charges or costs required to own or have possession of a property: rent, insurance, taxes, maintenance, and the like.

Fixed-Rate Mortgage: A mortgage in which the interest rate does not change during the term of the loan.

Fixture: Property that was originally personal in nature but converted to a real property category due to the intention and manner in which it was affixed to real property.

For a Valuable Consideration: A statement that reflects that money or some legal consideration is being given in exchange for the property. (This is a holdover from earlier times and is no longer necessary in a voluntary conveyance.)

Foreclosure: The nonvoluntary procedure to sell real property according to the terms and conditions of the deed of trust that identified the subject property as security for a lien.

Foreclosure Sale: The nonvoluntary selling of property (in default) that was used as security for a lien.

Forfeiture: The loss of a right, title, or interest in property as a result of neglect of a duty or nonperformance of an obligation.

Franchise: A privilege of a public nature conferred on an individual or group by a governmental grant; also, the right granted by a company to a dealer (franchisee) to conduct business under the company name within certain territory.

Fraud: Intentional deception with the intent to gain advantage, which results in injury to another.

Free and Clear: Title to real property that is unencumbered by liens.

Freehold Estate: An estate of indefinite duration; a fee or life estate.

Functional Obsolescence: A loss of value in property due to conditions regarding the property itself: style, age, size, poor floor plan, outdated heating/air conditioning, and so on.

Future Interest: An estate in real property that provides for the benefits of possession and enjoyment at some future date.

Garnishment: The process of attaching money or goods that are due a defendant and yet in the hands of a third party.

General Index: Matters affecting title to land that are maintained by a title company according to names of individuals and entities instead of by property description.

General Partner: The managing partner of a limited partnership or all partners in a general partnership; the one(s) who is ultimately liable for all obligations of the partnership.

General Plan Restrictions: Restrictions (attached to the grant deed) on the development and usage of all lots within a subdivision.

Gift: A voluntary transfer of property without compensation received in return.

Good Faith: Clear intention to fulfill one's obligations; a total absence of any intention to seek unfair advantage or to defraud another.

Gore: A small triangular piece of land.

Graduated Lease: A lease with provisions for changing and varying rental rates according to a time structure and/or other conditions.

Graduated Payment Plan: GPM. A fixed-rate, fixed-term mortgage that provides for reduced payments in the beginning year, with payments increasing to a set level in later years.

Grant: The operative word or conveyance in a grant deed; in general, the transfer of interest in real property by deed.

Grant Deed: A voluntary written instrument transferring title to real property.

Grantee: The party buying or receiving the property. The grantee's status (husband and wife, etc.) and legal method of acquiring title (joint tenants, tenants in common, etc.) comprises the vesting. In a public auction such as a trustee's sale or a tax sale, the successful bidder at said sale is the grantee.

Grantor: The party selling or transferring the interest in property.

Grants Are Condition Subsequent: Specific Use: In the land contract of sale, one provision specifies certain granting to occur automatically upon the completion of specified events (i.e., upon the recordation of a deed of full reconveyance, the vendor will grant title to the vendee).

Gross Income: Total income before any expenses are deducted.

Guaranteed Loan: A loan backed by a guarantee from a party other than the borrower.

Guarantee of Title: Evidence of title based solely on matters of public record.

Guardian: A person appointed by probate court to care for and be responsible for the person and/or property of a minor or incompetent person.

Habendum Clause: A clarifying clause in a deed that names the grantee and defines the limits of the estate to be granted; the clause begins with the wording "to have and to hold . . . "

Head of Household: One who is responsible for dependents; not necessarily a married person.

Heir: A person entitled by law to inherit property of a decedent who dies either testate or intestate.

Heir Apparent: The person who has the right to inheritance providing that he or she lives longer than the ancestor.

Hereditaments: Includes anything that can be inherited: real, personal, or mixed property.

Hereditary Succession: The passing of title according to the laws of descent.

Highest and Best Use: An appraisal term indicating the most productive and logical usage of land.

Holder in Due Course: One who has taken a check, note, or bill of exchange in good faith and for value, without notice that it is overdue or has been dishonored, and free of any claims to it or defenses against it by any person.

Holding: Possession of property to which one has legal title.

Holding Agreement: A form of trust where the trustee holds legal title to real property without active control or management responsibilities.

Holographic Will: A will entirely written, dated, and signed in the handwriting of the testator.

Homestead: The primary residence of a declarant who has filed a Declaration of Homestead that offers protection (within specific guidelines) against a forced sale.

Homestead — Pertinent Information: Sets forth the recording reference and the county where the Declaration of Homestead (which is being abandoned) was recorded.

Hostile Possession: Possession of real property without permission (of the owner in title) coupled with a claim, express or implied, of ownership.

HUD: The U.S. Department of Housing and Urban Development.

Hypothecate: To pledge property as security for a debt without giving up possession of the property.

Idem Sonans: Latin, meaning "items the same." The doctrine that if two names sound alike, any slight variance in spelling is immaterial, i.e. Lawrence and Lawrance.

Implied: Not explicitly written or stated. To say or address indirectly.

Impound Account: An account into which a borrower deposits periodic payments toward annual taxes and/or hazard insurance, usually at the insistence of the lender.

Improved Real Estate: Land upon which buildings and/or other improvements have been made.

Improvement: Any development of land or buildings.

Incapacity: The quality or status of being unable to care or act for oneself; incompetence.

Inchoate: Something that is incomplete, unfinished, not perfect.

Income and Expense Statements: An itemized statement of income received from a property and the expenses incurred in its operation.

Income Property: Property owned or purchased for the generation of income.

Incompetent: A person deemed by law incapable of caring for or managing him- or herself and/or property.

Incorporate: To combine together to form a whole; to incorporate writings together; to form a corporation.

Incorporeal: That which is intangible, without a physical existence.

Indefeasible: An estate that cannot be defeated or altered by any condition.

Indemnify: To secure against a loss or damage that may occur in the future, or to provide compensation for a loss already suffered.

Indemnity: Compensation that is given for a loss sustained.

Indemnity Agreement: An obligation to compensate. Also known as a hold harmless agreement. An agreement whereby one party agrees to compensate the other party for specific potential losses the second party sustains.

Indenture: A deed between two parties conveying an interest in real property wherein both parties assume obligations.

Independent Contractor: One who contracts to do a specific act and who is responsible to his or her employer only as to the results.

Indorsement: Signature written on back of an instrument with the intent and effect to transfer the right to the instrument to another; also, a rider attached to an insurance policy expanding or limiting the coverage. See *endorsement.*

In Esse: Latin; abbreviation of *id est*: "that is to say."

In Essee: Latin, meaning "alive, in being."

In Fee: Fee simple estate; absolute ownership in an estate in land.

Inference: A proposition or deduction based on the given facts; usually is less than certainty; however, may be sufficient to support a finding of fact.

Ingress and Egress: The entering upon and departure from, such as a landowner's physical right to enter and exit onto a public street; also contractual, such as the right of a lessee to enter and leave a leasehold.

Inherit: To take as an heir, originally by law of descent (intestate); however, modern usage includes devise (testate).

Inheritance Tax: A tax imposed on the right to receive property from a decedent, not a tax on the property itself.

Injunction: A court order restraining one or more parties from doing an act deemed unjust to the rights of some other party.

In Personam: Latin, meaning "against the person"; an action against the person.

In Propia Persona: Latin, meaning "in his own person; himself." Abbreviated as "pro per."

In Re: Latin, meaning "in the matter of"; usually used in legal proceedings where there is no opponent.

In Rem: Latin, meaning "against a thing/property"; signifies actions that are against property rather than actions against a person.

Insolvent: A situation where liabilities exceed assets; inability to pay one's debts: impoverished.

Installment Loan: A loan that requires periodic payments until both principal and interest are completely paid.

Installment Sales Contract: An agreement of purchase wherein the purchase price is paid in specific and timely installments and the title is not transferred until the final payment.

Institutional Lenders: Banks, savings and loans, and insurance companies that provide real estate loans.

Instrument: A formal, legal, and written document that records an act or agreement.

Insurable Interest: A sufficient interest in property so that loss or damage to said property would create a financial loss to the owner.

Intangible Property: Property that does not have value in and of itself; rather, it simply represents value.

Intangible Value: Goodwill, franchises, licenses, patents, trademarks, and similar benefits of an established business.

Intent Recital: A statement that clarifies the intent and purpose of the document and/or parties.

Interest: A share of, a right to, or a concern with something of value; also the premium paid for the use of money (based on an annual rate).

Interest-only Note: A promissory note that requires that only the interest by paid during the term of the note, with the principal amount due in a lump sum at the end of the term.

Interim Loan: A short-term loan while borrower is waiting for a subsequent long-term loan to be granted.

Interlocutory: Something that is temporary, not final; waiting for issues to be determined and resolved at some future time.

Interlocutory Decree: A degree that is temporary, pending the outcome of issues before it is finalized.

Intestate: To die without leaving a will; also, a decedent who did not leave a will.

Intra: Latin, meaning "within"; used in the formation of compound words.

Intrinsic Value: The actual, true, or inherent value of something that is not based on temporary economic swings.

Inure: To serve to the use or benefit of someone; to vest.

Investment: The amount of money put into property with the expectation of making a profit.

Involuntary Lien: A lien imposed upon property without the consent or choice of the owner; federal/state/property tax liens.

Irrevocable: Unchangeable, or incapable of being recalled or revoked.

Joinder: The uniting of several causes or persons into a single unit or suit.

Joint: A united combination in interest or action.

Joint Protection Policy: A policy insuring more than one party's interest; such as the interest of both the owner and the lender.

Joint Tenancy: A form of co-ownership by two or more persons, each with equal shares and the unique quality of the right of survivorship upon death of a cotenant.

Joint Venture: A form of business organization composed of two or more persons in which profits, losses, and control are shared.

Judgment: A final determination in a court (of competent jurisdiction) to an action or proceeding.

Judgment Creditor: Identifies the party (creditor) to whom the debt (court settlement) is owned by the judgment debtor. The identification of the creditor often includes his or her address.

Judgment Debtor: Identifies the party (debtor) who owes the debt (court settlement) to the judgment creditor. Certain identification information (of the judgment debtor) is usually declared: social security number, driver's license number, and address.

Judgment Lien: A statutory lien ordering the payment a of a sum of money, created by recording an abstract or a complete judgment.

Judgment — Pertinent Information: Sets out recording reference information including: date of entry, book and page numbers of the court judgment books, and the names of the judgment debtor and creditor.

Junior Lien: A recorded lien of inferior priority.

Jurat: The clause appearing at the end of an affidavit reciting the date, location, and person before whom the statement was sworn. A jurat is not the same as an acknowledgment, although the terms are often (mistakenly) used interchangeably.

Jurisdiction: The power of a court to hear and determine a case.

Just Compensation: The fair and equitable compensation paid to a landowner when the power of eminent domain is exercised.

Laches: Inexcusable delay in asserting a right; the doctrine suggests that long-neglected rights cannot be enforced.

Land: Real estate without any improvements attached to it.

Land Contract of Sale: Also known as a conditional sales contract and a contract of sale; title remains in the name of the vendor (seller) until the vendee (buyer) fulfills certain conditions of the contract. The vendee has possession and equitable interest.

Landlord: A lessor who leases or rents property to a tenant (lessee).

Land Usage: The uses being made or those allowable under zoning ordinances.

Lease: An agreement whereby the lessor (landlord) relinquishes the right of possession of the property (in exchange for rent) to the tenant, while retaining title and full ownership.

Leaseback: A sale arrangement wherein the buyer leases the property back to the seller.

Leasehold: The lessee's estate in real property that was created by virtue of the lease agreement.

Lease Option: A lease allowing the tenant the right to buy the property if and when certain conditions are met.

Legacy: A gift of personal property by a will.

Legal Advice Notice: A cautionary note suggesting that the trustor should seek legal advice from an attorney or government agency.

Legal Description: Legally describes the real property or interest being conveyed. Usually accomplished by lot/tract, metes and bounds, or U.S. Government Survey type or legal description.

Legal Rate of Interest: The maximum rate of interest that legally can be charged for the use of money.

Legatee: A person to whom personal property is given by a will.

Lessee: The person acquiring possession of real property by virtue of the lease agreement that creates a leasehold estate for the lessee.

Lessor: One who grants a lease and the exclusive right of possession of real property to another, subject only to rights expressly retained by the lessor in the agreement.

Less Than Interest Note: A promissory note that allows or requires the borrower to make periodic payments that actually are less than the accrued interest.

Let: To grant a lease to another.

Letters of Administration: The written approval from the probate court that appoints an administrator (administratrix) as the personal representative of the affairs of one who dies intestate.

Letters of Conservatorship: The written approval from the court that appoints a conservator to handle the affairs or care for the person who is a conservatee.

Letters of Guardianship: The written approval from the court that appoints a guardian for the person and/or estate of a minor or of an incompetent.

Letters Testamentary: The written approval from the court that appoints a personal representative of the estate of a testate decedent.

Levy: To assess, collect, gather: i.e., the seizure of property by judicial procedure.

Liable: Held responsible or accountable under the law.

Liability: An obligation or duty that must be performed, that which must be paid. The opposite of asset.

License: Permission by a recognized authority to act or engage in a business, profession, or other activity. A certificate or document that gives the right to receive or perform a specific activity. Also, a right to a use of real property.

Lien: A charge, hold, or claim of another for the purpose of securing a debt or obligation.

Lien Subordination ("Good Faith") Clause: Provides for the protection of the lien holder's value and position from any future reversion or forfeiture resulting in a breach of the restrictions attached to the agreement.

Life Beneficiary: A person entitled to receive specified benefits for the duration of that individual's life.

Life Estate: An estate measured in duration by the lifetime of a natural person.

Limitations, Statutes of: Statutes that limit the time within which parties having a cause of action must institute judicial proceedings or lose such rights.

Limited Partnership: A partnership arrangement in which some of the partners (the limited partners) have a limited investment, limited liability, and no management controls.

Lineal: Descent by a direct line of succession in ancestry.

Liquid Assets: Assets that are readily convertible to cash.

Liquidate: To convert property or other assets into cash.

Liquidated Damages: The amount of money agreed upon in a contract as payment or compensation for a breach of contract; thus eliminating further legal action.

Lis Pendens: Latin, meaning "action pending;" suspended or pending lawsuit.

Listing: A written contract between an owner (principal) and an agent (broker) authorizing the agent to sell, lease, or rent the owner's property in exchange for compensation.

Lite Pendente: Latin, meaning "while the action is ending."

Litigant: Party involved in a lawsuit.

Litigation: Civil action; a controversy in court to determine the rights of each party.

Living Trust: A trust that is operative during the lifetime of the person creating it.

Loan: Delivery of something of value with the expectation of repayment or return. Money given to another in expectation of return of the principal amount plus interest for given period of time.

Loan Policy: A policy of title insurance, which insures the interest of the lender on a particular debt obligation.

Loan to Value (LTV): The ratio of the amount borrowed to the property's appraised value or selling price.

Lock-in Clause: A loan provision specifying a time period during which no repayment or complete payoff is permitted.

Loss Payable Clause: An endorsement to a fire insurance policy identifying additional parties (lenders) entitled to participate in claims proceeds in the event of loss.

Lot Books: A title company's set of books reflecting every real estate document that has been recorded within the county.

Lot Split: The legal division or splitting of a parcel of land into more than one legal parcel of land.

Maintenance: The ongoing painting, cleaning, and repair work done to property and equipment to keep it productive, useful, and in good repair.

Maker: One who executes or endorses a note.

Management: The supervision of people or property for another.

Map Act: The Subdivision Map Act that sets forth the guidelines and regulations for the subdivision of land.

Margin: The amount that the lender adds to the index to determine the rate on an adjustable-rate mortgage (ARM) when it adjusts.

Marketability: The status and condition of title to property in relationship to its acceptability (for conveyance) to an informed and able purchaser.

Market Data: Information regarding the listed price, sales price rental fees, market time, and so on, of real property.

Market Data Approach: A method used in appraisal that determines the price of a home or lot by comparing it with other property similar to it that has sold recently.

Market Title: Title to a piece of property that a reasonable informed purchaser would be willing to accept.

Market Value: The price for a property that a willing buyer and a willing seller would agree upon when neither is under abnormal pressure.

Master Plan: A long-range general plan for physical development and usage of property within a community based on projected population changes and growth trends.

Material Fact: A fact that in all likelihood would affect the decision of an owner in giving his or her consent to an agent to enter into a particular transaction.

Maturity: The date at which time a note becomes due and payable; the same concept is valid with regard to when legal rights become enforceable.

Meander: To follow a variable and winding course.

Mechanic's Lien: A statutory lien to secure payment for persons contributing labor and/or material toward improvements upon real property when the compensation was not paid in a timely manner.

Mechanic's Lien — Pertinent Information: Sets forth the name of the mechanic's lien claimant, name of the party who requested the improvement work, and a recording reference for the mechanic's lien, including the county where said lien was recorded.

Memorial: A short written statement; a memorandum.

Merger of Title: The absorption of a lesser estate into a larger estate.

Meridians: The imaginary lines (north-south) used (along with base lines east-west) to measure and identify land.

Metes and Bounds: Measurement, angles, boundaries, and distances used in describing land perimeters.

Mineral Lease: A lease that permits a lessee to explore and extract minerals from an owner's land. Mineral leases usually are payable on a royalty basis.

Monument: A fixed mark or object used by a surveyor to fix or establish boundaries or land location.

Moratorium: The legal authorization to delay the performance of some obligation, especially payment of debts.

Mortgage: A two-party security instrument pledging land as security for the performance of an obligation.

Mortgagee: The creditor (lender) who takes a lien on the subject property in return for expected performance on the obligation by the mortgagor.

Mortgage — Pertinent Information: Sets forth recording reference, names of mortgagor and mortgagee, and the county where the mortgage was recorded.

Mortgagor: The debtor (borrower) who executes a mortgage, has possession of the property used as security, and promises the performance of the obligation.

Muniments of Title: Deeds and other original documents comprising a chain of title to a parcel or real property.

Mutual Consent: Agreement by two or more people.

Mutual Water Company: A company organized for the purpose of providing water to its members and customers.

Name of Assignee ("New Beneficiary"): Identifies the party receiving the beneficial interest under the deed of trust (assignee). The status and method of acquiring title to the beneficial interest also should be specified.

Name of Attorney: Specific use: The name and address of the attorney who is representing the party identified.

Name of Claimant: Specific use: Identifies the contractor (claimant) who is claiming the mechanic's lien.

Name of Contractors: Specific use: Identifies the original contractor for the work of the improvement. If there was no contractor for the work or improvement as a whole, insert "none."

Name of Court: Name and location of the court adjudicating a specific case.

Name of Deceased: Specific use: The nature of the court action is specified. For probate proceedings, the decedent's name generally is preceded by the wording "in the matter of the Estate of . . ." The name of the decedent will appear exactly as it appears on county records in order to provide a complete chain of title.

Name of Distributee: Specific use: Identifies the party (distributee) who is receiving the property described in the Decree of Distribution.

Name of Party Executing and Interest Held in Property: Specific use: Identifies the party giving the Notice of Nonresponsibility and indicates his or her interest in the property.

Name of Party Requesting Work Under Contract: Specific use: Identifies the party who requests, by agreement (contract), that work be performed and/or materials be supplied by the claimant. This is usually the owner of the property.

Name of Property Owner: Specific use: Identifies the owner, or supposed owner, of property on which the work or improvement has been completed.

Name of Subdivider: Identifies the subdivider (often the developer and/or owner of the tract) who is creating the restrictions for the tract development.

Naturalization: The conferring of rights and privileges of citizenship on one who was an alien.

Naturalized Citizen: One who has been legally proclaimed a citizen of the United States by an act of Congress.

Negative Amortization: Payment terms under which the borrower's payments do not cover the interest due. The "deferred interest" is added to the principal balance.

Negotiable: Capable of transfer between parties by indorsement of the holder in the ordinary course of business.

Negotiable Instrument: An instrument that contains an unconditional promise or order to pay a certain sum of money, payable at a definite time, or on demand, and is payable to order or to bearer.

Negotiation: The process of creating a meeting of the minds between two or more parties in order to reach an agreement.

Net Income: The amount of money from income property that remains after expenses and charges have been deducted.

Net Lease: A lease that requires the tenant to pay all the costs of maintaining the building, including the payment of taxes, insurance, repairs, and other expenses normally paid by the owner.

Net Listing: A listing that states the minimum amount the seller is to receive and stipulates that any amount above this goes to the broker as commission.

Net Worth: That which remains after subtracting liabilities from assets.

New Deed of Trust — Pertinent Information: Sets forth the amount of the note, date, and beneficiary of the new deed of trust, which is to record concurrently with the Subordination Agreement.

Nominee: A person designated to act in the place and stead of another.

Nonconforming Use: Actual use of land that lawfully existed prior to the enactment of a zoning ordinance (which now prohibits or restricts said usage) and, therefore, said usage may be continued.

Nondisclosure: Misrepresentation by silence.

Nonjudicial Foreclosure: Sale of property pursuant to the power-of-sale provisions contained in a security instrument.

Nonrecourse Loan: A loan that limits the lender, in the event of default by the borrower, to foreclosure on the property that was used as security. The lender cannot sue for deficiency of funds and cannot attach the borrower's personal assets.

Notarize: To provide proof of execution of a document by means of notary public's certificate of acknowledgment.

Notary Public: A public officer authorized to administer oaths to attest or certify certain types of documents, to take depositions, and to perform certain other civil functions.

Notary Seal or Stamp: The official seal of the notary public or other authorized official.

Note: A common reference to a promissory note.

Notice of Cessation: A recorded notice shortening the time for the filing of mechanic's liens when work has ceased prior to completion of the improvement.

Notice of Completion: A notice recorded within ten days of completion of a work of improvement signals commencement of the time period within which claims of mechanic's liens must be recorded.

Notice of Default: A recorded notice of a trustor's failure to perform his or her obligation under a deed of trust. It is the initial step in nonjudicial foreclosure.

Notice of Default Recording Information: Includes the book and page notation for the recordation of the Notice of Default in the official records. This statement also acknowledges that the legal procedures connected with the Notice of Default have been completed in a timely manner.

Notice of Intent to Sell: States intent to sell defaulted property at public auction to the highest bidder. Must be posted and published according to specific regulations.

Notice of Nonresponsibility: A recorded notice by an owner of real property that he or she will not be responsible for payment of costs of improvements contracted for by anyone other than the owner him- or her-self.

Notice Regarding Construction and Responsibility: Sets forth a statement of the nature of the improvement work being done on the property and demonstrates that the owner executing the notice has obtained knowledge of this work within the past ten days. Furthermore, a declaration is made that the owner will not be responsible for any material or labor furnished in regard to this specific improvement work project.

Notice to Current Beneficiary: Cautionary note concerning the possible use of new loan proceeds for reason other than improvement of the land.

Notice to Quit: Notice given by a landlord to a tenant to pay rent within three days or vacate the premises. This term also is used after a foreclosure to give notice to tenants (may be previous owner who was foreclosed) to vacate the premises and give possession to the new owners.

Notorious Possession: Possession of real property that is open and conspicuous.

Novation: The substitution of a new obligation for an old one, or the substitution of another party for one of the original parties.

Now Therefore ... : Sets forth various terms relating to the subordination agreement: priority levels, extensions, contingent agreements, and so on.

Nuncupative Will: A verbal will before sufficient number of witnesses; generally reduced to writing later, if ever.

Oath: A declaration appealing to God to be witness of the truth of a fact, statement, or act. A solemn affirmation or serious pledge.

Obsolescence: A loss of value or property due to its being outmoded.

Official Records: The books in which all documents filed in a county recorder's office are recorded that impart constructive notice of matters pertaining to real property.

Offset Statement: An owner statement, deposited into escrow, showing the status of rents, security deposits, and other balances and obligations connected with the investment property.

Omnibus Clause: As applies to the Decree of Distribution, this clause is intended to protect the distributee's interest by including property that may have been improperly or not specifically described. It is included so that it will not be necessary to reopen probate proceeding or to amend the decree. An example of the protective language: "The following described property and all other property of the estate, whether described herein or not, is distributed to ... "

Open-End Mortgage (Deed of Trust): Provision that allows for additional loan advances to be funded to the borrower while keeping the same security and security documents.

Open Listing: A listing given by a property owner that states that the first agent to secure a buyer on the terms and conditions agreeable to the seller will be paid a commission.

Operative Property: Property that is reasonably necessary to operate and conduct a specific type of business.

Operative Words of Conveyance: An essential part of any deed, which indicate an intent to transfer the title to real property. In a grant deed: The wording "hereby grant(s)" is qualified by ". . . without any covenant or warranty . . ." In a deed of trust (trust deed), the trustor conveys or transfers "bare legal" title to the trustee. The wording "hereby grants, transfers and assigns to trustee, in trust, with power of sale" is generally used.

Operative Words of Endorsement: The formal words that transfer the beneficiary's interest under a deed or trust to the assignee: ". . . has endorsed said note and does hereby assign and transfer to . . ."

Option: A choice, right, or consideration to do or not to do a certain thing, either now or sometime in the future; the option to lease or to buy property.

Optionee: The person who acquires or holds a legal option; the person who has the choice.

Optionor: The person who grants an option and is bound by the decision of the optionee during the lifetime of the option.

Order Confirming Sale: A court order confirming the sale of estate property by a personal representative or other fiduciary.

Ordinance: A legislative enactment of a city or county.

Original Trustee Under the Deed of Trust: Identifies the original trustee who is being replaced under the deed of trust by use of the Substitution of Trustee document.

Origination Fee: A charge made for obtaining and processing a new loan.

Ostensible: That which is or seems to be apparent.

Outlawed: A claim, right, or cause of action unenforceable due to lapse of time.

Owner's Equity: The value held by the owner that represents the difference between the market value and the existing liens on a property.

Ownership: The exclusive right to use and enjoy property.

Owner's Policy: A policy insuring the title of the owner of the property.

Paper: Slang for a note or mortgage used in lieu of cash.

Parcel: Any area of land contained within a single description.

Parol: That which is verbal rather than written.

Partial Reconveyance: A document that identifies a particular parcel of land and releases said parcel as security from a blanket deed of trust.

Partial Release Clause: A clause in a blanket mortgage allowing for the release of a portion of the property (as security for the lien) when certain conditions are met.

Partition Action: A judicial separation of the respective interests in land of co-owners; it may be a physical division into separate parcels or a sale of the entire parcel and a division of proceeds.

Partnership: As association of two or more competent persons to carry on as co-owners of a business for profit.

Party Giving Notice — Pertinent Information: Sets forth: the full name of the party (owner of property) giving notice on line 2; his or her full address on line 3; the nature of the interest held in the subject property on line 4.

Party Wall: A dividing wall located on a boundary line and used by both owners.

Patent: A federal or state government conveyance of public lands to a private party.

Payee: One who receives a payment.

Payor: One who makes a payment.

Pendente Lite: Latin, meaning "matters that are contingent upon the determination of pending litigation."

Per Annum: Latin, meaning "through the course of a year," "annual."

Per Capita: Latin, meaning "by the head," "by the number of individuals"; a method of reporting figures or statistics.

Percentage Lease: A lease that provides for the rental rate to be determined, in whole or in part, from the dollar volume of business conducted.

Percolation Test: A test that determines the ability of the ground to absorb and drain water.

Performance: The fulfillment of an obligation or promise.

Performance Bond: A bond posted by a contractor as a guarantee that he or she will satisfactorily complete a project and it will be free of any liens.

Periodic Tenancy: Tenancy for successive periods of equal duration (week to week, month to month, year to year).

Personal Property: Anything that is movable and not attached to real property; therefore, anything that is not real property.

P.I.T.I.: Abbreviation for principal, interest, taxes, and insurance in regard to a loan payment.

Plaintiff: The party who brought the court action or the party who is suing another.

Plat: A plot, map, or chart.

Pleadings: The formal writings filed in court containing the various claims and defenses of the opposing parties.

Pledge: The delivery of personal property as security for the performance of an obligation.

Plottage: The assemblage of adjoining land to increase the area of holding and often the inherent value.

Policy of Title Insurance: A contract indemnifying against loss resulting from a defect in title or outstanding liens on the real property insured.

Point: A charge (to borrowers by lenders) pursuant to obtaining a loan. One point is equal to 1 percent of the loan value.

Police Power: The power of the state and local governments to impose such regulations and restrictions upon private rights that are reasonably related to the promotion and maintenance of the health, safety, morals, and general welfare of the public.

Possession: Having, holding, or detaining property in one's command.

Possession (Actual): As concerns real property, actual possession is the physical occupation of the property or the direct appropriation of the property's benefits.

Possession (Constructive): The ability to have the power and the intention to exercise control over said property. Constructive possession does not include physical occupation.

Possessory Action: Lawsuits to obtain or maintain possession or real property.

Power of Attorney: A document authorizing a person (the attorney-in-fact) to act on behalf of another (the principal). To be directive in real estate, the power of attorney must be recorded.

Power of Attorney — Pertinent Information: Sets forth the recording reference and county where the power of attorney (which is being revoked) was recorded.

Power of Sale: A right granted in a deed of trust or mortgage that permits the trustee or mortgagee to sell the property at a public auction in the event the buyer defaults.

Powers: Specifies exactly the authority given to the attorney-in-fact.

Preceding Estate: A prior estate upon which a future estate is determined. An estate in remainder is based on a preceding life estate.

Preemptive Right: A right to purchase on the same terms as offered by another party.

Preliminary Report: A formal report that sets out in detail the condition of title to a particular parcel of land.

Premises: Basically, land and all its appurtenances; however, different entities have specific definitions.

Prepayment Clause: A clause within an agreement permitting payment of a debt prior to a due date; may be with or without a penalty.

Prepayment Penalty: A provision inserted in a note whereby a penalty is to be paid by the borrower in the event the note is paid off before the due date (or, usually, if more than 20 percent is paid off in any one year). Most prepayment penalties expire at the end of five years into the term.

Prescription: The securing of a property right by using the property openly, continuously, hostilely, and notoriously for a period of time prescribed by the civil code.

Presumption: That which is assumed without actual proof.

Prima Facie: That which is assumed to be correct until proven otherwise.

Primary Financing: The first note, mortgage, or trust deed.

Principal: One who has permitted or directed another to act for his or her benefit and subject to his or her direction or control. Power of Attorney: Identifies the person (principal) who is giving authority to the attorney-in-fact to act in his or her behalf. Generally, the name of the county and state of the principal's residence is also specified. Revocation of Power of Attorney: Identifies the party (principal) who is revoking the powers set forth in a previously recorded power of attorney. Also, the amount of loan to be repaid exclusive of the interest.

Priority: The relative positions of liens and encumbrances, usually according to recording date and time.

Private Mortgage Insurance (PMI): Insurance written by a private company that protects the lender against losses if a borrower defaults.

Probate: A period of time during which the court has jurisdiction over the administration of an estate of a deceased person.

Probate Court: The court that has jurisdiction over wills and estate settlements.

Probate Sale: A sale to liquidate the estate of a decedent for the settlement of the estate.

Processing: The preparation of a mortgage loan application and supporting documentation for consideration by a lender or insurer.

Procuring Cause: An action by an agent that originates a series of events that eventually finalizes in a sale.

Promissory Note: A document promising to pay a sum of money at a specified time in the future; an IOU.

Pro-Rata: Latin, meaning "directly proportional to a certain rate or amount of ownership or use."

Proration: Dividing something (income/expense, etc.) according to relative time or amount of use.

Public Domain: All federal government–owned land that is subject to the general land laws.

Public Report Subdivision: A report (prepared by the real estate commissioner on the details of a new subdivision) that must be given to each buyer in a new subdivision.

Purchase Money Loan: A loan originated at time of purchase for all or a portion of the purchase price.

Purchase Note Terms: Specific use: A promissory note specifying the terms and conditions of payment included within the displayed version of a land contract of sale.

Purchase Offer: A written document used to secure a firm offer to purchase property and provide a receipt for the buyer's earnest money; also known as a purchase agreement or deposit.

Purpose: Sets forth the purpose and intent of the contract of sale and specifies the vendor's security interest protection through the power of sale.

Purpose and Identification of Restrictions: Sets out the nature and purpose of the development restrictions, along with the "general plan" restrictions and the method by which the restrictions shall be imposed on the tract.

Qualified: Approval by meeting certain requirements. Legally competent or capable.

Quasi: That which is or has a similar nature.

Quasi-Community Property: Property acquired by either spouse that would be considered community property if the person had been living in this state; however, it was purchased while domiciled outside of the state.

Quasi-Contract: A contractual-type relationship based on conduct, which receives its power by implication of the law.

Quiet Title Action: A court action to establish clear title or to remove a defect or "cloud" on a title to real property.

Quitclaim Deed: A deed that transfers the grantor's rights and interest in property without any warranty or covenants of title.

Range: A column of townships running north and south in a row parallel to and east or west of a principal meridian.

Ratification: The alteration of a previously unauthorized act to an authorized act.

Real Estate Settlement Procedures Act (RESPA): A federal law that requires lenders to give borrowers advance notice of closing costs.

Real Property: Land and whatever is erected, growing, or affixed to the land.

Realtor®: A real estate licensee who is a member of the National Association of Realtors® and who has agreed to abide by the ethics and standards of that organization.

Recession of Contract: To rescind or annul a contract by mutual consent of all parties or, for cause, by any one party.

Recognized Gain: The amount of monetary gain (subject to tax) that is realized from the sale or exchange of real property.

Reconveyance: A document that returns the "bare legal" title to the owner (trustor) upon fulfillment of all obligations under a deed of trust.

Record: To give public notice of a document by placing the document on file with the county recorder.

Recorder's Office: The government office that publicly records deeds, mortgages, trust deeds, and all other legal documents as part of the public record process.

Recording Information: The book and page numbers of the official records where the document is entered, the file number (sometimes called the document or instrument number) is assigned by the county recorder, and the date and time of recordation are noted on the document.

Recording of Judgment — Pertinent Information: If the Satisfaction of Judgment is to be recorded, the recording reference information and the county where the judgment (or abstract) was recorded should be documented.

Recording Requested By: Identifies the party requesting that the document be recorded and often shows the names of title companies when they submit groups of documents to the county for recording.

Record Trustee's Acknowledgment: The signature of the trustee (being replaced) that certifies receipt of a copy of the substitution of trustee document.

Recourse Loan: A loan that allows the lender to seek a deficiency judgment in the event that money is still owed on a debt after a foreclosure sale.

Redemption: The time period during a nonjudicial foreclosure process in which the owner must pay the entire sum due and payable to the lender to prevent the final sale; also, the buying back of one's property after it has been lost through foreclosure (usually judicial foreclosure).

Redemption Right: The legal right of a debtor to reacquire title to property lost in a judicial foreclosure.

Refinancing: The process of taking out a new loan on property already owned; paying off the existing financing and retaining the cash balance, if one exists.

Reformation: An action to correct a mistake or modify a document.

Register Number: A trustee's cross-reference number used for quick file location of a "blanket deed of trust" whenever a partial reconveyance is issued for that specific trust deed.

Regression: An appraisal concept: When a property of a given value is placed in a neighborhood with properties of a lower value, the higher-value property will tend to be devalued to the level of the lower-valued properties.

Reinstatement: Restoration of a previous position or status after losing said position to default; also, the first three-month period of a nonjudicial foreclosure process of a deed of trust with a power of sale.

Release Clause: A clause in a blanket mortgage allowing for the release of a portion of the property (as security for the lien) when certain conditions are met; also known as a partial release clause.

Reliction: The gradual recession of a body of water leaving a body of land.

Remainder Estate: A future interest in property created in someone other than the grantor, which is or may become possessory upon the natural expiration of the prior particular estate.

Remainderman: The person who owns an estate in remainder; therefore, the person who will receive title upon termination of the prior, particular estate.

Renegotiable Rate Mortgage: A mortgage whose interest rate may be renegotiated periodically, typically every three to five years.

Renovate: To restore to a former condition or to upgrade the condition.

Rent: Income received for the use of property.

Replacement Cost: A method used in appraising whereby a property is given a value based on the estimated cost to replace a similar or equivalent property in the current market.

Request for Notice of Default: A request to receive a copy of any Notice of Default that may be filed against any lien encumbering said property. Contract of Sale: Both vendor and vendee request a copy of the Notice of Default that was in existence and either assumed or taken "subject to" as part of the contract agreement.

Request for Reconveyance: Written instructions from the beneficiary to the trustee to issue a reconveyance deed to the trustor because the loan obligation has been satisfied.

Reservation: A right or an interest retained by a grantor as part of a conveyance.

Reservation of Vendor's/Vendee's Right: Sets forth certain important and reserved rights of the vendor and vendee (from conveyance to the trustee) since title does not pass until the conditions of the contract are complete.

Restriction: A limitation on the use of real estate; may be part of the conditions, covenants, and restrictions ("CC & Rs") adopted by the developer, or it may be a governmental ordinance.

Revenue Stamps: Tax levied by the county (sometimes by the city) on the sale of real property; the same as documentary tax stamps.

Reversion: A future estate, generally reserved in the grantor, that becomes possessory at the end of a grantee estate.

Rider: A supplement or an addition to; an indorsement to a document.

Right of Survivorship: The right of a surviving joint tenant(s) to acquire automatically the interest of a deceased joint tenant.

Right of Way: A right granted by an owner (to another person) to pass over or through the owner's land.

Riparian Rights: The right of a landowner to a reasonable use of the water comprising a waterway either through or adjacent to said property.

Rule Against Perpetuities: The rule of law that places time limits on the vesting of future interest in real and personal property.

Sale Contract: An agreement entered into for the purchase and sale of real property. Also known as a purchase agreement and deposit receipt.

Sandwich Lease: A sublease that is subject to the original lease and that has been further sublet. An "in-between" lease.

Satisfaction: A paid-off debt. Also, a document recorded with the county recorder when a mortgage (satisfaction of mortgage), trust deed (deed off reconveyance), or lien has been paid in full.

Scheduled Rate: A list of prices for title insurance policies.

Seal: An embossed or stamped impression made to authenticate a document or attest to a signature.

Searcher: A person who collects all the facts and documents regarding the title to real property for submission to a title examiner.

Secondary Financing: Mortgages or trust deeds that are secondary in priority, or subordinate, to first mortgages and trust deeds; also known as junior liens.

Secondary Money Market: The market where existing secured notes are bought and sold. This is accomplished on the institutional and private level.

Section: A measure of land containing 640 acres, one mile square.

Security Deposit: A deposit made to assure future performance of an obligation.

Seller Carryback: Any situation in which a seller acts as a lender, holding or "carrying back" a part of the purchase price on a note.

Separate Property: All property owned prior to marriage or acquired after marriage by gift, will, inheritance, or acquired as rents, issues, or profits from separate property.

Servient Tenement: The estate burdened with an easement.

Setback Line: A line established by a zoning regulation prohibiting any building beyond a prescribed distance from the edge of the property.

Severalty Ownership: Sole or single ownership.

Shared Appreciation Mortgage: A loan, usually at lower-than-market interest rates, wherein the lender and the seller share in the future appreciation of the property.

Sheriff's Deed: The deed issued at a court-ordered sale of real property.

Short-rate Insurance: The rate of an insurance premium that is charged when one cancels a policy.

Signature of Assignor ("Old Beneficiary"): Signature of assignor with his or her name printed beneath the signature. This is the party releasing interest in the deed of trust.

Signature of Attorney: Signature of the attorney for the judgment creditor with his or her (attorney's) name printed beneath the signature.

Signature of Beneficiary: Signature of beneficiary with his or her name printed beneath the signature. Notice of Default: Either the beneficiary or the trustee may sign as the official on this notice. Notice of Recession: Beneficiary's signature indicates cancellation of Notice of Default. Substitution of Trustee: Beneficiary's signature causes change or substitution of trustee.

Signature of Claimant: Signature of claimant with his or her name printed beneath the signature. Claimant's legal capacity (individual, firm, corporation, etc.) is also designated. Mechanic's Lien: Signature of person setting forth claim. Release of Mechanic's Lien: Signature demonstrating the claim is being released.

Signature of Deputy Clerk of the Court: Signature of the deputy clerk with his or her official title printed beneath. Occasionally the deputy clerk of the court will acknowledge the document; his or her signature would be sufficient to take the place of the signature and stamp of the notary public.

Signature of Grantor: Signature of grantor with his or her name printed beneath the signature.

Signature of Judge: Signature of the judge of the Superior Court (who approves the document) with his or her name printed beneath the signature. Occasionally the name of the judge is simply stamped on the document.

Signature of Mortgagee: Signature of the mortgagee (lender) with his or her name printed beneath the signature.

Signature of Owner: Signature of the owner with his or her name printed beneath the signature. Notice of Nonresponsibility: Signature of owner giving notice. Abandonment of Homestead: Signature of declarants of the recorded Declaration of Homestead that is being abandoned. Subordination Agreement: Signature of owner receiving new financing.

Signature of Party Executing Document: Signature of the surviving joint tenant with his or her name printed beneath the signature.

Signature of Principal: Signature of the principal with his or her name printed beneath the signature.

Signature of Subordinating Party: Signature of the beneficiary of the deed or trust that is subordinating to a new loan. Name is printed beneath the signature.

Signature of Trustee: Signature of trustee with his or her name printed beneath the signature. Notice of Recession: Indicates receipt of the notice on a specific date. Full Reconveyance: Under directions from the beneficiary, the trustee reconveys or releases the subject property. Partial Reconveyance: Under directions from the beneficiary, the trustee reconveys or releases a specific property as security under a "blanket deed of trust."

Signature of Trustor: Signature of trustor with his or her name printed beneath the signature. Deed of Trust: Acknowledges security of note. Substitution of trustee: Occasionally the trustor may be involved in the decision (along with the beneficiary) to change or substitute the trustee and, therefore, the trustor would sign the document.

Signature of Vendee: Signature of vendee with his or her name printed beneath the signature.

Signature of Vendor: Signature of vendor with his or her name printed beneath the signature.

Soldiers' and Sailors' Civil Relief Act: Federal law initiated to protect members of the armed forces from loss of property to satisfy obligations incurred prior to service entry.

Solvent: Able to pay all of one's debts and financial obligations.

Special Assessments: Fees collected by the tax collector (along with taxes) that are to pay for improvements and other benefits (school district assessments, etc.).

Specific or Special Lien: A lien that affects only one specific asset, as opposed to a general lien, that affects a number of assets.

Specific Performance: A sale of real property that fulfills the terms agreed upon.

Spouse: A husband to a wife; a wife to a husband.

Starter: The base or policy of the last title order, used as a starting point from which examination of the current order is begun.

Statement of Identity: A questionnaire used by title companies to help establish the identity of a person in order to protect the title from liens on persons with similar names; also known as a statement of information.

Statement of Improvement Work Completed: An explanation of the work completed or material supplied by the claimant. Also, when appropriate, an itemized breakdown of expenses that are incorporated in the claims.

Statement Regarding Signatures: By affixing their signatures to this contract of sale, both the vendor and vendee agree to the Request for Notice of Default.

Status: The legal position of a person (minor, adult, incompetent, etc.).

Statute of Limitations: A law that requires that certain court actions be initiated before expiration of certain time period.

Straight-line Depreciation: A depreciation method that assigns an equal loss in value for each year of a property's useful life; paper loss for tax purposes.

Straight Note: A promissory note that requires that only one payment of principal and all accrued interest be paid at the end of the term.

Street Improvement Bonds: Interest-bearing bonds issued by a city or county to secure the payment of assessments levied against land for street improvements.

Subcontractor: An individual or contracting firm agreeing to perform all or part of a principal or general contract; someone hired by the general contractor on an independent contractor basis.

Subdivision: The division of a single parcel of land into four or more separate parcels.

Subject to: When one purchases property with existing loans and takes the responsibility to make the payments without accepting personal liability for said indebtedness.

Sublease: A lease, junior to and shorter than the original lease, made by the original lessee to a new lessee.

Subordinate: To make inferior in priority, position, and recognition.

Subordinating Beneficiary Declares, Agrees, etc.: Sets forth agreements of the beneficiary of the subordinating deed of trust; consents to subordinate to the new deed of trust; to new loan disbursements, etc.

Subordinating Deed of Trust — Pertinent Information: Sets forth recording reference, trustor, trustee, beneficiary amount of note, and the county where the subordinating deed of trust was recorded. Note: On this form, a legal description is inserted in between the above information.

Subordinating Party: Identifies the beneficiary (lender) of the existing deed of trust that is subordinating to a new deed of trust. The subordinating agreement and the new deed of trust are to record concurrently.

Subordination Agreement: A provision allowing a new agreement to move into a superior position of priority over an existing or concurrent agreement.

Subrogate: To substitute one person into a position for another; to substitute a claim against one person for a claim against another person.

Substitution: The appointment of a person to act in place of, or for, another.

Succession: The legal act of taking, or right to take, property by will or inheritance.

Summons: An instrument from the court (usually via the sheriff) notifying the defendant that an action has been filed against him or her.

Surety: A person or entity guarantees the performance on a obligation by another; often accomplished with the purchase of a bond.

Survey: The measurement of land and the establishing, or the ascertaining, of its area and boundaries.

Sweat Equity: Labor or services put into improving real property and used in place of money to gain title.

Take-off: The abstract of all instruments or other matters affecting title to real property that are filed each day in the clerk's and recorder's office. If full photocopies are used instead of abstracts, it is known as complete take-off.

Takeout Loan: A long-term loan that pays off and takes the place of the short-term construction loan.

Tax Deed: The deed conveying title to property purchased at a tax sale.

Taxes: As applied to real property, a charge assessed against the value of real property to pay the cost of governmental services.

Tax Lien: A statutory lien, in favor of the state or municipality, on the land of a person charged with unpaid personal or real property taxes.

Tax Statement Address: The party (and address) to whom statements regarding real property taxes will be mailed by the county tax office. It is usually the same party mentioned in the "And when recorded mail to" section.

Tenancy: The occupying of real estate under a lease or rental. Ownership of an estate less than freehold.

Tenancy in Common: A form of co-ownership of real property by two or more persons in undivided interests; the percentage of interests can be unequal and each tenant has the right to alienate or devise his or her interest.

Tenancy in Partnership: The interest held by two or more partners in property purchased by the partnership.

Tender: An unconditional offer to perform coupled with the ability to perform.

Tenements: All the land, rights, and benefits that are conveyed with said land.

Tentative Map: A proposed subdivision map that is placed before local planning commissions/building departments for approval, which leads to a final map.

Term: Provisions and conditions within a contract; also, the length of time of a contract.

Terminable Interests: An interest in property that is extinguished by death or the occurrence of a specified event.

Termite Report: A report of structural inspection concerned with wood-destroying pests. Also the common verbiage for a "structural pest control report" that identifies all wood-damaging situations.

Terms and Conditions of Sale — Contract of Sale: A distinction must be made between a contract of sale in the legal concept of the purchase agreement and contract of sale (as used in the real estate profession) as an alternative method of financing. The latter is the used in this text according to the following explanation. During the life of the contract, the contract of sale is unique in that possession and equitable interest is delivered to the vendee while the vendor retains title to the subject property. Therefore, it is necessary to set forth specific areas to rights and responsibilities as well as to identify the consequences for the violation of said agreements during the term of the contract.

Testament: As commonly used, the statements and wishes of a person in his or her will; however, in the literal sense, testament deals with the person's wishes as to the dispensation of personal property.

Testamentary Trust: A trust created by a decedent's will and testament.

Testator: One who died leaving a will.

Tier: A row of townships running east and west that are parallel to and positioned either north or south of a designated base line.

Time, Date, and Place of Sale: The actual time, date, and location of the trustee's sale is documented to demonstrate compliance with the original notice of sale.

Time Is of the Essence: A standard clause in real property contracts that indicates that punctual compliance is required.

Title: The basic rights of enjoyment and possession or interest in property; also used to describe a document that furnishes proof of ownership.

Title Insurance: Indemnification for loss occasioned by defects in the title to real property or to an interest in real property.

Title Plant: The lot books or property accounts, maps, general index, individual/corporation files, and other records necessary for the issuance of title insurance policies by a title company.

Title Policy: An insurance policy or contract indemnifying against loss resulting from a defect in the title to the interest or lien in the real property thus insured.

Title Search: The examination and research in the history of title to a specific property in order to develop the chain of title.

Topography: The physical appearance and elevations of land.

Torrens: A system under which the title to land is registered with a registrar of land title. After the first registration, theoretically it is unnecessary to go beyond the registry to investigate the validity of a title. This system is used in only a few states.

Township: In the U.S. Government Survey, a plot of land six miles square, containing 36 sections; also, a unit of local government.

Tract: A parcel of land that is subdivided into smaller parcels of land called lots.

Trade Fixtures: Articles of personal property that are affixed to real property, which, however, remain personal property due to their necessity to carry on a trade or business.

Trade Name: The name under which business is conducted.

Transferor — Pertinent Information: If the notice of completion is signed by a successor in interest of the party (previous owner) who initiated the work of improvement, the full name and address of the previous owner is documented.

Transfer Tax: Tax levied by the county (sometimes also by the city) on the transfers of title to real property.

Trust: A right of property, real or personal, held by one party for the benefit of another.

Trust Account: A special account wherein monies held in trust are maintained separately from other monies.

Trust Deed: A three-part security document conveying "bare legal" title to be held in trust as security for the performance of an obligation; also known as a deed of trust.

Trustee: Identifies the party (usually a corporation) who is receiving the "bare legal" title (to be held in trust for the trustor and the beneficiary). The trustee is usually given a "power of sale" pursuant to which a trustee's sale (nonjudicial foreclosure) may be conducted in the event of default by the trustor. Under a full reconveyance, the trustee is identified as the party "reconveying," or releasing, the subject deed or trust. Partial Reconveyance: Identifies trustee who is reconveying or releasing a specific property from the effect of the subject deed of trust.

Trustee's Deed: The deed issued to a purchaser of real property at a trustee's sale.

Trustee's Sale: Nonjudicial foreclosure sale, conducted by the trustee under a deed of trust with a power-of-sale clause.

Trustor: Identifies the obligor (trustor, usually the borrower) who is conveying the "bare legal" title of the property to the trustee who holds this title in trust for the benefit of the trustor and the beneficiary. Under a full reconveyance, the original trustor (on the deed of trust being reconveyed) is identified. Partial Reconveyance: Identifies original trustor (as shown on the subject deed of trust) for the specific property that is being reconveyed or released.

Trustor Under the Deed of Trust: Identifies the original trustor (borrower) as shown on the deed of trust that was foreclosed upon.

UCC: Abbreviation for the Uniform Commercial Code.

Undivided Interests: The unsegregated interest in the ownership of property by the various co-owners in joint tenancy and tenants in common.

Undue Influence: Taking undue advantage of another's need, distress, or weakness to further personal gain; using excessive persuasion to overcome the will of a vulnerable person.

Unilateral Contract: A contract in which only one party promises to do something or undertakes a performance and, therefore, only one party has an obligation.

Unities: Time, title, interest, and possession; the four basic elements of joint tenancy.

Unlawful Detainer: An action brought for recovery of possession of property from a person who is in unlawful possession.

Usury: Charging an interest rate higher than that allowed by law.

VA: The U.S. Veterans Administration.

Valid: Legally sufficient; authorized by law; effective.

Valuation: An opinion of an asset's worth; an appraisal.

Variable-Rate Mortgage: Any real estate loan in which the interest rate varies over time according to a prescribed formula or set of conditions; usually changes in economic conditions. Also known as an adjustable-rate mortgage.

Variance: A change of the zoning of a specific parcel from the zoning of the rest of the immediate area.

Various Restrictions Imposed and Enforcement: Specifies the development restrictions imposed (usually by the owner of the property or the subdivider/developer) and the means for enforcing said restrictions.

Vendee: Identifies the contractual purchaser (vendee) of property under a contract of sale. The status of the vendee (husband and wife, etc.) and the legal method of acquiring title (joint tenants, tenants in common, etc.) is also set forth.

Vendee Protection on Underlying Loan Payments: Specific use: The displayed land contract of sale has a provision for an all-inclusive deed of trust; therefore, the protection allows the vendee to make up any underlying loan payments not made by the vendor and the vendee. See *All-Inclusive Deed of Trust* for more information.

Vendor: The contractual seller (vendor) of property under a contract of sale.

Venue: The state and county where the acknowledgment is taken.

Verification: A confirmation of correctness, truth or authenticity of the contents of the attached document.

Vest: To give title to or to transfer ownership of property.

Vested Interest: Unconditional, fixed interest in a property, for both now and in the future.

Vestee: Present record owner.

Vesting: A statement of the name(s) of the owner(s) of property and the nature of said ownership: joint tenancy, tenancy-in-common, and so on.

Void: Null, having no force or effect.

Voidable: That which may be declared void but is not void itself.

Voluntary Lien: A lien created by choice.

Waive: To relinquish or set aside a right.

Warranty: An assurance or promise that certain defects do not exist or will be corrected.

Warranty Deed: A deed in which express covenants of good title and the right of possession are detailed and guaranteed.

Water Right: The right of an owner to use water adjacent to and below the surface of his or her property.

Water Table: The changeable level at which natural water is present, whether above or below the ground level.

Whereas … : Specific use: Sets forth the purpose and intent of the subordination agreement and generally establishes benefits and agreements.

Will: Written instructions on the disposition of the effects of one's estate upon death.

Without Recourse: A provision often found in endorsements of negotiable instruments that means that the endorser does not assume responsibility or liability for collection.

Wraparound Mortgage of Deed of Trust: A deed of trust (or mortgage) that "wraps around" or secures payment of a senior or prior deed of trust; also known as an all-inclusive mortgage.

Writ: A court order.

Writ of Execution: A court order instructing an official to carry out a judicial decision.

Yield: The profit or income that an investment will return; the rate of return.

Zone: An area, region, or district officially designated for specific types of use.

Zoning: Governmental regulations controlling the use of property according to specified areas within the community.

INDEX